T0320800

Financial Crises and the Limits
of Bank Reform

Financial Crises and the Limits of Bank Reform

France and Germany's Ways Into and Out of the Great Recession

EILEEN KELLER

OXFORD
UNIVERSITY PRESS

Great Clarendon Street, Oxford, OX2 6DP,
United Kingdom

Oxford University Press is a department of the University of Oxford.
It furthers the University's objective of excellence in research, scholarship,
and education by publishing worldwide. Oxford is a registered trade mark of
Oxford University Press in the UK and in certain other countries

First Edition published in 2021

Impression: 1

Published in the United States of America by Oxford University Press
198 Madison Avenue, New York, NY 10016, United States of America

British Library Cataloguing in Publication Data
Data available

Library of Congress Control Number: 2020950496

ISBN 978–0–19–887074–6

DOI: 10.1093/oso/9780198870746.001.0001

Printed and bound in the UK by
TJ Books Limited

To my family

Preface and Acknowledgements

The roots of this book reach back to the early phase of what became the biggest financial disaster in almost a century. It was back then, as an undergraduate student, that I realized how stunningly wrong things can go on a large scale. Collective failure was not bound to some distant past, it was happening at the centre of what was—and still is—the heart of global capitalism. Market segments grew based on the assumption of ever rising prices. Risk managers trusted in the sophistication of their tools and models, calculating down the cost of the risk until most of it was seemingly gone. Regulators based their reasoning on the premise of the efficiency of markets and the benefits of financial innovation, thereby overlooking the elephant in the room. Politicians wanted the economy (and the state) to profit from highly liquid markets and liberalized, innovative finance, helping the elephant become a mammoth.

Since banks were the profiteers of the bailout schemes in Europe and essential to the funding of the real economy, I decided to focus on their 'fate'. In the light of the crisis, how bank-dependent should our economies be in the future? When I started my fieldwork in France in 2013, the answer to this question seemed to be quite clear: Whether I talked to representatives from the business sector, the state, politicians, or the financial sector, the main message was that the French economy had to become more independent of the banks. Financial disintermediation and non-bank intermediation had to be strengthened as a consequence of the crisis and a series of measures was under elaboration to further this end. As ironic as it may seem, I concluded that classic bank intermediation, which had nothing to do with the outbreak and the propagation of the financial crisis, seemed to be its greatest victim. European economies would become more like Anglo-Saxon finance capitalism because of the crisis and despite the fact that the crisis emerged there in the first place.

Given the severity with which the crisis had hit the German banking sector, I returned to Germany expecting to discover a similar response. However, I quickly had to revise my expectations and I was puzzled to realize that the German counterparts saw things very differently: Hardly anybody seemed to agree that the time of financial intermediation had come and that bank credit would unavoidably play a lesser role in the future, even though new market segments had emerged on several regional stock exchanges since the beginning of the crisis. In the light of the failure of financial innovation and market-based forms of banking, strengthening classic bank intermediation along the three pillars, as had been practised in Germany for decades, was the collectively agreed answer. The reform proposals that were widely discussed at that time dealt with regulatory stipulations on how this could be realized. Since German businesses were, contrary to their French equivalents, highly satisfied with the banks, I refined my working hypothesis: The response to the crisis and the future economic role of the banks seemed to be mediated by the satisfaction of the corporate sector with bank intermediation.

With hindsight, while I was probably right in recognizing the role of the real economy in shaping the response to the financial crisis, I was mistaken in assuming that this was because bank intermediation worked inherently better in Germany. I owe this realization to a high-ranking French official and fine *connaisseur* of the German political economy, who was openly sceptical of the idea of any form of 'superiority' of German relationship banking. I began to look into a series of indicators on the availability and the cost of bank credit and realized that the story was more complex than I had thought. I found remarkably similar developments in both countries at different moments in time with respect to changing perceptions on bank lending, despite the organizational differences of both banking sectors. I realized that the collective response to the financial crisis had less to do with brute numbers, such as the availability of bank credit or the costs of the bank bailouts, but with how the crisis undermined widely shared beliefs about the functioning and the future development of the domestic financial sector, changes which I describe as a form of *social learning*.

Going back in time and extending the time horizon of the analysis turned out to be fruitful in several ways. It was a corollary against a too deterministic understanding of how institutions constrain or further political decisions. It was also helpful in realizing how political decisions are linked to economic developments and widely shared perceptions. As much as the technicalities of financial regulation take place behind closed doors and are the result of discussions among specialists, they are often rooted in what can be termed the predominant perception of the day. Finally, it made me rather sceptical about an overly instrumental and mechanistic understanding of the policy-making process, in which the most affluent players, such as the banks, automatically get what they want, where the ways issues are understood result from the strategic framing of policy entrepreneurs, and where stable advocacy coalitions oppose each other over time.

I argue that major moments of policy change are linked to changing perceptions on how things are and how they will develop in the future. This form of social learning not only concerns the cognitive foundations of a policy, but also how widely a specific understanding is shared. The French and the German responses to the financial crisis differed because the crisis led to the reassessment of different assumptions on the functioning and the future development of their respective financial sectors. Assumptions that were taken for granted before the crisis were now no longer deemed valid. While this form of social learning revealed the limits of bank intermediation in France, it lay bare the risks of asset securitization and financial innovation in Germany. As the book will show, the subsequent reform agendas resonated with these predominant, but not uncontested, crisis perceptions.

This endeavour would not have been possible without generous support from several sides. Firstly, I would like to thank Ellen Immergut and Cornelia Woll for the cooperative way in which both agreed to be involved in this project. It has profited hugely from their advice, support, and encouragement. Both have been role models in their ways of doing research in the social sciences and they generously supported this project well beyond their initial commitment. I would also like to thank Pepper Culpepper, who agreed to be a mentor. I have always felt a particular affinity to some of the themes of his research.

The research on which this book builds was realized thanks to a scholarship from the Berlin Graduate School of Social Sciences and was developed further during my stay as a Max Weber Fellow at the European University Institute. I would like to thank both institutions and their teams for the excellent working environment and their generous financial support. My thanks also go to the Centre MaxPo for having hosted me twice in such a cordial way. The library team at the Deutsch-Französisches Institut in Ludwigsburg helped me access their unique archival material. I am also indebted to all my interview partners for sharing their time and expertise with me.

I finished this manuscript at the Deutsch-Französisches Institut in Ludwigsburg (dfi) and would like to express my gratitude to the director Frank Baasner, who benevolently and generously supported the completion of this book manuscript. His ability to build bridges between the academic and the 'real' world is exemplary. Joanna Ardizzone with her fine understanding of what I intended to express was of great help with language editing.

This project would not have been possible without the company of great colleagues and friends during the various stages of this project, including the fellows at the BGSS, the Center MaxPo, the LIEPP, the EUI, the dfi, and beyond. My deep gratitude goes to Camille Allé, Monica Andriescu, Anna auf dem Brinke, Natalia Besedovski, Juliana Bidadanure, Kyu Jun Choi, Martino Comelli, Priska Daphi, Nadja Douglas, Franz Filaffer, Damien Gérard, Johanna Gereke, Nicolas Griesshaber, Dominik Grillmayer, Lukas Haffert, Mathijs Jansen, Hent Kalmo, Lisa Kastner, Michael Kozakowski, Merethe Leiren, Anna Lührmann, Nicolas Merz, Raphael Reineke, Julija Sardelic, Martijn Schoonvelde, Verena Seibel, Stefan Seidendorf, Florian Stöckel, Silvana Tarlea, Jan Ullrich, Kathrin Ulmer, Benedetta Voltolini, and Nan Zhang with whom I shared the pleasures and pitfalls of this endeavour in seminars and conferences, over lunch breaks, Feierabend beers and a lot more.

This project also profited from the input and advice of many colleagues with whom I discussed it. While this list is certainly not complete, I would like to acknowledge the support and advice of Hans-Jürgen Bieling, Sebastian Botzem, Isabelle Chambost, Ismael Erturk, Clément Fontan, Dieter Fuchs, Oscar Gabriel, Axel Görlitz, David Howarth, Marc Lenglet, Susanne Lütz, Huw Macartney, Elsa Massoc, Andreas Nölke, Stefano Pagliari, Richard Portes, Friedbert Rüb, Joachim Schild, Silvia von Steinsdorff, Matthias Thiemann, Henrik Uterwedde, and Konstantin Vössing. All remaining short-comings and weaknesses of this work are, of course, mine.

Finally, I would like to thank Dominic Byatt for having taken the time to consider my proposal. I greatly appreciated his understanding and reliable guidance through the final stages of this project. I would also like to acknowledge the feedback of the reviewers, who helped me articulate some aspects of the argument more clearly.

On the private side, Malte, Elian, and Alexandra have been great companions along the way, sharing a keen interest in debate. Albin and Sonja Keller have done everything in their power to support me all over the years. Their love, care, and 'good thoughts from afar' are the groundwork on which I stand. Rainer and Renate Hofmaier were always interested in and supportive of my work, and never tired of asking when they would finally get their dedicated copy. Their wait is over! This book also is in memoriam of Barbara Keller and Herta Kraft, who I am sure would have been amazed to see the opportunities available to their granddaughter compared to their experiences as young women. Finally, I am somehow at a loss for words to express my indebtedness and gratitude to Christian Hofmaier for whom no distance was too far to see each other, no time of the day too late to talk, and no aspect of this project too weird to be discussed. His patience, support, confidence, humour, and love have carried me through this project and beyond.

Crises—financial, economic, and political amongst others—have been ongoing ever since I started working on this project. Looking into our daughter's sparkling eyes, observing her happy smile, and feeling her gently (and often less gently) touch on my face, I realize how urgent it is that we are collectively up to the challenges of our time. We owe it to our children and future generations that we try our best to learn from past failure. I want her to know that nothing will ever matter more to me than her fate.

Ludwigsburg, July 2020

Contents

List of Figures

List of Tables

List of Acronyms

ACP(R) Autorité de Contrôle Prudentiel (et de Résolution) French prudential (and resolution since 2013) authority

AF2i Association Française des Investisseurs Institutionnels French federation of institutional investors

AFG Association Française de la Gestion Financière French asset management association

AFIC Association Française des Investisseurs pour la Croissance French association of private equity investors

AFTE Association Française de Trésoriers d'Entreprise French association of corporate treasurers

AMAFI Association française des marchés financiers French financial markets association

AMF Autorité des Marchés Financiers French financial markets authority

APCMA Assemblée permanente des chambres de Métiers et de l'Artisanat General Assembly of the crafts sector (now CMA France)

ASF Association Française des Sociétés Financières French association of financing societies and other specialized finanical institutions

ASMEP-ETI Mouvement des entreprises de taille intermédiaire (now METI) Association of family-owned and medium-sized enterprises

ASU Arbeitsgemeinschaft Selbständiger Unternehmer – Die Familienunternehmer Association of family-owned enterprises

BaFin Bundesanstalt für Finanzdienstleistungsaufsicht German federal financial supervisory authority

BAKred Bundesanstalt für die Kreditwirtschaft Previous German banking supervisor, replaced by BaFin in 2002

BCBS Basel Committee on Banking Supervision Global standard setter on banking regulation

BdB Bundesverband Deutscher Banken Federation of the German commercial banks

BDI Bundesverband der Deutschen Industrie Federation of German industries

BMF Bundesministerium der Finanzen German Federal Ministry of Finance

BMWi Bundesministerium für Wirtschaft German Federal Ministry for Economic Affairs

Bpi (France) Banque Publique d'Investissement French state development bank, successor of Oséo

BVMW	**Bundesverband mittelständische Wirtschaft** German association of the medium-sized economy
BVR	**Bundesverband Deutscher Volks- und Raiffaisenbanken** Federation of the German cooperative banks
CCIP	**Chambre de Commerce and d'Industrie de Paris** Paris Chamber of industry and commerce
CDC	**Caisse des Dépôts et Consignations** French public financial institution
CGFS	**Committee of the Global Financial System** Monitoring committee at the Bank for International Settlements
CGPME	**Confédération générale des petites et moyennes entreprises** French employer federation of smaller and medium-sized enterprises
DAI	**Deutsches Aktieninstitut** German organization of financial markets participants
DIHK	**Deutscher Industrie- und Handelskammertag** German federal chamber of industry and commerce
DSGV	**Deutscher Sparkassen- und Giroverband** German association of the savings banks
EBA	**European Banking Authority**
ECB(S)	**European Central Bank (System)**
ECOFIN	**Economic and Financial Affairs Council of the EU**
ECON	**Committee for Economic and Monetary Affairs of the European Parliament**
Erafp	**Etablissement de Retraite additionnelle de la Fonction publique** French public sector pension fund
EU	**European Union**
FBF	**Fédération bancaire française** French banking association
FFSA	**Fédération Française des Sociétés d'Assurances** French federation of insurance companies
FMSA	**Finanzmarktstabilisierungsanstalt** Financial markets stabilization authority
FSI	**Fonds Stratégique d'Investissement** French sovereign fund for strategic investments
GDV	**Gesamtverband Deutscher Versicherer** German insurance association
GFI	**Groupement des Fédérations Industrielles** Association of the sectoral industrial federations
GHOS	**Group of Governors and Heads of Supervision** Central oversight organ in the Basel Committee
GIAC	**Groupement des industries agricoles alimentaires et de grande consommation** Society of the agro-alimentary industries and wholesale trading
HCJP	**Haut Comité Juridique de la Place Financière de Paris** High-level legal committee of the Paris marketplace
HCP	**Haut Comité de Place** High-Level Committee of the Paris marketplace (replaced by the HCJP in 2015)

HCSF	**Haut Conseil de Stabilité Financière** French high financial stability council
IMF	**International Monetary Fund**
KfW	**Kreditanstalt für Wiederaufbau** German public development bank
Medef	**Mouvement des entreprises de France** Largest French union of employers
Minefi	**Ministère de l'Economie, de la finance et de l'industrie** French economic, finance, and industry ministry
SoFFin	**Sonderfonds Finanzmarktstabilisierung** Special German financial markets stablization fund
TSI	**True Sale International GmbH** Initiative to promote the German securitization market
VAB	**Verband der Auslandsbanken in Deutschland** German association of foreign banks
vbw	**Vereinigung der Bayrischen Wirtschaft** Bavarian trade organization
vdp	**Verband deutscher Pfandbriefbanken** German association of banks issuing Pfandbriefe, a form of covered bond
VÖB	**Verband Öffentlicher Banken** German federation of the public banks
WKÖ	**Wirtschaftskammer Österreich** Austrian economic chamber
ZDH	**Zentralverband des Deutschen Handwerks** German federation of the skilled crafts sector
ZGV	**Zentralverband Gewerblicher Verbundgruppen – Der Mittelstandsverbund** German central association of commercial groups

1

Financial crises and the limits of reforms

The new millennium began with the worst financial crisis in almost a century. From summer 2007 onwards, booming markets showed signs of a reversal, and when the US government decided in September 2008 not to bail out the investment bank Lehman Brothers, one of the major players in what has since become known as the subprime market, a chain reaction set in that triggered large-scale public interventions in the United States and in many European countries. Governments and central banks intervened to stop an uncontrollable crash, fearing the implosion of the global financial system. Given the depth of the financial crisis, the costs of the bailouts, which led to significant increases in public debt levels, and the economic recession that followed, the financial and economic crisis, which became known as the Great Recession, has had, and will have, long-lasting implications for the twenty-first century's socio-economic and financial development.

While events of this severity are rare, one thing is certain: the next financial crisis will come. It is only a matter of when, where, why, and how. The history of finance is one of reoccurring crises from its origins until today. Financial meltdowns and bursting bubbles have occurred in various places—in developed as in developing economies—and in different forms, but they have never been absent for long (Kindleberger and Aliber 2005). Years of above-average profits, global imbalances and current account deficits, excessive debt accumulation, and increased financial leverage have been followed by the conspicuously frequent bursting of bubbles and considerable collateral damage. Their build-up was often fuelled by technical innovation, irrational exuberance, and disproportionate beliefs that this time would be different and the insights from past experiences would not be applicable (Reinhart and Rogoff 2009). Since 1800, the world's most important financial centres—the United Kingdom, the United States, and France—have seen a banking crisis less than every 20 years on average, although most of them occurred before 1945 (based on Reinhart and Rogoff 2009, 150).[1] In Europe, the banking crisis

---

[1] The authors document 12, 13, and 15 episodes of crisis respectively.

Financial Crises and the Limits of Bank Reform: France and Germany's Ways Into and Out of the Great Recession. Eileen Keller, Oxford University Press (2021). © Eileen Keller. DOI: 10.1093/oso/9780198870746.003.0001

contributed to the depth of the sovereign debt crisis, throwing European Economic and Monetary Union into disarray.

After a period of financial moderation, which followed the Great Depression of the late 1920s and early 1930s and lasted until the breakdown of the Bretton Woods monetary and financial order, the process of financial globalization that took place from the 1970s onward has spurred the recurrence of crises (Kindleberger and Aliber 2005, 6). The lifting of various barriers to the free flow of money and competition among financial institutions has not, contrary to theoretical expectations, made the allocation of financial resources and investments more efficient on a global scale. Rather, it has made the financial system more fragile and crisis-prone, especially in the immediate aftermath of periods of financial liberalization (Kaminsky and Reinhart 1999). There have been crises from Asia to Latin America and Scandinavia, with neither the United States, the heart of global capitalism, nor supposedly boring German banking having been spared. Learning the lessons of a crisis and preventing the worst from happening, it seems, is a futile enterprise.

This book is about the nature of crisis responses and the politics of financial sector reform leading to their adoption. Drawing on an extensive study of French and German crisis responses with respect to their banks, it shows how competitive concerns, the selective reconstruction of the crisis in terms of its causes and implications for the future, and the balancing of competing and partially conflicting policy aims shaped the responses observed in the aftermath of the Great Recession. Since financial regulation has always been 'a-theoretical' and more of an ad hoc response to observed dysfunctionalities during moments of crisis (Goodhart 2010, 165), understanding the conclusions drawn from a major crisis are crucial. While it is certainly true that crises are unavoidable, a partial answer as to why this is the case lies in the nature of crisis responses, which cannot, however, be resumed to financial industry power.

1.1 The rhetoric of crisis responses

Despite the reoccurring observation of financial crises, the Great Recession generated considerable expectations regarding the momentum it created for a significant overhaul of the international financial architecture. Political decision-makers around the world seemed determined to engage in major reforms. Nicolas Sarkozy, the French President at that time and one of the initiators of the global post-crisis reform agenda, for instance, argued that 'a certain idea of globalization, which built on a financialized version of capitalism that had imposed its logic on the economy and contributed to its perversion, had come to an end'.[2] Given the experience of the drastic crisis, he argued, we had to change our way of thinking and our behaviour. According to Sarkozy, the crisis must be an incentive to refound capitalism by rebalancing the power of the state and the market, ending laissez-faire capitalism and relinquishing the assumption of the superiority of markets. 'If we want to rebuild a viable financial system', he emphasized, 'the moralization of financial capitalism must remain the priority' (Sarkozy 2008; own translation).

Have politicians and regulators finally got it right and made finance a safer and less crisis-prone place? Has the global financial crisis laid the groundwork for a new financial architecture based on a different set of economic and moral principles as was the case after the last big financial and economic crisis, the Great Depression? 'If an event with widespread and severe economic and social consequences keeps on repeating itself', Markus Brunnermeier, Andrew Crocket, Charles Goodhart, Avinash Persaud, and Hyun Shin (Brunnermeier et al. 2009, xi)—some of the most distinguished financial experts—write, 'the onus is surely on the authorities to change something'. Crises reveal dysfunctionalities and therefore prompt reforms, so common wisdom goes.

From a theoretical perspective, the preconditions for major political change with lasting legacies for future developments indeed seemed to be united: A drastic, highly visible, and extremely costly crisis laid bare various dysfunctionalities of the pre-crisis international financial architecture. Given its depth, the crisis should allow even the most powerful entrenched interests to be overcome. A failure to do everything to avoid such a situation from happening again seemed to be tantamount to political suicide: Private financial institutions, where some of the political economy's highest returns on equity were achieved, the biggest salaries paid, and the largest bonuses attributed, had to be bailed out with the money of the collective.

---

[2] 'Une certaine idée de la mondialisation s'achève avec la fin d'un capitalisme financier qui avait imposé sa logique à toute l'économie et avait contribué à la pervertir. . . . Nous pouvons sortir plus forts de cette crise. Si nous acceptons de changer nos manières de penser et nos comportements. . . . Un nouveau rapport doit s'instaurer entre l'économie et la politique à travers la mise en chantier de nouvelles réglementations. L'autorégulation pour régler tous les problèmes, c'est fini. Le laissez-faire, c'est fini. Le marché qui a toujours raison, c'est fini. Il faut tirer les leçons de la crise pour qu'elle ne se reproduise pas. Nous venons de passer à deux doigts de la catastrophe, on ne peut pas prendre le risque de recommencer. Si l'on veut reconstruire un système financier viable, la moralisation du capitalisme financier demeure la priorité.'

The crisis was halted thanks to the investment of taxpayers' money, creating tremendous liabilities that have to be paid back with state income to which any child buying sweets on the way home from school contributes with the taxes paid on them. One of the most fundamental laws of capitalism had been broken on a large scale with the bank bailouts, namely that profits are primarily private, but so are losses, and that entrepreneurial risk taking is financially highly rewarding if things work well and punished by bankruptcy in the worst case. Unlike hundreds of smaller banks, which did not survive the crisis, the rule of (limited) liability was not applicable to larger and highly interconnected banks because of the devastating consequences their bankruptcy would have for the financial system and the societal costs that would have followed from it. In communism you nationalize banks and they go bankrupt, in capitalism, the banks go bankrupt and then you nationalize them, was the realization with which many decision-makers had to live.[3]

Governments in Europe committed up to 39 per cent of GDP and effectively spent 11 per cent of GDP to bail out the banks (European Commission 2011a). The true costs of the crisis are, however, even higher as a result of the economic downturn—the Great Recession—that followed. Public expenses rose because of the trigger of automatic stabilizers, such as unemployment payments, while tax revenues diminished as businesses made lower profits. In the years following a banking crisis, government debt rises by 86 per cent on average (Reinhart and Rogoff 2009, 142). Banking crises thus usually almost double public debt levels. Indeed, in the decade following the global financial crisis, global government debt relative to GDP has more than doubled (Lund et al. 2019).

Evidently, policy-makers would not have committed taxpayers' money to the banks and to economic stimulus packages if what was at stake had not been a central public good. Financial sectors perform vital economic and societal functions. They provide the payment system, which allows salaries to be paid into one's bank account every month and enables us to withdraw cash on (still some) street corners. Financial sectors manage the monetary wealth of our societies. Pension funds play an important role in old age provision, and insurance companies provide protection against various hazards of life by managing compensation funds. Financial sectors contribute to economic growth by financing investments and assuming part of the entrepreneurial

---

[3] Peer Steinbrück, German finance minister at that time, reported that a little note containing this observation circulated among decision-makers in an international meeting on the crisis (Steinbrück 2010, 169).

risk. If, from one day to the next, the functionality of the financial infrastructure was severely hampered, parts of public life would come to a standstill. Financial sectors and public authority ultimately are—and have always been—closely intertwined (e.g. Calomiris and Haber 2014; Gerschenkron 1962; Zysman 1983).

1.2 The contours of the post-crisis reforms

The Great Recession did lead to considerable reformatory efforts. In autumn 2008, in the immediate aftermath of the financial meltdown, the G20 Forum of heads of government and states was created—a new format to discuss and to coordinate financial issues at the highest political level. The institutional architecture for financial regulation and supervision was modified on various levels, creating new institutions, such as financial stability councils, and strengthening existing ones. At the global level, the Financial Stability Board was created, an upgraded version of its predecessor. In the United States, the Consumer Financial Protection Bureau was established amongst others. Within the European Union, a systemic risk board was implemented, and the Lamfalussy Committees were transformed into regulatory agencies.

Substantially, the global G20 reform agenda left hardly any area of finance aside (see G20 2008, 2009, 2010). Banks, credit rating agencies, clearing houses, hedge funds, stock exchange operators, and operators of trading platforms all faced regulatory and supervisory changes. Accounting standards were modified and various financial products and practices, such as derivatives and asset-securitization, were reformed. A financial transaction tax, stricter rules on executive compensation, and the prohibition of certain forms of speculation were discussed. Existing regulations, such as capital requirements, were tightened, new regulatory principles, such as liquidity rules or macroprudential regulation, were added, and even structural reforms, such as ring fencing, the purpose of which is to lower the risk of regulatory arbitrage and the exploitation of regulatory loopholes, were envisaged (Haldane et al. 2010).

In addition to the internationally coordinated reform efforts, action was taken at the national level. Some governments decided to introduce bank levies to make sure that the banks contributed collectively to pay off the financial burden they had caused. This was, for instance, the case in Germany (Bankenabgabe) or in France and the United Kingdom with an additional one-year tax. Governments also decided at least on some aspects, to go beyond the reforms that had been agreed upon internationally. The British rules on ring fencing and the Volcker rule on speculative investments in the United States are both examples for how governments defined stricter boundaries for the activities banks may pursue within one legal entity in the future.

The domestic response to the crisis was, however, not limited to the adoption of new financial sector fees and regulatory reforms that result from highly technical and complex discussions among financial experts and regulators behind closed doors. The depth of the crisis, the various dysfunctionalities of the pre-crisis financial architecture revealed by it, and the huge costs it had created for taxpayers, and thus for generations of ordinary citizens, led to broader political and societal discussions on the purpose of finance and its place within the domestic economic and societal order. What conclusions have been drawn from the crisis beyond the highly technical discussions in regulatory and supervisory fora and what was their impact on shaping reform outputs?

Contrary to the global regulatory reform agenda, which dealt with fundamental, encompassing principles of regulation and supervision, domestic discussions tended to focus on the national financial sector's behaviour in the years prior to and during the crisis. Beyond regulators and supervisors, these discussions involved other societal forces more directly, including parliamentarians and representatives of the business associations. Looking at the conclusions drawn from the crisis on the future of banking in France and Germany—two major European economies where banks play an important economic role—we will see how strikingly different these debates were, depending on the domestic experience of the crisis. If we want to understand the impact of the crisis and the conclusions drawn from it, it is necessary to broaden our view and take this facet of the crisis response into account.

1.3 Lessons learnt?

Despite the regulatory effervescence and the breadth of the reform options discussed, the reforms actually implemented in response to the crisis have failed to meet the expectations of many. Compared to the rhetoric of change, the new rules have been marked by 'limited ambitions' (Mügge and Stellinga 2010) and a 'status quo orientation' (Helleiner 2014). A 'business as usual' approach has often prevailed, leading to marginal (Hellwig 2010 on banking) or incremental adjustments (Moschella and Tsingou 2013) and 'symbolic, but largely ineffective, reforms' (Rixen 2013). Many observers warned about the risk of 'wasting a crisis' (Froud et al. 2010), observing the 'strange non-death' of the pre-crisis intellectual—or ideological—foundations (Crouch 2011; similarly Schmidt and Thatcher 2013).

The lack of reform ambition was attributed to the facts that the power of the financial industry persisted because the locus of authority on economic thinking was unchanged (Blyth 2013, 211). Elite ideas about the centrality of a large financial sector were unchallenged (Bell and Hindmoor 2014b) and the club-like elite networks, in which major decisions were made, were still in place (Tsingou 2014, 2015). An alternative explanation holds that competing technocratic and political elites could not agree on a shared diagnosis of what had to be done (Engelen et al. 2011). Some have come to conclude that the recurrence of crisis is inevitable in the light of the adjustments made (Kay 2010, 233).

Comparing the post-crisis responses to those implemented in the aftermath of the Great Depression, Barry Eichengreen (2015) argues that encompassing regulatory change became the victim of effective crisis management by preventing the worst from happening in terms of social misery. In a similar vein, Renate Mayntz (2012b, 25 f.) explains that limited change was due to the fact that '[n]othing short of a popular revolution' would have been necessary in order to bring about radical change—too intrinsically entrenched are the processes of financialization and credit-based growth with the institutions of western capitalist democracies.

If fundamental, radical change was out of reach, what can explain the adjustments that were actually made? Do crises lead to any form of social learning, that is a process that prompts the adjustment of the so-called 'rules of the game' in the light of better and more appropriate knowledge or information? Or is the idea of learning the lessons from a crisis no more than a well-cherished illusion because the monetary strength of the financial industry translates into political power, which in turn prevents any form of true learning if it goes against the financial interests of the big transnational players whose financial capacities easily outreach those of many states? In other words, is crisis politics—as politics in general—only about powering or is there at least some room for true learning?

Limited change in response to a major crisis may incline us to respond to this question in the affirmative. On closer inspection, however, the answer is more complex than the famous dichotomy of powering versus puzzling (Heclo 1974) suggests. On the one hand, power can operate through different mechanisms—it can, for instance, operate on the level of intellectual discourses and worldviews or, alternatively, 'buy' regulatory decisions—while on the other hand, social learning is difficult to detect. Given the complexity of the financial system, the limits of human cognition, and the contingency of human behaviour, the process of learning from a crisis is unavoidably socially constructed. The answer to the question of the drivers of the post-crisis reforms therefore requires thorough empirical research that deals with the different aspects and facets of the crisis responses and the identification of the causal mechanisms that have led to their adoption.

Focusing on the conclusions that have been drawn from the crisis in both France and Germany, this book shows that a financial power perspective is insufficient in accounting for them. Social learning actually did occur, and its nature, its substance, and its effect on the subsequent policy-making process explain the policy outcomes observed. The reforms priorities identified regarding the future role of the banks resonated with widely shared crisis perceptions. This form of learning is not a pure cognitive process that takes place in closed-shop events among top financial experts. Rather, it is a social process that involves a revision or updating of common-sense knowledge, of what is taken for granted regarding the functioning of the economy and future developments among larger societal groups.

1.4 Negotiating the future of banking

What conclusions have been drawn from the Great Recession regarding the future of banks, institutions that have a long-standing reputation as being 'more dangerous than standing armies' (Thomas Jefferson)? Banks are an essential part of any modern financial system because of the specific functions they fulfil and the services they offer. They play a central role in the provision of a payment system and are usually essential to the transmission of monetary politics through their access to the central bank rediscounting facilities. In addition, banks are a special type of financial intermediary because they create money by issuing debt claims on themselves when they lend money (Bossone 1999, 12).

One of the reasons that may have contributed to Jefferson's distrust of the banks, despite the essential economic functions they fulfil, is their vulnerability to crises and the resulting societal costs. Banks engage in maturity transformation, transforming short-term financial resources—deposits in the traditional view—into long-term credit. They transform, in other words, liquid resources into stable resources with a longer maturity bearing considerable economic risks with this form of financial intermediation because of the devastating consequences the diminishing of trust levels in a bank's solvency—or liquidity—can have. If this is the case, a bank run can cause a bank's bank(!)ruptcy[4] even if the rumour was wrong in the first place. When customers massively withdraw their savings because they fear the freezing of their bank accounts because of the bank's shutdown, this can actually lead to a self-fulfilling prophecy and only be stopped—or avoided in the first place—if a liquid third party, such as the public hand, steps in, guaranteeing the concerned bank's liabilities.

During the crisis, several banks—and market segments as a whole—saw bank run-like movements. In September 2007, the British mortgage bank Northern Rock saw a depositor run, following refinancing problems on the capital markets and the granting of an emergency loan by the Bank of England.[5] In March 2008, the US-American investment bank Bear Stearns came under pressure. When rumours spread that the bank was unable to meet its payment obligations because of its maturity spread combined with high leverage, its capital base dropped drastically. Bear Stearns would have filed for bankruptcy if the Fed had not stepped in, organizing the bailout. With the loss of confidence generated by the bankruptcy of Lehman Brothers, the subprime crisis turned into a fully-fledged systemic liquidity crisis. In order to both prevent further runs and to defreeze the capital markets, central banks stepped in and governments in Europe extended their public guarantees.

While banks are an integral part of any modern financial system, they perform a special economic role in many of continental Europe's intermediated economies. Many businesses, especially smaller ones, strongly depend on bank credit in order to fund their activities, holding lower levels of other forms of debt. While debt securities made up only about 11 per cent of all debt liabilities of non-financial corporations in the Euro area in 2005, their share amounted to 27 per cent in the United Kingdom and to 39 per cent in the United States (ECB 2007, 17). The special role of banking in Europe not only translates into a higher share of credit-based funding, it has also come with a specific funding culture—relationship banking—that relies—to varying degrees—on close long-term relations between banks and their customers (Keller 2019).

---

[4] The word bankruptcy goes back to Italian *banca rotta*, meaning that the money dealer's table was broken. It is said to refer to an old custom that breaks the bench of an illiquid money dealer, but this may only be a figure of speech without a corresponding actual practice. https://www.etymonline.com/word/bankrupt.

[5] In that sense, Northern Rock does not conform the model of the classic bank run, because the run occurred *after* the announcement of public aid (Shin 2009).

The German banks have traditionally been the closest to the ideal type of a bank-based financial system with high levels of bank intermediation and an active participation of the large universal banks in corporate decisions via strategic shareholdings (Beyer 2002; Beyer and Höppner 2003). While the dense network of financial participations between the big banks and the German industrial corporations has largely imploded since the late 1990s, many banks have maintained close relations with their customers (Keller 2019). France, continental Europe's second largest economy, also opted for a bank-based financial system after the Second World War. When the banks were privatized from the 1980s onwards, the building of a form of relational capitalism was encouraged by the French authorities, before it also dissolved.

Banking has, as these examples show, undergone major changes over the past decades and these changes contributed to the build-up and the depth of the Great Recession. Banks were, indeed, at the very centre of the financial crisis. Changes in their business models from classic bank lending and relationship banking towards market-based and transaction-oriented forms and the ominous links they had established to what has become known as the shadow banking sector made them vulnerable to movements in the markets and triggered the subprime crisis in the first place (Hardie and Howarth 2013b). High bank leverage, that is little equity capital in relation to a bank's overall activities, contributed to the banks' vulnerability and implied high risks for third parties when the turmoil began, while the owners of the banks, mostly shareholders, only had relatively little 'skin in the game'.

Finally, the high degrees of interconnectedness among major banks, mutually lending to each other on a short-term basis, greatly contributed to the propagation and the depth of the crisis with the freezing of the interbank market. In autumn 2008, the equity price of the major global banks had fallen by 50 per cent, equalling a market loss of roughly 640 billion US dollars (Haldane et al. 2010, 88). In the light of these shortcomings, bank reforms included three broader areas: bank resolution, bank structure, and the regulatory and supervisory treatment of bank activities via new rules on bank capital, bank liquidity, and bank leverage (Quaglia and Spendzharova 2017).

Given the tremendous losses banks incurred during the crisis and the massive public support schemes taxpayers had to shoulder in order to stabilize the banks, did politicians and regulators really care about the fate of their banks? How far did they go—or feel obliged to go—in their search for financial stability and the avoidance of future bank bailouts that were so costly for taxpayers? Did the French and the German governments decide to implement measures in favour of financial disintermediation that would make their economy less dependent on the banks in the future in order to avoid such a situation from happening again? Or did they stick to their banks because of the prominent role they have always had, a lack of experience with alternatives, or bank lobbying influence?

The comparison of French and German crisis responses leads to a puzzling observation: Even though bank-dependence was relatively high in both countries and even though both were considerably affected by the financial crisis, the lessons learned from the crisis collectively and the adjustments made as a reaction to them differed significantly. Focusing on both French and German participation in international and European banking reforms— Basel III and the CRR-CRDIV—and the domestic responses to the crisis, the book shows how different both the interpretation of the crisis and the subsequent policy responses were. While both followed a rather similar logic when participating in global banking reforms, taking into account fundamental interests of their banks, they developed diametrically opposed approaches towards the future role of the banks in their respective financial systems. Whereas France pushed for greater independence from the banks by strengthening financial disintermediation and non-bank intermediation, Germany sought to strengthen classic bank intermediation, based on the three-pillar banking system.

Depending on the policy setting in which they were articulated, and the specific socio-economic context in which they emerged, the conclusions drawn from the crisis were remarkably different. No consensus has emerged on whether European economies should be less bank-dependent in the future, despite the high levels of bank-dependence and the costly bank bailouts. This opposition is at the heart of the current debates on banking, and shows that no unified solution has been found, much to the regret of all advocates of a coherent and more resilient European financial architecture. Despite the wealth of analyses and unprecedented efforts to build a unified international reform agenda, learning from the crisis ultimately was a selective and fragmented process.

1.5 The argument in brief

The responses observed in the aftermath of the Great Recession show a pattern that is not easily explained by major existing approaches to the study of political decision-making. On the one hand, theoretical approaches that expected encompassing reforms, leading to path-breaking change were inadequate, as the previous discussion has shown. While the financial crisis had the potential of becoming a critical juncture with lasting legacies for future developments (Pierson 2000), it did not turn out to be the window of opportunity many had expected. On the other hand, approaches that attribute limited regulatory change to the special power of finance (e.g. Kwak 2014; Strange 1988) have their own limits in the post-crisis context: Regulatory capture misses the focus since the cornerstones of the reforms were not decided behind closed doors between regulators and bankers. Cognitive capture is insufficient since there were clear advances in some areas of banking regulation, including macroprudential regulation and the new rules on liquidity and leverage. The same applies to cultural capture: French top bankers are known to have excellent access to political decision-makers because they are all part of the same elite, but despite their access and lobbying power, they were the biggest losers of the French reforms. In turn, structural power arguments can neither explain the lack of support for the large French universal banks nor the favourable outcome for the small regional German savings and cooperative banks.

The problem with 'fundamental change' approaches is that they under-estimate the selectivity that characterized the lessons learnt in response to the crisis. The approach that informs this book takes up this selectivity with a learning-based argument that has implications with respect to the substance of the conclusions that are likely to be drawn from a major crisis and their impact on the subsequent policy-making process. The weakness of 'power of finance' approaches in turn is that they are usually neither sensitive to questions of timing nor to the specific socio-economic context in which reforms are made—both of which proved to be decisive, as this analysis shows.

Identifying the drivers behind the post-crisis reforms compels us to analyse the process leading to their adoption. Nobel Prize winner Robert Shiller (2013) has rightly pointed out that 'once we focus on economic policy, much that is not science comes into play. Politics becomes involved, and political posturing is amply rewarded by public attention.' While Shiller is right to highlight the role of politics in explaining the contours of post-crisis banking reforms, he is probably wrong to reduce it to political posturing and he misses the actual impact the public understanding of the crisis has had on financial sector reforms. As this book shows, the reforms implemented in the aftermath of the global financial crisis can be attributed to the interplay of competition struggles, trade-offs between competing legitimate policy aims, and the selectivity and the nature of social learning.

I argue that the reform priorities pursued in France and Germany in response to the crisis cannot be separated from the specific institutional set-up and socio-economic context in which they were made. Domestic reforms are different from international negotiations. In the process of negotiating banking reforms internationally, French and German regulators paid attention to the impact of the reforms on their domestic banks relative to foreign competitors, which can be attributed to the logic inherent in international negotiations. At the domestic level, the reform priorities identified are difficult to understand without the specific historic socio-economic context in which they emerged: For instance, the overwhelming majority of French businesses are highly bank-dependent because of their small size. Inversely, Germany is the country with the highest number of middle-sized enterprises that could quite easily find alternatives to bank credit. It is difficult to understand from this perspective why France strengthened financial disintermediation and non-bank intermediation whereas Germany supported traditional bank lending.

Financial sector reforms—as any reform that passes parliament—take place in the public sphere and politicians must be able to justify them, especially if the interest in a topic is high. This poses a political risk unless decision-makers can be sure that the reforms will be perceived as appropriate—and this in turn has much to do with whether they resonate with widespread beliefs amongst the broader public. These beliefs can be seen as the wealth of usually unwritten knowledge that informs human behaviour. Like a map, these beliefs give orientation in a complex world. They are influential because people take them for granted as constitutive features of the environment they live in. Individuals can trust them because they are widespread and usually underpinned by formalized dispositions like laws. This in turn furthers faith in them since they cannot be diminished easily.

While these beliefs often appear quite stable in the short run, they do change over time—gradually up to a tipping point in some cases and rupture-like in others. This can be due to societal, scientific, or technological progress, but also, as in the present case, due to a crisis. I call such changes or updates of beliefs moments of *social learning*—social because this process concerns a larger social group, learning because it leads to a reappraisal of the way things are, of what can be taken as a given. Empirically, social learning can be traced through a three-stage process that begins with the questioning of existing beliefs—something was proven wrong, not as expected—the search for a new consensus concerning the implications for the future and, finally, its consolidation through political reforms.

Social learning did occur in France and Germany in response to the crisis, but it was related to different aspects of banking. While new beliefs centred on bank lending in France, they were related to the potential and the risks of market-based banking compared to traditional banking in Germany. These changes can be attributed to the ways in which the crisis led to a questioning of beliefs that were influential and widely shared in the pre-crisis years. In Germany, efforts to modernize the financial sector were ongoing and the conviction that asset securitization was a promising means to boost the banking sector began to spread from the early 2000s onwards, whereas traditional banking organized along the three pillars appeared increasingly outdated. The massive losses incurred by several German banks during the crisis provoked a collective awakening in this regard. This was not the case in France, as financial sector reforms had been made more than a decade earlier, including a—tightly regulated—framework for asset securitization at that time.

In France, in contrast, the early 2000s were characterized by a considerable expansion of bank credit. When the French banks tightened their lending standards in response to the crisis—as did banks everywhere in Europe—this provoked a collective awakening, especially among smaller business owners. The insight that bank credit can be gone from one day to the next and the belief that time for financial disintermediation had come were widely shared in the business community and beyond. In Germany, the crisis did not lead to the same reaction because beliefs on the conditions and the availability of bank lending had changed with a banking crisis in the late 1990s and regulatory changes appearing at the horizon with Basel II—changes that had, as will be shown, largely passed unnoticed in France at that time.

Studying the responses to the financial crisis through the lens of social learning helps us understand both their substance and their selectivity: The lessons drawn from the crisis politically were influenced by the ways in which the crisis was widely perceived. These perceptions must make abstractions from a complex reality, highlighting selectively specific aspects of the crisis at the expense of others, which creates bias. At the same time, the perception of the crisis eases access for interest groups, whose proposals are in line with social learning while hampering it for others. Practically, policies that resonate with social learning and which are supported by a broad 'financing the economy-coalition' have good chances to be adopted.

Overall, the institutional dispositions in place, such as the set-up of the banking sector and the organization of different parts of the financial industry, did have some influence on the ways in which beliefs were questioned and the solutions that were feasible. Nevertheless, the dynamics engendered by social learning are powerful and can overcome the distribution of power built in the institutions in place, leading to developmental paths that are more malleable than many institutionalist analyses suggest. The French and the German crisis responses were different because the patterns of stability and change with respect to the conditions of bank lending and financial sector reform in the decade prior to the crisis were different. The drivers of the reforms only become fully comprehensible by placing politics in time, recognizing how the collectively shared understandings of what specific aspects of the political economy were like and how they would develop in the future changed.

1.6 Methodology and data

The present research is case-oriented, putting 'significant historical outcomes' (Ragin 1987, 11)—multi-level, interrelated adaptation processes as a reaction to the global financial crisis—at its centre. They deserve scholarly attention because of the societal impact they have. France and Germany are continental Europe's most important political economies and they have been key cases for theory building (e.g. Culpepper 2003; Hall 1986; Hall and Soskice 2001b; Immergut 1992; Schmidt 2002; Streeck 2009; Thelen 2004; Zysman 1983). The focus of the analysis is on the identification of the concrete constellation of causes that contributed to the empirical variation of interest—divergent adaption processes within similar settings that cannot sufficiently be explained by existing approaches—building on the in-depth study of two cases. The aim thereby is to generate a precise understanding of the processes at work in each of them by combining cross-case and within-case analysis.

Methodologically speaking, the comparative method is the best practical means to causal inference since experiments, the 'gold standard', are often not applicable to phenomena of interest for social scientists (Schmitter 2008, 276). However, as this route to causal inference, which operates through the intentional choice of differences and similarities among cases in a way to exclude logically the causal role of certain factors (Mill 1882), has increasingly been criticized owing to the imperfections in the set-up of many comparisons (e.g. Lieberson 1991), it is combined with within-case analysis, studying the causal role of different factors and tracing the process through which the differing policy responses came about (e.g. Beach and Pedersen 2013; George and Bennett 2005; Hall 2008).

In the limits of the imperfections any comparison among countries implies, the present set-up can be considered a most similar systems design. In such a setting, the cases analysed vary unexpectedly on an outcome—the responses to the Great Recession—because they are similar on one or several variables one would generally attribute a strong causal role in the study of the phenomenon of interest (Gerring 2007). In the present case, this applies to the economic role of universal banks and bank lending in financing the economy. In this respect, France and Germany have similar political economic orders. The differing crisis responses are a puzzle as they are, as we will see, not easily explained by existing approaches, such as state structure, or bank power.

Despite their idiosyncrasies, the French and the German socio-economic orders share several commonalities: Both are embedded in the various dispositions of European Economic and Monetary Union including banking and financial markets regulation, the Euro and monetary policy, besides certain fiscal policies. Both countries have a strong tradition of governance arrangements that rely on the coordination outside markets—either within privately organized settings or by state authorities (e.g. Hall and Gingerich 2004; Schmidt 2000, 2002). Their financial systems have both been bank-based and universal banks have played an important role in financing the economy. Finally, they both belong to the civic law tradition, which has shaped the functioning of financial sectors, especially regarding the role of financial markets, as a result of lower levels of investor protection (La Porta et al. 1996, 1997).

Empirically, the book builds on descriptive quantitative evidence, document analysis, and 70 mainly face-to-face expert interviews with 84 persons in total. The material collected in the interviews was coded and analysed using the software atlas.ti. The coding scheme was developed semi-inductively starting with broader categories that were identified because of their analytic merit. Their content was systematically cross-checked with other sources of information, including press coverage, official reports, and statistics. The average time of the interviews was about an hour. Both the questionnaire and the individual questions were semi-standardized. One block of questions was similar for all interviewees and dealt with the experience of the financial crisis, the conclusions drawn from it, the positioning of the interviewee's organization on key reforms, and their diagnosis of post-crisis developments. A second set of questions related to the specific expertise of the respective interviewee and the organization (s)he[6] represented. This block covered a broader spectrum of issues, reaching from bank internal management practices to coordination procedures in public administrations.

---

[6] Among the 84 experts I met, 14 were female. In Germany I conducted three interviews with women *only*. In France, this was nine times the case; in two additional cases male assistants represented their female superiors, since the latter were not available on the day of the interview.

Table 1.1 Interviews according to sector affiliation

	France	Germany
Public sector	ACP(R), AMF, Assemblée nationale, Banque de France (6), CDC, Ministère de l'Economie et de la Finance, Oséo, Trésor (3)	BaFin, BMF, BMWi (2), Bundesbank (2), Deutscher Bundestag (2), KfW
Banking sector	FBF (3) 5 individual banks: BNP Paribas (3), Crédit Agricole, Groupe Banque populaire et Caisse d'épargne	BdB, DSGV, BVR (2), VAB, vdp, VÖB 7 individual banks: Commerzbank, Deutsche Bank, DZ Bank (2), Société Générale CIB, one savings and one cooperative bank
Other financial sector	AF2i, AFG, AFIC, ASF, FFSA, Europlace, Finance Innovation	Börse Stuttgart, DAI, Deutsche Börse, GDV, TSI
Corporate sector	AFTE, APCMA, ASMEP-ETI, CGPME, CCIP, Medef, Middlenext	ASU, BDI, DIHK, ZDH, ZGV
Total	37	33

Source: Own elaboration.

Most of the interviews took place between April and December 2013, mainly in Paris, Frankfurt, Stuttgart, and Berlin. Seven of them were conducted by phone. Table 1.1 gives an overview of the distribution according to the interviewees' affiliation. The interview partners worked in the relevant public administrations and political institutions, they represented central employer federations from the financial, the banking, and the business sector, and they worked for individual banks. A complete list of the interviews by organization and division without reference to the interviewed person, in order to guarantee their anonymity, is provided in the appendix.

1.7   Chapter outline

The core of the book is on how the future of banking was negotiated in the aftermath of the global financial crisis, and the reasons behind the choices made. Before coming to this, two chapters lay the groundwork for the subsequent analysis. Chapter 2 studies the adjustment process to financial globalization in the decades prior to the financial crisis. In brief terms, it sketches the emergence of modern finance and the changes financial globalization has brought about. The chapter synthesizes the main characteristics of the French and the German financial sectors and discusses how both adjusted to financial globalization, financial innovation, and increased competition. The chapter shows that despite their institutional specificities, both entered the crisis in a comparable situation when considering the fundamental adjustments made.

Chapter 3 moves on to discuss how these changes have shaped the study of increasingly integrated financial sectors. It summarizes key insights from comparative and international political economy, synthesizes the progress that has been made, and highlights remaining conceptual difficulties. The subsequent sections spell out the ontological foundations and the theoretical building blocks that inform the book's analytic prism of social learning, which is the answer I provide to the difficulties identified in the first part. The chapter closes with the causal chain that underlies the mechanism of social learning. It begins with the collective questioning of the status quo, the realization that at least one taken for granted assumption on the functioning of the economy is no longer deemed valid. This opens up a discursive space, in which a new consensus can emerge. The new consensus then needs to be consolidated through political reforms in order to increase the trust level in it.

With Chapter 4, we enter into the dynamics of the global financial crisis and the reformatory efforts that followed from it. The first of the four empirical chapters gives a brief overview of the origins and the spread of the financial crisis and spells out key elements of the global G20 reform agenda on banking. It discusses the implications of major reform elements on bank capital, liquidity, and leverage for the future of banking. The chapter moves on to analyse how representatives from France and Germany participated in these negotiations. Comparing French and German priorities to the positions of representatives from the United States and the United Kingdom, it shows that representatives from more intermediated financial systems supported bank lending in a specific way. Overall, international negotiations tend to bring a specific pattern of preference formation in favour of the domestic financial sector to the fore, providing a partial explanation as to why regulatory change in response to the crisis was more limited and piecemeal than expected.

Chapter 5 moves on to explore the domestic lessons that were drawn from the crisis in both countries. At this level, the implications of the crisis that were discussed were strongly influenced by the behaviour of the domestic banks prior to and during the crisis. The chapter therefore explores how the French and the German banks were affected by the crisis and it compares the governments' responses. It shows that surprisingly different dynamics developed in both countries, despite an initially rather similar situation.

Whereas the financial crisis became a veritable bank lending crisis in France, in Germany it was primarily perceived as a crisis of Anglo-Saxon finance capitalism and the failure of individual banks' business models that had drifted away from traditional bank lending. The chapter traces the dynamics that brought about the differing understandings of the crisis and the corresponding reform agendas that were derived from it. While the French focus was on strengthening alternatives to bank intermediation, the Germans focused on the opposite: means to strengthen classic bank lending.

With the empirical puzzle spelled out and illustrated by various statements from reports and the author's fieldwork, Chapter 6 explores the pre-crisis developments that triggered the differing reactions. In order to gain analytic leverage, the chapter provides original empirical data that shows why some intuitions on the banks' behaviour during the crisis cannot account for the observed outcome. The second half of the chapter lays out the empirical narratives behind the differing learning processes observed. It does so by systematically comparing and cross-checking the diverging dynamics in the two cases. Simply put, while social learning was about the conditions and the availability of bank lending in France, it was related to the risk and the benefits associated with market-based banking and financial innovation in Germany.

Chapter 7 deals with the final stage of the causal mechanism behind social learning: In order to be successful, its insights need to be consolidated through political reforms. This increases the trust level in the newly found consensus because it adds a formalized component to it. At this stage, the insights of social learning interact more strongly with the formal institutions in place, shaping the concrete policy output. Depending on how successful this final step is, social learning can be more or less consequential in shaping future developments. While the success of the French initiatives ended with the limits of state influence and voluntary self-interested cooperation by various market actors, the coalition in Germany profited from the institutional dispositions in place and even found EU-wide support as the measures fell under European legal competence.

Chapter 8 takes stock of the previous chapters and discusses the findings. It summarizes the book's main argument and examines the nature of social learning with respect to true learning, the institutional dispositions in place, the role of politics, and contingency. The chapter presents additional empirical evidence that confirms the findings in a comparative perspective and tests the validity of the argument by using Bayesian updating. Next, the relevance of social learning is demonstrated by applying it to the US-American and the British crisis responses and to reforms of bank structure from a comparative perspective. The chapter closes with a brief discussion of the theoretical merits of the social learning approach developed in this book. It highlights its contribution to ideational scholarship in institutional analysis, public policy-making, and economic sociology and spells out promising areas for future research.

The book concludes by discussing the policy implications of the findings for the future management of the financial sector and banking crises (Chapter 9). It highlights major developments in banking since the financial crisis and discusses the nature of the political responses to it. The insights from the previous chapters relate to the selective reconstruction of the crisis and its consequences for political reform, competitive concerns, competing policy aims, and a bias of contemporary capitalist democracies towards the promise of future growth. Given the limits of financial regulation and the expectation of future bank bailouts, the chapter encourages a broadening of the fora in which financial knowledge is constructed.

2

Adjustments to financial globalization

In many ways, the Great Recession can be seen as an outgrowth of the process of financial globalization, which has gathered pace from the 1970s onwards. Since then, the framework in which financial institutions operate has changed dramatically. Overall, the change has been one from relatively autonomous, predominantly national settings with relatively high levels of state control over the flow of money towards a much more integrated and significantly liberalized financial environment where banks and other financial institutions have many more business opportunities. Financial globalization can be understood as a process that leads to both transnational market integration and the harmonization of key regulatory stipulations designed to (partially) level the playing field.

On the monetary side, the emergence of financial globalization was triggered by the rise of offshore foreign currency markets, the so-called Eurodollar markets, and the end of the Bretton Woods regime of coordinated, fixed exchange rates. On the technical side, the process was fuelled by the development of new information and communication technologies and rapid product innovation, leading to new financial practices that were increasingly computer- and algorithm-based. On the regulatory side, a significant number of barriers to competition and constraints on business practices were abolished with the so-called financial services revolution (e.g. Coleman 1996; Helleiner 1994b; Moran 1991; Underhill 1997).

As a consequence of these processes, banks and other financial institutions increasingly entered into competition with each other in a growing array of activities and the realization grew that the issues of regulation and competition were 'inextricably linked' (Kapstein 1994, 104–5). Regulatory harmonization became necessary in order to level the playing field and avoid regulatory arbitrage among global financial institutions. As a reaction, an increasing number of international organizations and private bodies were created, endowed with the task of elaborating global standards. In 1974, the Basel committee of central bankers, the global standard setter for banking regulation, was founded. Various other global standard setting bodies

Financial Crises and the Limits of Bank Reform: France and Germany's Ways Into and Out of the Great Recession.
Eileen Keller, Oxford University Press (2021). © Eileen Keller. DOI: 10.1093/oso/9780198870746.003.0002

followed, dealing with accounting standards (1973), securities markets (1983), and the insurance business (1994).

Within the European Union, the integration of financial markets was realized as a part of the European Single Market Program and eased by the introduction of the single currency. The liberalization of financial services was boosted by the White Paper on the Completion of the Internal Market in 1985. The process of financial integration was relaunched with the Financial Services Action Plan in 1999 (Mügge 2010, 53, 93; Schildbach 2008, 12; on the history of European financial integration also see Quaglia 2010; Story and Walter 1997). Within the European Union, so-called European passports were introduced for a growing array of financial services. With these passports, financial institutions that have obtained a licence for a certain business in one country can offer this service within all EU member states without prior authorization by the host country regulator as long as certain requirements are met.

The following sections deal with the implications these changes have had for both the French and the German financial sector and their banks in particular. In what ways did both adjust to the new market environment? How did banking develop from relatively autonomous national towards highly integrated and significantly liberalized financial settings? Have French and German banks lost their specificities during this process and to what extent has this changed their business models? In order to gain a better understanding of the adjustments made up until the financial crisis, the following sections trace the emergence and the development of both banking sectors from their origins in the late nineteenth century. In a next step, the implications of the financial services revolution are discussed. Finally, their effect on banking is estimated by looking at a series of indicators regarding the banking business and the banks' role in financing the economy.

The chapter shows that France and Germany have converged from different starting points, following different trajectories towards a similar form of universal banking and a comparable role for the banks in financing the economy despite the persistence of highly different configurations of their respective banking sectors. While the importance of financial markets has increased considerably in both countries, classic bank intermediation has remained a more important activity for the banks in both countries than is the case for banks in what are traditionally considered market-based financial systems.

2.1 The development of banking in France and Germany

The idea of banking is old. Rich individuals and organizations that specialized in financing operations emerged from the thirteenth century onwards in merchant circles. Their main purpose then was to finance international trade. These institutions took over additional functions, such as deposit taking, the issuance of bills, and the granting of credit, successively. Up until the nineteenth century, the development was one of gradual territorial as well as social inclusion. By the late nineteenth century, encompassing banking sectors had emerged in many western countries, fuelled by the industrialization process (Braithwaite and Drahos 2000, 90–1; also see Grossman 2010; Kindleberger 1984).

While the general pattern of inclusion and diversification is true for the development of banking in general, the historical trajectories and the specific constellations of banks and other financial services providers that have emerged in different countries are remarkably different. The history of German banking in the twentieth century was marked by an incremental adjustment process that was driven by the competitive dynamics between three different banking sectors—the private, the cooperative, and the public banks. Liquid financial markets have only played a secondary role, as the German banks used to be highly integrated in the productive sector, holding and managing equity participations in addition to the granting of credit.

The French banking sector, by contrast, underwent greater changes and its history was full of discontinuities as '[t]here was no smooth evolution of institutions and structures that could be traced from the present back to the origins of capitalism' (Loriaux 1991, 98). Whereas the French stock exchange played an important role in the nineteenth century—in 1914, Paris was the second most important marketplace in the world after London (Hautcœur et al. 2011, 10)—financial markets only played a limited role in the early post-war decades. Changes not only apply to the relative role of banks and financial markets, but also to the set-up of the French banking sector. Overall, there was a switch from separate banking in the late nineteenth century to state-dominated banking after 1945, with separate banking being structurally largely maintained, and then to universal banking from the 1980s onwards.

2.1.1   France: From separate over state to universal banking

The development of a more encompassing banking system in France goes back to the nineteenth century. At that time, the banking sector was largely composed of the *haute banque* and small, local *banquiers*. The former consisted of roughly 20 rich and politically influential families, like the Rothschilds, who invested their private fortune in industrial corporations, public debt titles, and international trade. The local bankers, on their part, offered loans to craftsmen and smaller local businesses, refinancing their activities with the local branches of the French central bank. In the second half of the nineteenth century, the big French banking groups began to develop. In 1859, the Société générale de crédit industriel et commercial was founded; Crédit Lyonnais followed in 1863. Compared to their German counterparts, the French commercial banks were, however, more reluctant in making long-term commitments to non-financial corporations (NFCs). From the 1880s onwards, the banks focused on deposit taking and the granting of short-term credit (Bouvier 1973, cited in Pastré 2006, 70). By the end of the nineteenth and at the beginning of the twentieth century, the cooperative and mutual banks (*caisses régionales* and *banques populaires*) were created in order to end the shortage in the supply of credit many farmers, small firms, and craftsmen suffered from (Plessis 2003; also Thiveaud 1997, 27–44).[1]

After 1945, the French authorities opted for a bank-based, but state-dominated form of financial intermediation. It was informed by an overall statist approach to the steering of the economy that characterized the first decades after the war (Schmidt 2002). The political elites sought to promote the structural transformation of the economy in that way, privileging state interventions over the free play of market forces (also see Hall 1986; Hayward 1986; Loriaux 1991). With respect to banking, the measures taken to achieve this aim included price, credit, and exchange controls, the nationalization of the large French banks, the control of funds for investment, interest rate subsidies, and state support for industrial restructuring (Cerny 1989, 170–1). In order to achieve this large-scale modernization process, a politico-economic regime was established that was characterized by the close integration of the financial sector, banks in particular, in an

---

[1] Mutual banks offer their services only to members who hold a share in the bank. Cooperative banks are subjected to the cooperative principle of 'one person, one vote', but they may accept non-members among their clients (also see Noyer 1990, 38).

overall pattern of monetary and industrial policies, which became known as the overdraft economy (*économie d'endettement*).

The financing of the economy was largely credit-based in that period.[2] The allocation of credit itself was informed by political priorities. Certain banks that were close to the state—the Caisses de Dépôt et de Consignations (CDC), Caisses d'Epargne, the Crédit National, the Crédit Foncier de France, and the post offices—had to deposit parts of their funds with the Treasury as a part of the Treasury circuit. These funds were used to finance state deficits and industrial investments, often at subsidized interest rates (*crédits bonnifiés*; Loriaux 1991, 149–52). Regulated savings schemes allowed certain banks to collect tax-exempt deposits, which were transferred to the CDC and allocated according to government priorities (Pastré 2006, 81). With the permanent establishment of quantitative credit restrictions in 1971 (*encadrement du crédit*), the state defined global as well as bank-level targets for credit growth.

Regarding the allocation of credit, the relevant public authorities defined investment priorities by selectively excluding certain firms and economic sectors from the lending restrictions which were imposed on the banks (Loriaux 1991, 24–45). Competition in the banking sector was further restricted by price administrations, the existence of cartels, and other legal restrictions. Prior to the reforms of the 1980s, more than 30 different legal statuses and more than 200 privileged procedures for the allocation of credit coexisted in France (Cassou 2001, 14, n. 3).

In 1983, in the context of deteriorated macroeconomic conditions, the changing international monetary order, and the deepening of European integration, the socialist government under President François Mitterrand radically changed its political course and decided to introduce a financial regime in which securities markets would play a more important role and where banks would be more strongly subjected to market forces (Coleman 1996, 107; for a broad overview see Uterwedde 1988). State control over credit was dismantled successively, many of the subsidized credit regimes were phased out. The banks were re-privatized in two waves between 1986 and 1988, and from 1993 onwards (Loriaux 1991, 218–27).[3]

---

[2] For a more extended, excellent account of corporate financing in the age of the overdraft economy see Loriaux (1991).

[3] The nationalization of the French banking sector between 1945 and 1982 is not described in detail as there is good reason to assume that given the overall omnipresence of the state, state ownership as such did not significantly alter the conditions under which the banks operated in their everyday business. The government was indeed reluctant to go beyond changing the ownership structures and the banks were granted the freedom to operate like private banks (Fabra 1985, 173; Lacoue-Labarthe 2001, 46). Fabra concludes that '[i]t is quite possible to argue that on a very

Structurally speaking, the banking system of the early post-war period was relatively fragmented. The laws of 1941 and 1945 distinguished between, firstly, deposit taking institutions (*banques de dépôts*) which were allowed to take sight deposits but were restricted in their ability to discount short-term commercial papers and to hold equity participations in NFCs above 10 per cent; secondly, merchant banks (*banques d'affaires*) which could only take time deposits and were active in corporate financing; thirdly, banks that were allowed to offer loans with a maturity of two years or longer (*banques de crédit de moyen et de long terme*) and, hence, were capable of sustaining industrial development; and, fourthly, other financial institutions (*établissements financiers*) which offered loans but did not collect deposits (Loriaux 1991, 111–12; Noyer 1990, 7; Thiveaud 1997, 45–6).

The Décrets Debré from 1966/1967, the first major banking reform after 1945, allowed for some de-specialization of the different banking groups and, hence, for some degree of competition among the deposit taking institutions and the merchant banks. The former were allowed to hold equity stakes of up to 20 per cent in NFCs and to collect deposits with a maturity of two years and more. The latter were allowed to collect deposits. In addition, bank lending rates were deregulated and bank branching was liberalized. Cartel-like arrangements on deposit interest rates, by contrast, remained in place (Coleman 1993, 130–1; Lacoue-Labarthe 2001, 14; Story and Walter 1997, 192; Thiveaud 1997, 49–50).

With the Banking Act of 1984—in many respects the regulatory fundament of the current banking system—many dispositions that supported the segmentation of the banking sector and the restrictions of competition in the credit market were abolished and universal banking was introduced. The Banking Act built on an encompassing definition of credit institutions, including not only the different banking groups—the savings, mutual, and cooperative banks, which had until then not been included in the regulatory parameter of the commercial banks (so-called AFB-banks[4])—but also financial holding companies, money market brokers, finance houses, and securities firms, leading to a harmonized set of regulatory and supervisory stipulations for all of them (Noyer 1990, 36–48; Pastré 2006, 44). The savings banks were deregulated and special state subsidies abolished. From 1987

---

fundamental issue—the relationship between the lender and his clients, the borrowers—the change has not been of major significance' (Fabra 1985, 173).

[4] AFB-banks are the French commercial banks which used to be represented by the Association Française des Banques.

onwards they were allowed to engage in corporate lending (Coleman 1996, 110–11; Lambert 1996).

With respect to the role of the banks in financing the economy, the Banking Act opted for some form of insider control, incentivizing banks to hold equity stakes in NFCs. The intention of the then finance minister, Jacques Delors, and Jean-Yves Haberer, the Director of the Trésor, the prestigious French unit for economic planning and decision-making, was to establish a universal banking model that paralleled the German one regarding the closeness of bank–industry relations (Coleman 1996, 110; Story and Walter 1997, 200–1). The law reduced more obstacles to universal banking, allowing banks to engage in foreign exchange operations, securities related activities, asset and portfolio management as well as leasing (Coleman 1993, 132). With the privatizations between 1986 and 2002, the banks were encouraged to take over large parts of the equity participations in NFCs the French state had held until then (also see Coleman 1996, 111–12).

The transition from the state-led financial system in which competition among the banks was strongly circumscribed by state regulations towards a more liberalized financial system was associated with considerable adjustment costs. The French banking system was strongly hit by a banking crisis in the early 1990s. The crisis was linked to the bursting of a bubble on the commercial real estate markets and the global recession, which hit large parts of the world economy in the years following the 1987 Krach. The crisis hit the French commercial banks strongest, but had a rather limited impact on the cooperative banks as they had maintained a strong deposit base and invested less in mortgages (Aglietta 1997, 2).

According to the Lambert Report submitted by the Committee on Finances to the Senate, the severity of the crisis and its durability were due to the fact that the necessary adjustments, such as market-exit of non-competitive banks and bank restructuring, which should follow from increased competition were not made (Lambert 1996). In the light of increased competition, many banks focused on increasing their market share at the expense of pricing the credit risk correctly. Many banks did not pay enough attention to profitability and they often offered loans at rates that did not price the associated risk appropriately. As a consequence, middle- and long-term interest rates on bank credit were below those usually paid on the capital markets (Lambert 1996; similarly Conseil National du Crédit 1995, 92)—a clear sign that the pricing was not appropriate. The crisis fuelled the necessary adjustments and the French banks became more profitable.

2.1.2   Germany: The universalization of universal banking

The origins of the specific structural configuration of the German banking sector, the three pillars consisting of a commercial (*Kredit- or Privatbanken*), a cooperative (mainly *Volks- und Raiffeisenbanken*), and a public banking sector (nowadays *Sparkassen* and *Landesbanken*) go back to the age of industrialization in the nineteenth century. The three different banking types developed gradually in response to the specific financial needs of different types of debtors. The commercial banks developed out of the private banks and provided the funds needed to finance large-scale industrialization processes. The cooperative banks responded to the financial needs of craftsmen and small entrepreneurs by pooling resources, guided by the principle of mutual self-help. The savings banks collected deposits, they granted loans and financed the public sector (Deeg 1999, 33–5; also see Edwards and Ogilvie 1996; Guinnane 2002; Pohl 1976, 1982; Shonfield 1965).

In contrast to the savings and the cooperative banks, the German commercial banks were universal banks from the outset and as such involved in both investment banking and the granting of credit to the real economy.[5] They only started taking deposits on a larger scale from the 1880s onwards (Edwards and Ogilvie 1996, 432). The large universal banks were closely interwoven with and had a significant influence on the productive sector. They were represented on the supervisory board of listed non-financial joint-stock corporations either because of their own equity participations or those of their customers, whom they represented via so-called proxy votes (Edwards and Ogilvie 1996, 428–30). The big universal banks were considered to have played a strategic role in the German industrialization process and were unparalleled in their role as financial intermediaries at that time (Gerschenkron 1962; Zysman 1983; sceptical: Edwards and Ogilvie 1996; Guinnane 2002).[6]

---

[5] There is, however, not only one way in which a universal bank can be organized. The highest degree of integration would allow within the same legal entity bank, securities, insurance, and other financial activities. The German model only allows for a joint exercise of banking and securities activities; insurance and mortgage related activities, by contrast, need to be organized in separate subsidiaries (Story and Walter 1997, 123).

[6] The authors argue that the role of German universal banks providing funding to industrial joint-stock companies and exerting control over business decisions has been overestimated in their importance for German industrialization—for the period up to 1914 at least. They highlight the role of the savings and the cooperative banks, which financed the economic activities of farmers, craftsmen, and small businesses, the importance of public companies in railway construction, and the availability of internal sources of funding (Edwards and Ogilvie 1996; Guinnane 2002).

At the beginning of the twentieth century, competition between the different banking groups in the German banking system was relatively low.[7] The cooperative banks were constrained to serve the interests of their members. The savings banks followed a public interest mission and were only allowed to perform the tasks they were authorized for by law. Both the cooperative and the savings banks profited from tax benefits, but they were in return more restricted in their business activities. In addition, the public banks profited from a maintenance obligation according to which the state intervenes in case of liquidity problems (*Anstaltslast*) and a guarantee obligation by which the state is liable (*Gewährträgerhaftung*; see also Hackethal 2004, 78). Intra-group competition has also been rather low for both the savings and the cooperative banks as they usually operate on the basis of territorially segmented markets (Deeg 1999).

The segmented structure of the market for banking services was contested throughout the twentieth century, leading to fierce political struggles over the services that any of the three banking groups was allowed to offer and the regulatory settings required to allow for fair competition among them (Deeg 1999, 37–42). On the one hand, the cooperative banks and the public banks challenged the limitations of their business practices. The private banks on their side were increasingly opposed to the privileges of the banks belonging to the other two banking groups and the prohibition of taking them over (Deeg 1999).

During the twentieth century, many legal restrictions that maintained the distinctiveness of the three banking groups were abolished and the banks began to compete directly for clients on a growing array of financial services. In 1908, the savings banks were allowed to offer checking and payment accounts (Guinnane 2002, 88; Staats 2006, 32). Legal changes in 1915 and 1921 allowed them to underwrite and to sell securities. With these modifications, they were put on equal footing with the universal banks regarding their activities (Guinnane 2002, 88–9). In 1971, the savings bank group founded the DGZ International, which became the fourth German bank to operate in Luxemburg. The aim was to strengthen the engagement of the group on the Euromarkets.[8] In 1975, the central institution of the cooperative sector (Deutsche Genossenschaftskasse) abandoned its status as a public business

---

[7] For a more extended, excellent description of the development of the German banking sector up to the 1990s, see Deeg (1999).

[8] Homepage of the savings bank group: https://www.dekabank.de/db/de/konzern/geschichte/geschichte.jsp, accessed 14 July 2013.

development bank to become more flexible for mergers and engagements abroad (Stappel 2010).

Direct competition between the banking groups was further fuelled by the respective organizational structure of both the savings bank and the cooperative banking sector. Both are organized in financial federations (*Finanzverbünde*) with a relatively high degree of group integration. In order to profit from scale effects, certain services have been pooled within special entities which belong to the group. This allowed the individually much smaller savings and cooperative banks to compete with the big universal banks on services like investment banking, investment funds, and foreign activities (also see Deeg 1999).

With the lifting of restrictions regarding the activities the savings and cooperative banks were allowed to pursue, certain tax reliefs they profited from no longer seemed justified and were dismantled successively (Deeg 1999, 49). As a consequence, but also as a result of government efforts to increase competition and the widespread willingness to counter the economic power of the commercial banks, competition among the banking groups increased steadily (Deeg 1999, 19, 31, 49, 51).

All in all, the three-pillar structure of the German banking sector has proven to be remarkably resilient and it has had an important effect on the functioning of the German market for banking services, even though it was contested throughout the twentieth century. The savings banks were not privatized, contrary to the developments in many European countries during the 1990s.[9] Even the agreement in 2001 between the European Commission and the German government to end state guarantees for the public banking sector by 2005 because they were deemed incompatible with European competition law did not fundamentally alter the three-pillar structure of the German banking sector in the years prior to the financial crisis.[10]

Figure 2.1 illustrates the overall stability of the pillar structure in terms of balance sheet totals regarding the German market. The commercial banks lost some market share, from 38 per cent in 1950 to 23 per cent in 1967. In 2012, their market share amounted to 39 per cent again. The cooperative banks increased their market share from 9–10 per cent in the 1950s to 17 per cent in the 1980s. In 2012, their balance sheet volume amounted to

---

[9] In France, the savings banks were mutualized in 1999; in Sweden and Italy, the savings banks were privatized from 1992 onwards and in 1998, respectively (Polster 2004a, 2004b, 2005).

[10] On the dispute between the European Commission and the German government see Grossman (2006) and Seikel (2011, 2013). The effects of the decision were laid bare by the global financial crisis and the affectedness of several Landesbanken (see Chapter 5).

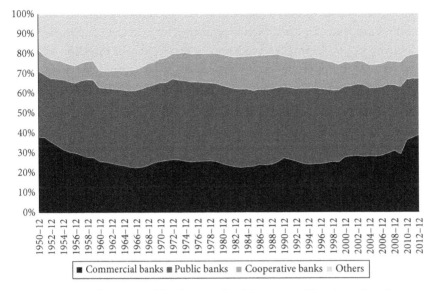

Figure 2.1 Development of the German banking groups (fraction of total bank assets)

Source: Bundesbank data, balance sheet totals, own calculations. Assets and liabilities of banks in Germany, excluding central bank and money market funds. The commercial banks include foreign banks. Other financial institutions include Realkreditinstitute, Bausparkassen, Banken mit Sonderaufgaben.

12 per cent. The public banks increased their market share from 33 per cent in 1950 to 40 per cent in the 1970s. In 2012, their market share had fallen to 28 per cent (Bundesbank data, own calculations).

2.2 Financial market reforms in bank-based financial systems

One of the most important developments in finance from the 1980s onwards concerned the freeing of financial markets from various restrictions. Financial markets were desegmented and liberalized, deregulated and modernized. This revolutionary overhaul began in the United States and led to a sweeping initiative of reforms in many European countries, fuelled by a 'competitive deregulation and liberalization dynamic' (Helleiner 1994a, 302). The so-called financial services revolution led to 'the most extensive legislative overhaul of financial services policy since the Great Depression, if not the greatest set of changes ever' (Coleman 1996, 2).

Within Europe, the financial services revolution reached Great Britain first. In 1986, the British 'Big bang' led to the liberalization of the London Stock

Exchange in one fell swoop, abolishing exchange controls and fixed brokerage commissions, and admitting foreign securities firms at the London exchange (Moran 1988, 1991). Smaller 'big bangs' and steps in this direction followed in many other European financial centres and Japan. The modifications made in many European countries in this period included the dismantling of restrictions to investment services, the admission of foreigners to stock exchanges, the abolishment of stamp fees, and the introduction of new financial intermediaries, financial products, and market segments (for detailed country accounts of this period, see Busch 2008; Cerny 1989; Coleman 1996; Lütz 2002; Moran 1991; Underhill 1997; Vogel 1996).

These changes were considered to be particularly consequential for economies like France and Germany, where financial intermediation by the banks had played an important role in the post-war decades. With the liberalization of financial markets, bank credit entered more directly into competition with market-based forms of financing. The following subsections trace the process of reforming financial markets in France and Germany, outlining major changes that have been realized in both countries—somewhat earlier in France, but fuelled by the willingness to catch up with the developments elsewhere in Germany from the 1990s onwards.

2.2.1   France: From starvation to reanimation

After 1945, the French financial market was 'abandoned to its fate of death by starvation' (Loriaux 1991, 111). High inflation rates had made investments in securities unattractive, all the more so as credit was abundantly available and cheap. The nationalization of major French industrial companies and banks after the war had further reduced the volume of listed shares. First efforts to liberalize and promote financial markets go back to the period of 1966–1969, when the French central bank obtained more flexibility in its interventions. In addition to that, the money markets were strengthened with the introduction of an auction-based mechanism for the issuance of treasury bonds, which replaced the existing mechanism for price setting by government officials. This allowed for some market discipline and reduced bank dependence on the central bank (Loriaux 1991, 175–6; Melitz 1990, 395). Some strengthening of financial markets was also realized with the Loi Monory in 1978, which introduced an income tax deduction for new purchases of French shares with the aim of creating some sort of popular capitalism (Cerny 1989, 177).

During the 1980s, financial market reforms intensified. The reforms were initiated by the economic minister Bérégovoy and the Trésor, in the face of opposition from the banks and other ministry officials. The aim was to make the Parisian marketplace an important financial centre (Story and Walter 1997, 214). Even though the reforms were sometimes presented as necessary, they are better interpreted as a 'deliberate choice' (Melitz 1990, 394), and 'clearly derive[d] from state policy' rather than the demands of domestic market actors (Cerny 1989, 176; similarly Perez 1998, 762). The foremost, although not exclusive, aim of the 1980s reforms was to reanimate financial markets in order to finance the *public* debt (Lambert 1996; similarly O'Sullivan 2007, 418).

The reforms cannot, in other words, be interpreted as a strong preference for financial liberalization as an end in itself. Rather, 'financial deregulation was perceived as the sine qua non of the French policymaker's ability to recover monetary policy-making powers of which [s]he had been deprived by the overdraft economy'. By liberalizing finance, 'the Socialists were not simply complying with or submitting to the dictates of the market, but were trying to regain control over the economy' (Loriaux 1991, 238; for a similar argument on the link between financial liberalization and macroeconomic adjustment in formerly interventionist states see Perez 1998).

In 1983, a second exchange with less strict listing conditions for smaller businesses was created and money market mutual funds were introduced. In 1985, a more liquid and more open money market for debt securities was created.[11] In contrast to the previous period, during which the money market was only open to the banks and certain non-banks (the *établissements non-bancaires admis au marché monétaire*, ENBAMM), the new market was inclusive and allowed NFCs to participate (Lambert 1996). The commissions on the issuance of bonds by the private and the public sector also became freely negotiable that year (Cerny 1989, 184). In 1986, MATIF, a futures market, opened and became an immediate success (Melitz 1990, 396). One year later, MONEP, the French options market, opened. In 1988, the Bourse de Paris merged with six regional stock exchanges and the Stock Exchange Reform Act was passed. With the Reform Act, the monopoly of the brokers (*agents de bourse*) was gradually phased out until 1992, when their special

---

[11] So-called *titres de créances négociables* (TCN). They include the *bons du trésor négociables*, the *certificats de dépôts, billets de trésorerie*, and the *bons des institutions financières et des sociétés financières* (Lambert 1996).

legal status was abolished and the oversight moved from the Trésor to a self-regulatory arrangement (Cerny 1989, 185–6; Coleman 1996, 109).

At the beginning, government policies, especially the realization of the privatization programmes as well as the emission of bonds and commercial papers, played an important role in boosting financial markets. Private non-financial firms, by contrast, reacted to the end of subsidized credit with an increased use of internal sources of funding. It was only by the late 1990s that NFCs turned increasingly to the markets in order to finance aggressive external growth strategies through acquisitions (O'Sullivan 2007). Between 1986 and 2000, 18 per cent of all proceeds from public share offerings were through privatizations (O'Sullivan 2007, 408). The fraction of bonds issued by the state rose from low levels in the mid-1970s to 25 per cent in 1980, 40 per cent in 1990, and 70 per cent in 1993; the share of bonds issued by private NFCs, in contrast, was roughly 5 per cent in 1993 (O'Sullivan 2007, 414–15).

2.2.2   Germany: Liberal but reluctant to liberalize

Capital markets used to be less developed in Germany than in many other countries and for a long time, equity and bond markets only played a minor role in financing the economy. Germany also opened and liberalized its financial markets in some respects later than many other western economies, despite the fact that the German regulatory regime for the oversight over the financial sector had shown some relatively liberal features early on: The role of direct state oversight had been relatively light and many regulatory and supervisory tasks had been delegated to privately organized settings (Lütz 2002). Referring to a study by Williamson and Mahar (1998), Mügge (2010, 35) emphasizes that Germany was more liberal than the United States and the United Kingdom at the beginning of the 1970s regarding public interventions in the financial sector.

Despite these liberal characteristics, by the late 1980s, Germany was lagging behind the developments of financial markets elsewhere. German financial markets were perceived as narrow and relatively illiquid. Their organization was fragmented, with the coexistence of eight regional, mainly self-regulated stock exchanges. The infrastructures and financial instruments available—no computer-based trading, no options and futures—appeared outdated in this period (Lütz 2002; Story and Walter 1997).

The willingness to launch stock exchange reforms gained momentum when Andrew Hugh-Smith, chairman of the London International Stock Exchange, proposed creating a single European equity market in London in 1989. In response to these challenges, German politicians wanted to make sure that Frankfurt would become the most important continental marketplace (Story 1997, 257, 260). Part of the pressure for reform came indeed from foreign competition—notably from Paris and London, where German mark (DM)-markets and trade in futures and options had developed (Moran 1992, 146, 148). However, a more open attitude towards capital markets also arose with German Reunification, for which additional financial resources were required. Government officials did not want to collect these by raising taxes, intending instead to turn to the capital markets. In addition, the Maastricht Treaty, which limited the amount of central bank balance sheet credit to governments, further contributed to the need for stock exchange reforms (Story and Walter 1997, 172, 180).

Financial markets were gradually liberalized in the 1980s and 1990s by several rounds of reforms. They were strongly promoted by the so-called Frankfurt Coalition composed of the big banks, the government of the Land Hesse, and, to some extent, the Bundesbank. Strengthening financial markets was supported by the Finanzplatz Deutschland Campaign, which was launched by the German Ministry of Finance in 1992 (Deeg 2005, 180). Many of the reforms were realized as a part of the so-called Financial Market Promotions Laws (Finanzmarktförderungsgesetze I–IV), adopted between 1990 and 2002.

These reform efforts resulted in various changes to the utilities in place. In 1990, the Deutsche Terminbörse, an electronic trading platform for futures, was founded. In 1992, 30 securities were traded on an electronic system, but floor trading remained in place (Story and Walter 1997, 179–81). In addition, a variety of new financial instruments was introduced, including money market funds in 1994, interest rates and currency swaps in 1998, and hedge funds in 2002. The reform laws also deregulated the investment forms in place, notably investment funds and their administering societies, they eased access for foreign market participants, centralized and modernized securities' trading, and introduced tax incentives for financial market related activities. The coupon tax was abolished in 1984 and the stock exchange turnover tax in 1990 (also see BaFin 2002, 10, 35, 49–50; 2003, 54; 2004, 210; BAKred 1997, 8; 1998, 35; 1999, 51; Franke 2000; Lütz 2002, 145).

Adapting German financial markets to the developments elsewhere implied more than deregulation, the opening of markets to foreign participants, and the introduction of new financial products. It also required the strengthening, or more precisely, the expansion and centralization of public oversight over the stock exchanges and other trading platforms. In order to attract foreign investors, but also to conform to the internationally predominant regulatory model, investor protection had to be strengthened, regionally organized forms of self-regulation had to be replaced by more rigid and centralized forms of public oversight, and transparency had to be enhanced (Lütz 2002, 237–40). In 1994, the Bundesamt für Wertpapieraufsicht was founded, which established, for the first time, a central oversight agency over securities markets in Germany. Prior to this, the work of the regional public oversight bodies had been coordinated by a state-level working group on stock exchange and securities-related issues (Arbeitskreis der Länder für Börsen und Wertpapierfragen; Lütz 2002).

Transforming Frankfurt into an internationally competitive financial marketplace required significant changes to the governance structures in place, shifting competences from the regional level to the federal government, giving up the decentralized, regionally oriented stock market structure (Coleman 1996, 138–42). Abandoning the regional principle in stock market organization and allowing for a fully computerized exchange platform was a significant modification of the federalist settings in place and was the most significant institutional change of the settings in place by then (Moran 1992, 147).

2.3   Banking and corporate finance in the free market era

Both the French and the German financial sectors have undergone considerable changes over the decades prior to the crisis. Some were due to domestic political dynamics; others were triggered by technological innovation and the competitive dynamic which liberalized, connected financial sectors brought about. Some features of both financial orders saw major revisions. This is true for the rules applied to banking in France as much as for the rearrangement of the German regional landscape of stock exchanges and changes in corporate governance. How did these changes affect how banks have operated from the 1990s onwards? In the following subsections we will turn to a series of empirical indicators that illustrate how banks in both countries adjusted to the new market environment. A comparison will be made to the United Kingdom and the United States and their financial systems that used to be more market-based.

Figure 2.2   Development of total bank assets (in mio.)

Source: European Central Bank (ECB). Balance sheet volume of MFIs, excluding the ECBS. Outstanding amounts at the end of the period (stocks), total maturity, all currencies combined, denominated in million Euros.

2.3.1   French and German banking compared

One remarkable development since the onset of financial globalization has been the strong increase of monetary financial institutions' (MFIs) balance sheet volumes.[12] The Bundesbank time series, which go back to the 1950s, show that the total balance sheet volume of German banks increased from 20 billion Euros at the end of 1950 to 372 billion in 1970. In 1980, the total balance sheet volume of German banks was roughly three times the volume of 1970, it was six time its volume in 1990, 16 times in 2000 and 23 times the volume of 1970 in 2010 (Bundesbank data, own calculations). In absolute terms, French and German banks have converged towards a similar overall volume. Taken together, the banks in both countries managed assets with a value of roughly 8,000 billion Euros in 2013 (Figure 2.2). UK banks have grown even more strongly, especially from the early 2000s onwards. Their

---

[12] Monetary financial institutions (MFIs) are defined as 'resident credit institutions as defined in Community Law and other resident financial institutions the business of which is to receive deposits and/or close substitutes for deposits from entities other than MFIs and, for their own account (at least in economic terms), to grant credits and/or make investments in securities'. They include money market funds. http://www.ecb.europa.eu/stats/pdf/money/mfi/mfi_definitions.pdf?b7a62313c3e772b5 1d86ec-804f0b1e4d, accessed 11 July 2013. The MFIs roughly equal what is commonly understood as banks. Separate data on credit institutions is not available for the period up to 2006 and monetary market funds only make up for a small fraction of MFIs' overall volume.

total balance sheet volume remains higher than that of French and German banks, despite a stronger contraction since the financial crisis.

Overall, the most outstanding difference between the French and the German banking sectors is the degree of sector concentration. In France, the five largest banking groups made up 77 per cent of all bank assets in 2008. In Germany, the share of the five largest banks only accounted for a market share of 27 per cent (CGFS 2018, 86). The German banking sector is the least concentrated in Europe, with a relatively high number of independent banks despite ongoing consolidation efforts (Sachverständigenrat 2008, 89). At the end of 2011, there were roughly 1,900 credit institutions operating in Germany—less than half the number of 1990 (Dialogforum Finanzstandort Deutschland 2012, 23). The relatively small cooperative banks—roughly 1,100 in total—make up the largest share of independent banks (Deutsche Bundesbank 2012, 3–4). In France, 659 banks were active in 2011 (Autorité de Contrôle Prudentiel 2013, 51) compared to 2,001 banks in 1984 (Lacoue-Labarthe 2001, 341).

Regarding the control of the domestic banking market, the effects of financial liberalization have been rather limited. In both countries, domestic banks have continued to control the domestic banking market, despite the liberalization efforts of the 1980s and 1990s. As a fraction of balance sheet totals, the market share of foreign banks amounted to roughly 15 per cent in both countries in 2006 (Schildbach 2008, 5). In France, the market share of foreign banks even decreased between 1997 and 2006, the result of a relatively strong decline in the presence of non-European banks (Schildbach 2008, 13). While there is some variation according to the financial service offered—especially in investment banking, where US-American banks have a considerable (but varying) market share in Europe—banking sectors have remained organized along national lines to a significant degree, despite financial liberalization, European financial integration, and varying degrees of foreign banks' market share (e.g. Epstein 2017; Grossman and Leblond 2011).

Figure 2.3 shows how the overall profitability of the banks has evolved since the late 1980s. In France, the return on equity (ROE) decreased after Mitterrand's liberal change of course up to the mid-1990s with the bursting of a real estate bubble. Profitability then rose until the outbreak of the financial crisis. In that sense, the French banks managed the adaptation to a more open and more competitive financial regime after an initial phase of disruptions fairly well. German banks used to have rather low profitability levels, but they remained relatively stable during the 1990s, despite the changes in the market environment. They then began to decrease with shortcomings in bank risk management and

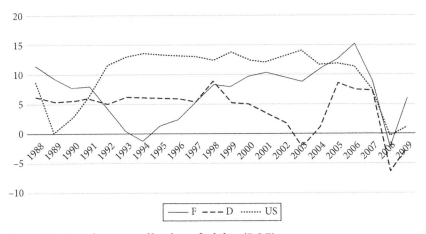

Figure 2.3 Development of bank profitability (ROE)

Source: OECD bank profitability database, own calculations. The ROE is calculated as the net income after tax divided by equity (capital and reserves). The database has not been updated since 2009 due to a lack of resources. Data on the UK is not available. The OECD bank profitability statistics cover financial institutions involved in deposit taking and financing activities.

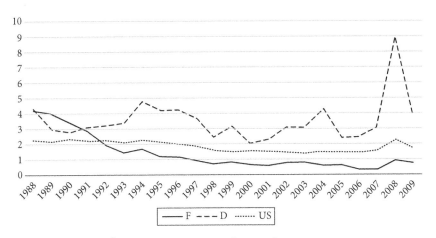

Figure 2.4 Ratio of net interest to net non-interest income

Source: OECD bank profitability database, own calculations. For further information also see Figure 2.3.

increased competition from foreign banks. The rates of return of US-American banks rose strongly at the beginning of the 1990s and were stable at a significantly higher level than in France and Germany. Thus, they seem to have profited disproportionately from the liberalized market environment.

Figure 2.4 illustrates the relative importance of different bank activities in terms of net income. Net interest-based income reflects the importance of the classic lending business for banks; net non-interest based income, by contrast, is generated by fees and reflects the role of investment banking as well as other financial services. The graph shows that the income structure of the French and the German banks was relatively similar in the late 1980s and early 1990s, with net interest-based income being almost four times the sum of non-interest-based income. Since then, the development has been different. Whereas interest-based income has remained the most important source of income for German banks, its role has decreased in France, where non-interest-based income has become the primary source of income since the late 1990s. Considered from this perspective, the French banks have moved more towards a market-based business model than their German counterparts (also see Howarth 2013). The overall higher ratio in the United States compared to France is primarily because US investment banks are not included in the database, contrary to European universal banks which may be active in deposit taking and investment banking within one legal entity.[13]

Overall, the French and the German banking sectors have converged from quite different starting points towards a universal banking model that allows for a broad array of financial services within one legal entity. At the same time, the institutional configuration of the banking sector has remained different, with the predominance of five large banking groups in France and a high number of independent banks in Germany, organized in three pillars and profiting from high levels of group integration as far as the cooperative and the savings banks are concerned. In both countries, the adjustment to financial globalization has been accompanied by significant consolidation as well as cost reduction efforts.

2.3.2 Effects on the banks' role in financing the economy

What were the implications of these changes for the banks' role in financing the economy? Figure 2.5 shows the development of the volume of outstanding corporate credit. It grew in France and the United Kingdom during the years preceding the crisis and was relatively stable in Germany over that period. Since the crisis, global corporate credit volumes have converged towards similar absolute levels in France and Germany. Relative to the size of the economy, corporate credit is thus more important in France than in Germany. The divergent post-crisis evolutions between France and Germany

---

[13] The database contains US-American domestic depository institutions, including commercial banks, savings institutions, and credit unions. Investment banks were not considered as banks prior to 2007/2008.

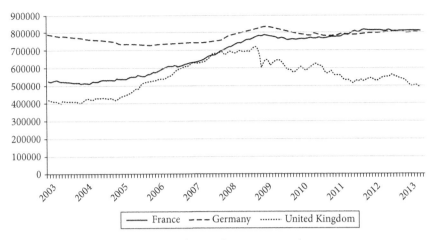

Figure 2.5 Development of the volume of corporate credit

Source: ECB data. Outstanding amounts of loan to NFCs at the end of the period (stocks), MFIs excluding the ESCB, all maturities, denominated in million Euros.

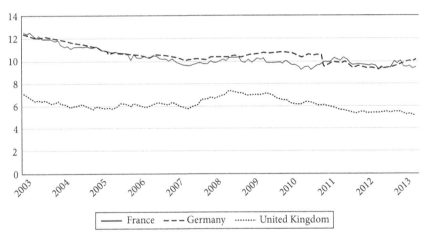

Figure 2.6 Corporate credit as a fraction of all assets

Source: ECB data, own calculations. Credit to NFCs as a percentage of total bank assets. For further explications, see Figures 2.2 and 2.5.

on the one hand and the United Kingdom on the other suggest that the engagement of British banks in corporate lending in the years prior to the crisis was more strongly driven by securitization opportunities than in the other two countries.[14]

---

[14] Unfortunately, data on corporate credit does not reach back very far, even the Bundesbank data only starts in 1999. Data for the UK on loans adjusted for securitization is not included in the ECB database.

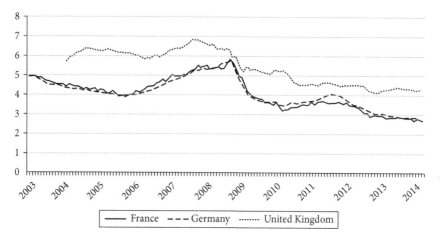

Figure 2.7   Interest rate development of corporate credit
Source: ECB data. Totals, original maturity between one year and five years.

Figure 2.6 displays the importance of corporate credit from the banks' perspective. As a fraction of total bank assets, corporate credit has had a similar importance in France and Germany, amounting to roughly 10 per cent respectively. Its importance is lower for UK banks (roughly 6 per cent). According to an estimation by McKinsey, corporate banking was the least profitable activity for European banks in 2004. The estimated ROE was 8 per cent for commercial banking compared to 16 per cent for retail banking, 20 per cent for investment banking, 28 per cent for asset management, and 35 per cent for private banking (cited in Pastré 2006, 50). This suggests that there was indeed significant cost pressure for banks on corporate lending in the years preceding the crisis.

Interest rates are another interesting indicator, since they reflect the cost of bank credit and, consequently, its attractiveness from a borrower's perspective.[15] Figure 2.7 displays the interest rates NFCs pay on average for bank credit with a maturity between one and five years. As the graph shows, interest rates are relatively similar in France and Germany. From a cost perspective, bank credit is equally attractive in both countries. This also holds for credit with other maturities and other lending volumes (ECB data). Taking

---

[15] The interest rate a client has to pay is composed of several elements. The starting point are the refinancing costs of the bank. Banks then add a charge for operating costs plus a fee for the credit risk that the bank assumes, which in turn depends on the statistical default probability of a specific borrower. Finally, the bank adviser adds the margin, hence the profit she intends to make with her engagement. This latter component is influenced by strategic considerations regarding the importance of the client, the bank-lending relationship, competitive pressures, and potential other business opportunities with that client (interview 2013092405D).

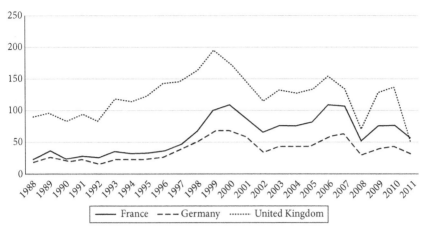

Figure 2.8 Development of stock market capitalization as a percentage of GDP

Source: World Bank Data. Market capitalization is the number of shares outstanding times their price. GDP is calculated at purchaser's prices.

all sizes and all maturities of credit together, bank credit tends to be slightly less costly in France than in Germany.[16] In the United Kingdom, interest rates that NFCs pay are usually higher; credit is, in other words, a more expensive source of external funds than in continental Europe.

Turning to the development of market-based forms of corporate funding, Figure 2.8 displays the development of stock market capitalization as a percentage of GDP. The difference between France and Germany on the one hand and the United Kingdom on the other is considerable, in particular for the period up to the 2000s. Stock market capitalization relative to the size of the economy was quite similar for France and Germany at the end of the 1980s but the increase since then has been somewhat stronger in France. The difference between Germany and France on the one hand and the United Kingdom on the other is also apparent regarding the number of listed companies, which amounted to 665 in Germany, 862 in France, and 2,179 in the United Kingdom in 2012 (World Bank data).

The contribution of stock markets to corporate finance is best captured by NFCs' net issues, that is the amounts of new shares issued minus the funds that were paid back, e.g. in the form of redemptions. Figure 2.9 shows that raising money on financial markets is strongly cyclical with a huge increase in net issues around the year 2000, in Germany in particular. With the new economy crash, however, stock market capitalization returned to its

---

[16] Comparable data on credit totals for the UK is not included in the ECB database.

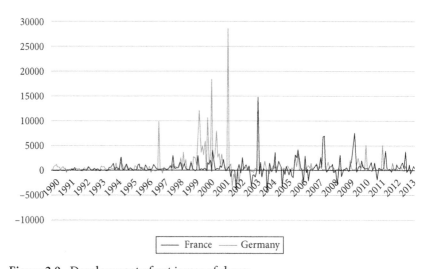

Figure 2.9 Development of net issues of shares
Source: ECB data. Net issues (flows) of quoted shares of NFCs, denominated in million Euros.

pre-boom levels in Germany and the Neue Markt, a market segment for new, innovative firms with riskier profiles founded in 1997, was shut down (also see Vitols 2004). Patterns for debt raised on financial markets are similar to those of equity, even though the volumes raised are somewhat higher, especially in France.

Table 2.1 compares the net issues of shares, bonds, and bank credit. The table shows that the relative importance of market-based forms of funding has been stronger in Germany than in France from the 1990s onwards up to the crisis. In the years prior to the crisis (2000–2007), market-based forms of funding (equity and debt) contributed with 20.5 billion net per year to the funding of the real economy in France. The amount of credit was roughly twice as much. In Germany, by contrast, financial markets contributed more than banks in net terms to the funding of the economy—and this even stands when we omit the strong increase in stock market capitalization around the year 2000. Between 2002 and 2007, financial markets contributed with a yearly 13.9 billion Euros of additional financial resources to the funding of the real economy. Net bank credit, by contrast, only amounted to 5.3 billion Euros per year.

Interestingly—and we will come back to this in Chapter 6—the financial crisis led to the inversion of the pre-crisis dynamics in both countries. In France, net issues of credit decelerated by 50 per cent compared to the pre-crisis period. In other words, credit grew only half as fast as in the years

Table 2.1 Net issues of equity, debt, and credit by NFCs (in bio. Euros)

	Period	France	Germany
I. Shares (equity)	1990–1999	4.5	10.9 (6,3)*
	2000–2007	7.1	14.7 (4,6)*
	2008–2013	8.2	5.9
II. Debt securities	1990–1999	11.8	2.6
	2000–2007	13.4	9.3
	2008–2013	35,3	8,7
III. Credit	2003–2007	42.3	5.3
	2008–2014	20.6	7.9

Source: ECB data, own calculations. Net issues in billion Euros. Shares: net issues of quoted shares by NFCs; debt securities: securities other than shares, excluding financial derivatives; credit: financial flows with domestic NFCs, all loan sizes, maturities, and currencies combined. Data on credit flows is only available from 2003 onwards.*Data in brackets on net issues of equity in Germany leave the stock exchange euphoria of around the year 2000 out, calculating averages for the periods 1990–1998 and 2002–2007.

before. In Germany, the opposite is true: Credit grew more strongly after the crisis than before. Regarding market-based forms of funding, net issues remained relatively stable in Germany. In France, by contrast, net issues of debt securities increased strongly. Overall, French enterprises have relied more strongly on external sources of funding than is the case in Germany.

Despite financial liberalization, the size of French and German financial markets relative to the size of the economy has remained below the levels found in Anglo-Saxon countries. In addition, granting corporate credit has remained a more important activity for French and German banks compared to their British counterparts and interest rates are significantly lower, which makes bank credit a more attractive source of external funding. Overall, the share of bank assets in total financial institutions' assets is considerably higher in France and Germany than in the United States and the United Kingdom (73 per cent and 62 per cent compared to 18 per cent and 49 per cent in 2006; see CGFS 2018, 80). In these respects, both the French and the German banks have maintained distinctive features compared to Anglo-Saxon finance, despite the increase of market-based banking (Hardie et al. 2013).

2.4 The changing character of the bank–firm relationship

The previous sections have traced the development of the French and the German financial sectors from their origins in the nineteenth century over their expansion in the twentieth century to the adjustment processes in the light of financial globalization. They shed light on the implications this process has had for the functioning of the markets for banking and financial services until the turn of the millennium and up to the financial crisis. Compared to their specificities in the early post-war decades, both have converged towards a model of financial intermediation that shares several important similarities. Both have opted for universal banks; both have implemented new financial market infrastructures and introduced new financial products to their marketplaces, attempting to compete with London and New York for financial resources. Nevertheless, in both countries banks and bank credit have retained an important role in financing the economy.

At the same time, the universal banking system itself and the relationships between the banks and firms have not been left unchanged. One of the specificities—if not *the* specificity—of the German model of financial intermediation, and the most debated one in the academic literature, has been the close integration of the banks into the productive sector, their presence on supervisory boards, and their potential influence on corporate decisions. Up to the 1980s, close bank–industry relationships were embedded in a net of cross-shareholdings that included the banks, insurance companies, and the big NFCs (also see Beyer 2002; Beyer and Höppner 2003; Culpepper 2005; Höpner and Krempel 2003). A similar model of interlocked directorship and insider control was also present in France and reinforced during the 1980s when the hitherto nationalized corporations were successively privatized (also see Morin 2000).

In both countries, these networks dissolved during the 1990s and early 2000s. Beyer argues that for Germany, the change resulted from a strategic reorientation of Deutsche Bank and Allianz away from industry participation. According to him, one major reason for the shift of Deutsche Bank, but certainly also for others, was that industry participation was incompatible with investment banking activities, M&A engagements in particular (Beyer 2002). A similar process of disorganization could also be observed in France, where corporate governance had undergone a rapid transformation from state control to cross-shareholdings and then to a regime of outsider control with the massive participation of Anglo-Saxon institutional investors holding larger amounts than in any other country: 35 per cent compared to 9 per cent in the United Kingdom in 1997 (Morin 2000, 42; also Culpepper 2005).

Even though the close integration of firms and banks via equity participations, proxy votes, and the presence on supervisory boards has always been only true for a small number of large businesses, this is much less the case today. The special relationship between banks and the real economy in intermediated economies is essentially based on a creditor–debtor configuration (plus additional services) and there is evidence that many German banks have succeeded in maintaining close relations with many of their customers (Keller 2019). In order to understand this relationship, it is not the interaction between the banks and the big corporations, which have largely turned to the financial markets in order to raise funds, that is decisive, but the vast majority of small and medium-sized firms and their interactions with the banks.

3

Studying the development of integrated financial sectors

The environment in which banks and other financial institutions operate has undergone tremendous change over the last decades. Understanding and making sense of it has been at the core of much work in comparative and international political economy. This chapter argues that both institutionalist and financial power perspectives are insufficient in accounting for the post-crisis reforms because they underestimate the relevance and the nature of politics: Politics is as much about puzzling as about powering, especially when the interest in a topic is high. This implies that we can neither deduct individual political decisions from the institutions in place nor from the powerfulness of certain interest groups.

Many important developments in financial sectors and the timing of when they become fuelled by political reform can be tied to processes of *social learning*, namely the collective realization that at least one up to then widely shared assumption on the functioning of the economy was no longer deemed a valid depiction of the future. This process involves people and organizations outside the policy-making community and ties political decisions back to broader societal developments.

The patterns of stability and change and the extent as well as the direction of political change can be linked to the ways in which and the timing of when unwritten, but widely shared assumptions on the functioning and the future development of the political economy are questioned and adapted collectively. Conceptually speaking, these unwritten shared assumptions on fundamental functioning principles of the political economy as of other societal subsystems can be described as *informal institutions*. Informal institutions are not formalized by laws or treaties and contrary to formal institutions, they cannot be enforced by a third party. They are influential because they are widely shared as valid depictions of the way things are. Informal institutions inform human behaviour because they are taken for granted.

When the world around us changes because of technological and scientific progress or changes in fundamental societal norms, the collectively shared

Financial Crises and the Limits of Bank Reform: France and Germany's Ways Into and Out of the Great Recession.
Eileen Keller, Oxford University Press (2021). © Eileen Keller. DOI: 10.1093/oso/9780198870746.003.0003

understandings usually do so at some point as well. This can happen in a gradual way over longer periods of time, but it can also occur more rupture-like in response to unforeseen events, such as crises. When a specific feature of the political economy is questioned collectively, a particular process of sense-making sets in, which aims at the restoration of a shared, but not necessarily uncontested, understanding of what the situation is about and how to deal with it. If this social learning process is successful, corresponding adjustments in the formal institutions follow, stabilizing the new consensus. As Victor Hugo (2010 [1877]) stated long ago, nothing is as powerful as an idea whose time has come.

The following sections discuss the merits and limits of institutionalist and power perspectives in studying financial sector development and they introduce the social learning argument that informs this book. The chapter details the specificities of informal institutions, on which the notion of social learning builds, it discusses its ontological assumptions and spells out the behavioural implications such an approach to political decision-making has. In a next step, the causal mechanism that underlies social learning is presented, discussing the empirically observable implications. The chapter closes with a short reflection on the notion of developmental paths, foreshadowing some of the empirical observations that follow in the subsequent chapters.

3.1 The limits of institutional design

Much research on political economies in general and financial sectors in particular has dealt with the considerable transformation both have undergone due to the interlinked processes of globalization, liberalization, de- and re- egulation, and international regime building (e.g. Busch 2008; Campbell 2004; Coleman 1996; Helleiner 1994b; Kapstein 1994; Moran 1991; Ruggie 1982; Vogel 1996). Studying and explaining these developments has been a challenging enterprise. Up to the 1990s, financial sectors were not a major research focus in the social sciences outside economics. An interest in the characteristics of financial sectors developed in Comparative Political Economy (CPE), stimulated by the works of Alexander Gerschenkron (1962) and John Zysman (1983), who showed that the financing options financial sectors provided had an important impact on economic growth strategies, industrial development, and the effectiveness of governments' economic policies.

Considered from a historical perspective, financial sectors developed relatively autonomously from each other over long periods. National financial sectors emerged gradually in response to different financing needs and under differing socio-economic conditions (Gerschenkron 1962). Consequently, they differed significantly from each other. They were more market- or more bank-based, they relied on arm's-length market interactions or on private inside information and stable relations over time. There were few big financial institutions in some countries and many smaller ones in others, and to varying degrees, they included public and cooperative or mutual banks, universal banks, savings banks, investment banks, and standalone investment firms.

A growing interest in the institutional foundations of market economies and their respective comparative advantages began to spread from the 1980s onwards, fuelled by the breakdown of the Soviet Union (Crouch and Streeck 1997a, 1). Various typologies described the existing differences among financial sectors in market economies as embedded in their broader national economic context (e.g. Amable 2005; Crouch and Streeck 1997b; Hall and Soskice 2001b; Schmidt 2000, 2002; for an overview Jackson and Deeg 2006). Besides characteristics of the financial sector, these typologies typically included the role of the state and state economic policies, production and growth strategies, corporate governance, industrial relations, and the welfare state. The different elements of these economic orders were considered to stand in a functional relationship, mutually reinforcing and complementing each other.

The most influential approach has been Peter Hall and David Soskice's 'Varieties of Capitalism' (VoC). Herein, they developed two ideal types of economic orders composed of sets of complementary institutions that allowed for the efficient resolution of coordination problems from a firm's perspective. While financial markets played an important role in so-called liberal market economies, providing risk capital for rapid, disruptive innovation, bank intermediation was central to so-called coordinated market economies. Thanks to the close and stable relations banks maintain with their clients over time, they dispose of private inside information, which in turn favours long-term commitment and a high-quality production strategy, relying on incremental innovation processes (Hall and Soskice 2001a).

With the intensification of financial globalization, which had lifted many obstacles to the free flow of money and various barriers to competition, financial sectors began to compete more directly with each other. Much of the subsequent research, therefore, focused on how the once territorially bound national financial sectors developed under these conditions, how stable their fundamental characteristics and financing patterns were, and whether or not they would converge towards similar functioning patterns (e.g. Allen et al. 2004; Allen and Gale 2000; Busch 2004, 2008; Coleman 1994, 1996; Deeg 2009; Hall and Soskice 2001b; Lütz 2002, 2003; Nölke 2011).

One of the implications of the interest in differing sets of institutional orders and their stability over time was that the issue of the relationship between institutions and interests had been insufficiently addressed. Given the high degree of interdependence or complementarity between major institutions of the political economy, actors were considered to have a strong orientation towards the 'institutional recreation of comparative advantage' (Hall and Soskice 2001a, 63). Since the institutional settings allowed for the (efficient) coordination among economic actors and had, by this, a direct impact on economic performance, they were considered to have a strong, if not deterministic, impact on policy preferences in favour of the solutions facilitated by the institutions in place. Institutional complementarities were understood as an at least implicit argument for path dependency because of the positive feedback the existing institutional configurations provided (Deeg and Jackson 2007, 158).

While analytic pre-eminence was given to stability, Hall and Soskice (2001b, 64) acknowledged the crucial role financial deregulation might play in this context, arguing that it could be the 'string that unravel[led] coordinated market economies'. Liberal and liberalized integrated coordinated market economies were predicted to converge towards a market-based financial system in a variegated world economy (Jessop 2014). The specific patterns that had emerged over the past century would gradually dissolve. The convergence hypothesis fuelled an interest in the commonalities and common trends in capitalist market economies, including financialization, commodification, privatization, and deregulation (Streeck 2009, 2010). This happened at the expense of a more nuanced approach to the differential developments in financial sectors and political economies, which touches upon the question of whether one can read the policy preferences of actors and the outcome of political reforms from the organizational settings in place.

Empirically speaking, the cumulated evidence of more than 30 years of research suggests that neither the persistence nor the convergence thesis fit the evidence well. The insights from various countries and features of political economies studied reveal a complex and sometimes perplexing picture of stability and change. Convergence on some aspects has gone along with divergence on others, depending on the features, the countries, and the time horizon considered (e.g. Berger and Dore 1996; Coleman 1996; Crouch and Streeck

1997b; Djelic and Quack 2003a; Kitschelt et al. 1999; Lane and Wood 2012; Morgan et al. 2005; Röper 2017; Schmidt 2002; Streeck and Thelen 2005).

One of the consequences of the process of financial globalization, the lifting of barriers to competition and the abolition of restrictions on business practices, was that the internal diversity of political economies increased (Deeg 2009; Lane and Wood 2009, 2012). Internal diversity thereby refers to the banks' business models (Hardie et al. 2013; Hardie and Howarth 2013b), the emergence of transnationally oriented fractions of capital (Macartney 2009), corporate government and management practices (Deeg 2009), the presence of new financial service providers, and new industry federations amongst others. Overall, the observation that 'in all parts of the financial system change and continuity exist side by side' (Krahnen and Schmidt 2004, 486) has become relatively uncontroversial, not only for Germany to which the authors of the quote were referring. This observation is not very satisfying from an institutionalist perspective because it raises the question of why some features of financial systems have proved more resilient to change than others.

The financial crisis added new puzzles for institutionalists since the varying degrees of affectedness cut across major analytical distinctions. The most severely affected financial systems included both so-called bank and market-based political economies, and they affected individual countries from both groups to different degrees. The crisis hit concentrated as well as fragmented banking sectors and small open economies besides larger political economies where domestic markets play a more prominent role. Why was Germany with its supposedly special banking culture so heavily affected and why were the large French banks less involved in the crisis than other large and internationally active universal banks?

Even after the fact, the existing distinctions of CPE do not help us understand what happened during the financial crisis (Hay 2020). The institutional dispositions in place and their effects are insufficient in accounting for the developments the financial crisis revealed. Given these shortcomings, the crisis has led to a renewed interest in a comparative approach to financial sector development that seeks answers to the 'dynamic patterned diversity of actually existing capitalisms' (Hay 2020, 303) and financial sector development in particular (e.g. Bell and Hindmoor 2015; Hardie and Howarth 2013b; Mayntz 2012a; Thiemann 2018; Woll 2014). In order to understand the empirical variation observed, the analytic categories developed by past generations of scholars are no longer sufficient. New tools building on the recognition of institutional frictions, politics, the importance of creative agency, and their ideational abilities are needed (e.g. Campbell 2010; Djelic 2010; Hall and Thelen 2009; Jackson 2010; Jackson and Deeg 2008; Mahoney and Thelen 2010; Schmidt 2002; Streeck and Thelen 2005).

3.2 The limits of financial power

An alternative approach to the development of financial sectors focuses on the special power of finance in shaping public policies.[1] Financial power perspectives highlight that finance is in a special position that leads to a disproportionate influence over the policy-making process. Contrary to pluralist views of policy-making, financial power perspectives highlight the special role of finance because of its privileged position and its resource endowment, including money, access, and expert knowledge. Considered from this perspective, limited regulatory change in response to the crisis can thus be imputed to the power of finance. As the crisis showed, large financial players have little interest in seeing the regulatory burden increase since they can count on state support if they are too big to fail.

At the structural level, the particular strength of finance has been attributed to the 'structural dependence of the state on capital' (Przeworski and Wallerstein 1988), financially but also in terms of investment decisions that generate economic welfare. Since a flourishing economy makes winning an election an easier task, the theory considers that politicians make business-friendly decisions, especially when the enterprise concerned makes plausible threats to leave the country otherwise and invest elsewhere (Bernhagen and Bräuninger 2005; Lindblom 1977). The more restrictions to the free flow of money are removed, the more easily large financial actors should be able to exert political influence and obtain favourable political decisions (Frieden 1991; Germain 1997; Strange 1988).

Theories of regulatory capture have identified further mechanisms of how finance gains political influence. Since business interests are usually more narrowly defined than those of other societal groups such as voters or consumers, and losses or gains more concentrated, business actors can overcome collective action problems more easily (Stigler 1971). They are more likely to mobilize, and they have more resources at their disposal to invest in their lobbying activities. According the revolving door hypothesis, representatives of the finance industry, like other business actors, have privileged access to regulators and legislators because of the personal benefits they can offer.

---

[1] A partially similar argument has been made in Keller (2018).

They gain influence through financial contributions or the promise of a well-paid job in the future (Dal Bo 2006; Hall and Deardorff 2006). Business representatives capture political decision-makers when they obtain consistently or repeatedly political deals in their favour that intendedly diverge from a contrafactually posed public interest (Carpenter 2014, 58; Carpenter and Moss 2014, 13 ff.).

While the traditional view of regulatory capture is relatively straightforward—money directly or indirectly buys favourable regulatory decisions—given that countervailing forces are limited, a more sophisticated approach has been developed through socio-cultural and cognitive perspectives. According to these accounts, the particular prevalence of finance, as of other privileged societal groups, lies in their shared background with political elites. Both are part of a network that cuts across the private–public divide thanks to their similar educational background, their biographies, and the societal events they attend. In these networks, individuals with similar worldviews meet and mutually support each other (also see Kwak 2014).

The transnational financial policy community has been characterized as a particularly close club-like community where 'financial policy becomes apolitical for those within the community, with regulators and supervisors becoming aligned with market participants' (Tsingou 2015, 228). The inner circles of the French elite, dominated by the graduates of the Grand corps and the Grandes Ecoles are a particularly homogeneous circle, whose members do not necessarily have conflicting interests (Bourdieu 1989; Jabko and Massoc 2012; Kadushin 1995). This fostered a 'symbiotic mode of coordination between state and bank elites through mechanisms of group identification and trust' (Massoc 2020, 148). Lobbying, therefore, is not necessarily about changing a decision-maker's mind, it can also function as a kind of 'legislative subsidy' that supports a position the concerned decision-maker was willing to defend in the first place (Hall and Deardorff 2006).

An alternative account of cognitive capture attributes the special influence of finance to the highly technical character of the policy field. Given the complex models that are used in banks when investment or lending decisions are made or financial risk appraised, their specialists, including mathematicians and financial as well as legal specialists, possess expertise regulators may find hard to keep up with. This knowledge gives them privileged access to decision-makers and a special say about regulatory politics. Given the high salaries paid in the financial industry, developing an independent public authority is a particularly difficult endeavour (also see McCarty 2014). When regulators follow proposals that come from the finance industry, they may consequently be convinced that what they do is the right thing to do—or, at least, they may not know of a better solution. Financial sector influence is thus a function of its centrality in the production of knowledge that is relevant for regulators.

The different forms of capture have been widely stated as root causes of the Great Recession (e.g. Baker 2010; Barth et al. 2012; Igan and Lambert 2019) and central to the explanation of bank bailouts (Culpepper and Reinke 2014; Woll 2014). Prominent representatives of this view include Nobel prize winner Joseph Stiglitz, Citigroup's former chief economist Willem Buiter, and the former executive chairman of the British Financial Services Authority Adair Turner (see Kwak 2014, 78 for an overview). Willem Buiter (2008, 106), for instance, considered that the Fed had been 'co-opted by Wall Street' because 'those in charge of the relevant state entity [were] internalising, as if by osmosis, the objectives, interests and perception of reality of the vested interest they [we]re meant to regulate and supervise in the public interest'. Thus, financial power perspectives attribute limited regulatory change in response to the crisis to the fact that rather little has changed regarding the banks' monetary power, their expertise, and the networks in which regulatory decisions are made.

However, the more attention power of finance approaches have rightly attracted, the more it has become clear that the translation from valuable resources and favourable predispositions into political influence that can be traced through the policy-making process is more circumscribed. This is true for all three perspectives. Empirical evidence has increasingly cast doubt on the policy- or vote-buying effect of financial contributions and employment perspectives. If existent at all, it seems to be rather weak (Ansolabehere et al. 2003, 112 ff.; Hall and Deardorff 2006, 70; Hall and Wayman 1990, 798; Morton and Cameron 1992). Overall, interest groups spend much more money on other lobbying activities than on direct financial contributions (Figueiredo and Richer 2013, 5).

Recent research on structural power has highlighted that its influence is far from operating automatically because it is contingent on other factors, including ideas, institutions, and issue attention (Bell 2012; Bernhagen and Bräuninger 2005; Culpepper 2011; Macartney et al. 2020; Vogel 1987). Political decision-makers must interpret the signals and evaluate their threat potential (Bell and Hindmoor 2014a). Massoc (2018) has highlighted that even the mobility of the business with money is limited. Despite the fact that huge sums can be transferred from one continent to the next in just a fraction of a second, not all activities can be relocated easily. While certain operations can be carried out from the Cayman Islands or other tax havens, the bank activities that involve regular contact with clients, such as retail or corporate banking, are much harder to relocate and the threat to leave the country is more circumscribed. The volume of taxes paid by the banks reflects this fact. When a French newspaper invited the CAC 40 corporations to reveal the amount of taxes and other duties paid in France, three banks were among the five largest contributors (Fay 2019).[2]

Regarding access and expertise, Pepper Culpepper (2011) has shown in the context of corporate governance reform that business representatives are most likely to profit from their special power resources in the form of access and expertise when the general interest in a topic is low. In these circumstances, politicians and journalists have few incentives to develop their own expertise and voters do not care much. Political decision-makers thus have little to lose when adopting business-friendly policies. If Culpepper is right, the influence of finance should be the lowest it can ever get in the aftermath of a crisis as severe and consequential as the Great Recession.

Finally, Matthias Thiemann's (2018) work on the regulatory and supervisory treatment pre-crisis of what has become known as the shadow banking sector shows that cultural or cognitive capture is not automatic. Analysing the practices of regulators and supervisors in the United States and several European countries, he documents that they were more or less likely to develop an independent expertise vis-à-vis the financial sector depending on how competences were institutionally attributed with respect to bank regulation and accounting norms. In a similar vein, Young (2012) argues that access does not equal influence and shows that the members of the Basel Committee often took a more critical distance towards financial industry input than is commonly acknowledged. All these pieces show that regulatory capture is far from given. The processes by which policies are defined and adopted subsequently merit closer empirical analysis with respect to the mechanisms leading to their adoption.

3.3 The politics of financial sector reform

The previous discussion has shown that we cannot read off the results of individual historical decision-situations from the institutional dispositions

---

[2] The amounts of 5.8 billion for Crédit Agricole, 4.2 billion for BNP Paribas, and 3.3 billion for Société Générale in 2017 include their contributions to the deposit insurance scheme and the European Single Resolution Fund.

in place. Nor can we deduce them from the powerfulness of financial sectors. This is because their effect depends on the specific political context in which they are made and it cannot be separated from it. Both approaches may have considerable explanatory power when considering a larger group of cases, but none of the two is influential enough not to be overcome by the specific circumstances in which a political decision is made—and this context can be more or less conducive to their effects. Ultimately, their strengths and weaknesses boil down to the recognition that they depend on *politics*.

Changes in financial sectors follow different trajectories. Some result from the decisions of influential private actors that have nothing to do with political reforms. This is, for instance, the case if a new business opportunity is exploited within the regulatory framework in place or if many actors begin investing in certain activities while abandoning others. Major moments of financial sector change have, however, been shaped by political reforms. The latter usually involve Parliament and consequently take place in the public sphere. This poses a political risk, especially if the interest in a topic is high, because political decision-makers will be held accountable for the positions they defend. From a political decision-maker's perspective, it therefore matters whether or not a political decision will be perceived as *appropriate*, i.e. that it will be widely seen as the right decision, given the situation at hand.

Appropriateness as a yardstick for political decision-making does not characterize all political decisions to the same extent. At peak moments of the financial crisis in autumn 2008, for instance, there was not much leeway to think about the electoral consequences or the perceived appropriateness of the decisions to be made. When the bank bailouts were set up over the course of a weekend before the stock exchanges opened on Monday morning in Asia, there was no room for such considerations. Given that the decisions were taken in small expert circles in a very short period, there was no political debate and the public—as were most politicians—was only informed ex post about the decision made. It was therefore only in the aftermath of the acute crisis management that questions of appropriateness, blame avoidance, and the management of reputational risks (Hungin and James 2018) began to play a more prominent role.

If political decision-makers are sensitive to how their decisions are perceived, in situations where they are not under acute pressure to react, the decisive question is how they will know if their decision will be deemed appropriate. Appropriateness has much to do with how a political decision relates to the general understanding of the circumstances and the specific situation in which it is made. In other words, it depends on whether it resonates or not with beliefs that are widely held outside the policy-making community among the concerned or the general public. These beliefs describe widely shared understandings of the way things are and how they develop and can be seen as constitutive features of the specific socio-economic context in which actors operate. They are influential because most people take them for granted as the way things are.

Along these lines, Röper (2017) has shown that the German financial sector reforms of the 1990s were not an issue behind closed doors. Presented as financial modernization, financial liberalization was seen as a measure against bank power and obscure insider control—and consequently compatible with the social market economy. This allowed for the emergence of a broad cross-partisan coalition for change. The reforms were considered as the precondition for competitiveness, economic growth, and the management of private household wealth. The privatization of the German telecommunication company Telekom was successfully framed as the people's shares, an equity euphoria began to spread, and shareholder value became the 'buzzword of the year'. In short, 'public approval facilitated the political emergence of finance capitalism in the 1990s' (Röper 2017, 383).

In abstract terms, such beliefs about the functioning and the future development of the economy can be seen as widely shared cognitive features, which are an important element of the political as of the social world. The environment humans live in cannot be reduced to its brute material reality (Adler 1997; Wendt 1999). Important features of the social world are mental constructs. This is true for norms, laws, and identities as much as for concepts like money or sovereignty and also holds for shared cognitive patterns on how the economy works. Humans are creative beings that are able to imagine alternative states of the world (Beckert 2013) and to develop sophisticated tools and technologies to achieve them. What makes these inventions powerful is not the fact that human beings are able to conceive them: their strength lies in the fact that they may attain intersubjective qualities because they are *widely shared*. Currencies, norms, and changing beliefs as a trigger for political reform only function on the premise that a larger social group agrees on their properties.

These shared understandings on the functioning of the social world in general and the political economy in particular can be characterized as *informal institutions*. Contrary to other institutions, they are, as their name indicates, not formalized by laws or specified in written documents, such as decrees, statutes, or treaties and they are usually not formally enforced by a third party (but see Helmke and Levitsky 2004). As other institutions, they have a social besides a cognitive reality. People trust in them as essential features of the world they are living in (Searle 1995). Their implications may well be codified by law, but their substance, the fact that they are considered trustworthy ultimately is not. Informal institutions comprise the fundamental, historically rooted, and collectively shared functioning principles of political economies. They transport the heritage of history (Djelic 2010) and reflect the unwritten collectively shared rules and beliefs, which complement and on which relies the functioning of other formalized dispositions.

Informal institutions are a form of common knowledge or a cognitive roadmap that guides individuals through the world (Goldstein and Keohane 1993b). They take interpretational ambiguity from decision situations, providing orientation on the way things are. Culpepper (2008, 2) describes common knowledge creation in the context of wage bargaining as a process, which alters 'socially agreed facts about the character of the economy'. This has an independent effect on preference orderings and bargaining power.

Informal institutions can be understood as the shared cognitive patterns that describe important features of the social world. They comprise all the aspects of our living environment that exist thanks to the fact that there is a shared agreement on their characteristics. This does not mean that they are uncontested—indeed, accounting for change requires that they are contested, at least by some people. However, when this happens, the fact that the disposition at hand is considered a valid pattern for most people must be taken into consideration. Contrary to other types of institutions, informal institutions do not influence human behaviour because they are coercive and defection can be punished by a third party, or because they are a resource in fulfilling specific needs. Informal institutions are influential because they are taken for granted as a constitutive feature of the social world. In that sense, they are pre-strategic and usually exogenous to strategic manipulation by actors. Creative actors may well try to do so, although success is usually beyond their control.

That informal rules can have a decisive, and in some cases even a more immediate impact on the development of political economies than change in the formal institutional dispositions has convincingly been shown by Pepper Culpepper (2005). His research on the development of cross-shareholdings and patient capital in France, Germany, and Italy shows that the maintenance of this form of strategic coordination was primarily conditioned by the commitment of relevant players to the informal institutions that underpinned it.

When a key player defected from it, as it was the case with Axa in France, the whole arrangement unravelled due to a 'joint belief shift' (Culpepper 2005, 181 ff.) because the previous arrangement was not taken as a given any more without any formal change occurring at this specific moment.

Political reforms are, as Hugh Heclo pointed out long ago, not only about powering, but also about puzzling—namely the struggle to find out what the right or best decision is, given the circumstances. This is particularly true in a quickly changing world, given the limits of knowledge, human capacities and psychological predispositions in processing information, and arbitrages between competing legitimate goals that political decision-making usually involves (e.g. Jervis 1976; Kahneman et al. 1982; Kertzer and Tingley 2018; Simon 1955, 1983).

High degrees of complexity and ongoing change are especially true for the realm of the economy where technological change and scientific progress have revolutionized our working and living conditions over the last decades. Personal computers, which were hardly present in German households in the 1980s, could be found in almost 40 per cent in the late 1990s and in 90 per cent in 2017 (Statistisches Bundesamt 2018). About 16 million people world-wide had access to Internet in the mid-1990s. In 2017, this was true for more than half of the world population (Deutscher Bundestag 2007 and internet-worldstats.com). Such changes—as encompassing as they may be—usually begin at the fringes before they become encompassing societal phenomena. These changes resonate with how we think about the world we are living in and what we deem appropriate.

Major political reforms often have to do with the collective realization that the world around has changed and that there is a need to adapt to it. Decision-makers have to deal with these transformative processes that can be gradual or rupture-like, slow at some points and in some areas and fast-changing in others. Cornelia Woll's (2008) work shows convincingly that even large resourceful companies struggle to make sense of a changing environment. In the context of international trade liberalization during the 1990s, she shows how firms had to learn about their preferences in discussions with government representatives, trying to get a grasp of what was going on 'and whether this was important enough to invest their time and resources' (Woll 2005, 19).

In many cases, these individual and collective realizations will lead to political reform. If this is the case, they will ease access for those interest groups whose suggestions are in line with the substance of social learning, while limiting the impact of other actors whose suggestions are not. Their legitimacy results from the fact that they relate to widespread, salient beliefs that transcend the policy-making community and resonate with perceptions and convictions among the broader public.

3.4 Social learning and political change

When the functioning and the future development of certain aspects of the economy are widely perceived to change through technological progress, crises, or other triggers, the collectively shared understandings will usually do so as well. This can be understood as a social learning process (Hall 1993) that leads to the 'reconstitution of social reality' (Rathbun 2007, 551). It is a form of *learning* because it leads to a reappraisal of existing beliefs on the way things are, of what can be taken as a given, in the light of new and deemed better information. It also is a *social* process because it entails an interactive component.[3] The following subsections discuss the theoretical underpinnings and the observable implications of this approach to political reform.

3.4.1 Agency and change

The realization that important features of intersubjectively shared social facts on the functioning of the economy have changed and are no longer deemed valid can take different forms. In some cases, the process of change is slow and gradual. Taken for granted rules may evolve continuously and in a very slow and incremental way over relatively long periods of time. This may lead to a tipping point, when the realization spreads that things have changed and that there is a need to adapt (Pierson 2004). Alternatively, this may remain largely unperceived and it is only by looking back that the change will be noticed. In other cases, crises, catastrophes, and scandals or other unforeseen events lead to a very abrupt process of collective reassessment of previously largely shared social facts. In this case, restoring shared knowledge on the way things are and consolidating it through political reform is essential.

If the validity of one essential assumption on the functioning of the economy is questioned collectively, actors cannot follow routine behaviour as it is conceptualized by the most influential action theories both in sociology and

---

[3] The notion of social learning is strongly associated with the work of Peter Hall (1993). I will come back to his and other conceptualizations in Chapter 8.

economics. Both sociology's 'social man' with a focus on internalized norms, roles, and identities and economics' 'economic man' with a focus on preferences, alternatives, and utility to maximize one's welfare (Granovetter 1985), have strong explanatory power in situations that characterize routine behaviour, like the appropriate behaviour at the workplace, voting behaviour, or consumer choices. Despite their conceptual differences, they build on the same ontological foundations, treating the world as relatively unambiguous and objectively assessable (March 1994). Actors may be unsure of what the right behaviour or decision is, but this is depicted as a problem of the availability of information or human capacities in processing it, not as one of the constitution of the world per se (Beckert 1996; Blyth 2002; Hay 2010).

When widely shared beliefs about the functioning of the economy change, the decision-making context does not conform to the premise of relative stability on which the previous approaches build. When one essential feature of the political economy is questioned collectively, it is the objectivity of the context itself that it is stake. In other words, decision-making contexts are structured in different ways and what informs human behaviour differs with it (also see Beckert 1996). Table 3.1 gives an overview of different structural characteristics and their implications for human behaviour. Considered from the perspective of the structural clarity of the decision-situation—and consequently the extent to which we can treat the external world as an objective given— three states can be distinguished: Situations of risk, situations of uncertainty, and situations of confusion. Overall, the more a situation is unclear to an individual, the more of what happens is endogenous to the decision-situation and determined by the interactions among individuals and groups.

Table 3.1 Situational characteristics and their behavioural implications

	Situations of risk/ Routine situations	Situations of uncertainty	Situations of confusion
Degree to which the decision-situation is known by an individual	High	Intermediate	Extremely low
Logic of the interaction	Strategic Guided by mutual expectations	Consensus-oriented	Truth-oriented
Mode of the interaction	Bargaining Norms-based	Coalition building	Arguing

Source: Own elaboration; on the logic of arguing see Risse (2000); on preferences in situations of risk see Frieden (1999).

At one extreme, the decision-making context is well known to the concerned individuals and the relevant parameters of the decision-situation can be identified fairly easily. Rationalist action theory has termed these moments situations of risk. Much of the above described explaining in economics and sociology deals with this assumption. From a rationalist point of view, the interactions are shaped by strategic considerations. Actors try to maximize their welfare, bargaining with others. Considered from the perspective of classic role theory, the interactions are guided by the mutual expectations actors have towards each other, given their respective social roles and the interactions are guided by internalized norms.

At the other extreme are situations of confusion, which are characterized by an extremely low degree of clarity regarding what is at stake. We can think about such a situation as an extreme type. It may emerge if all central taken for granted assumptions on the functioning of the economy or the society are suddenly questioned collectively. Such a situation would probably be true for a (time) traveller, who ends up in a wholly unfamiliar epoch or society. Under these conditions, an individual's grasp of the environment is extremely low, and the traveller would be truly baffled. In such a case, the interactions are best conceptualized as being guided by a truth-orientation. Ideas and arguments come to the fore and power and predefined interests retreat (Risse 2000). The inherent persuasiveness of ideas plays a prominent role (Yee 1996, 87).

Situations of uncertainty are in between situations of risk and situations of confusion regarding the structural clarity of the decision situation and are characteristic for many real-world decision situations (e.g. Beckert 1996; Blyth 2002; Nelson and Katzenstein 2014). Situations of uncertainty are special because the situation under consideration is unique and not comparable to other instances (Knight 1921, 233). They are ambiguous because they lack 'clarity or consistency in reality, causality, or intentionality' (March 1994, 178) because the existing institutions have lost their capacity to coordinate expectations (Blyth 2002, 30–3).

Uncertainty results from interpretational ambiguity, which emerges when at least one central taken for granted assumption on the functioning of the political economy is questioned collectively. The observations at stake can be an indicator for one thing, but there are equally good reasons to consider them as an indicator for something else. Uncertainty in that sense is understood as indeterminacy (Rathbun 2007, 550). From an actor's perspective, this is a very uncomfortable situation since it increases uncertainty about what the situation is about and what the right or the best behaviour is. When at least one key taken for granted feature of the economy is questioned collectively, it is precisely the presumed stability of the social context that is at stake.

In this case, logically, behaviour and decision-making cannot follow pre-established scripts in the form of social roles and existing assumptions about means–end relationships. Instead, the logic of the interaction is guided by consensus building, aiming at the restoration of a collectively valid depiction of what the situation is about. This process operates through a mixture of per-suasion and more strategic considerations, depending on how different actors relate to a given issue. While some actors will have lived a moment of true learning given the experience they have had or observed in their environ-ment, other actors may support their claims for other reasons such as elect-oral concerns or economic profit. If a relevant number of actors shares a specific idea, it becomes a social fact even for those who may dispute the validity of a certain claim. It has a social besides a cognitive reality. Social learning has occurred.

3.4.2   Observable implications

Three empirical stages can be distinguished when at least one taken for granted assumption on the functioning of the political economy is questioned collectively: the questioning of past developments, the fostering of a new con-sensus on its implications for the future, and its formalization by political reforms. Social learning begins with the realization that something is not the way it was predominantly perceived up until then. In the light of new infor-mation, a specific assumption is no longer tenable. One specific informal institution on the functioning of the political economy that was previously taken for granted is no longer deemed valid, having lost its capacity to coord-inate expectations. The situation at hand reveals something that is fundamen-tally incompatible with what would commonly be assumed. This realization brings a specific feature of a complex social phenomenon to the fore.

When fundamental features of the political economy are questioned col-lectively, the situation is ambiguous. The developments at hand can mean one thing but they can also be an indicator of something else. One observable implication of this is that different reasonable interpretations about what the situation is about and how to deal with it may coexist. For any actor this implies that the evidence at hand can mean one thing, but it can also be con-sidered as being an indicator for something—or several things—else. This is consequential, since the interpretation of one's interests and defining the optimal (or the appropriate) behaviour crucially depends on which of the different reasonable interpretations is at stake.

The early stage following the collective realization that one informal institution is no longer valid is driven by a largely uncontrolled situational dynamic. Various actors immediately concerned by the changes that have become manifest respond to what they perceive is going on in a largely uncoordinated way, trying to get a grasp of what the situation is about. The situation is highly open with respect to the implications for future developments. Media coverage often plays an important role since it leads to the diffusion of information and may amplify perceptions and moods. This process of questioning at least one taken for granted assumption opens a political space (Berman 2013, 227).

Just as the abandoning of a taken for granted assumption is a collective enterprise, so is the reduction of interpretational ambiguity that follows from it. Ambiguity can only be reduced collectively, not individually, because whether one rather than another interpretation is at stake also depends on *how widely* a specific interpretation is shared or accepted as the relevant interpretation of a given situation. The ambiguity inherent in such situations is reduced not only by the cognitive appeal or the 'innate qualities' (Hall 1989, 369) and the 'objective merit' (Yee 1996, 87) because reality is, as James March (1994, 85) put it, 'certified by a shared confidence in it'.

While the initial phase following the collective questioning of the validity of an informal institution is largely driven by an uncontrolled situational dynamic where many people react in a rather uncoordinated way to what they observe, stabilizing the situation needs a more structured and coordinated process. In order to deal with the situation, it is necessary to develop an understanding of what the implications for the future are. Following the initial questioning, social learning requires the fostering of a new consensus on the implications of the collective puzzlement for the future. This process will often lead to a more systematic reassessment of past experience and the integration of new information deemed relevant (Hall 1993, 278), making a judgement on future expectations (Bennett and Howlett 1992, 278). The second stage can also be influenced by more strategic advances of groups of actors whose interest resonates with the initial questioning of past experience. This process leads to 'a particular way of understanding a complex reality' among competing reasonable understandings (Mehta 2010, 27) by 'attributing cause, blame, and responsibility' (Stone 1989, 282). The understanding of such a situation is the result of an interactive social reconstruction process.

In order to restore such a consensus, a physical location and formats for exchange that allow discussions among relevant actors need to be found. This process of consensus building often takes the form of working groups, where experts from relevant organizations regarding the issue at stake come together to discuss the matter and how to deal with it. Elaborating reports is often part of this process of building the cognitive grounds for future policy proposals and delimiting what is collectively feasible. While the central loci of the policy-making process in a narrow sense are laid down in the constitution and other procedural laws, consensus (or agenda) building as a pre-stage can be realized in different settings. Problems can be defined within public institutions, but also in privately organized settings, parliamentary committees, or informal or ad hoc working groups. The initial dynamic that follows the questioning of a taken for granted assumption may thereby give an impetus on the fora and the settings that are feasible.

Practically, since this process is not about cognitions only, it implies coalition building, whereby the ways in which a specific assumption is questioned collectively are decisive for the coalition that is likely to emerge. While the core of a coalition is often composed of actors deeply convinced about the accuracy of a specific interpretation, others may join such a coalition more for strategic reasons, such as business opportunities or voter turnout. The coalitions that may emerge from these interactions are more malleable than what we know from the advocacy coalitions framework (Sabatier and Jenkins-Smith 1988, 1993) and resonate with salient attitudes, convictions, and experiences outside the policy-making community. If this process is successful, the emergence of a coherent reform agenda can be observed, structured by one specific understanding of what the situation is about and, consequently, how to deal with it.

Finally, the new consensus needs to be consolidated through political reforms. This has a stabilizing effect because it adds a formalized component, which punishes defection or provides positive incentives to what has become a new belief. If this process is successful, the situation stabilizes, and routine behaviour can develop within the new collectively shared framework. Social learning may be more or less influential in shaping future developments, depending on the extent to which the formalization of its implications is successful. Formalization contributes to the fact that a taken for granted assumption is indeed taken as a given that cannot easily be diminished, adding an external constraint or incentive to an internalized feature. This in turn increases the likelihood of the regularity with which a specific pattern can be observed (Clemens and Cook 1999, 447).

Table 3.2 summarizes the essential observable characteristics of the three stages of social learning and the role of the institutional context in each of them. In general terms, it can be hypothesized that the relevance of the institutional settings is all the more restricted, the more open and contingent the situation is. At the initial stage, when past developments are questioned collectively, the observable institutional imprints may be vague and only involve basic features of the political economy, such as a consensual vs. an adversarial style of interactions. At the second stage, institutional venues where problems can be discussed in a more structured way and agreement fostered are decisive. However, as existing venues can be used or ad hoc solutions found, the influence of the institutional settings in place must be considered an empirical question.

Once problems are defined and the corresponding political agenda established, the process of policy-making in a narrow sense begins and the institutional dispositions in place play are likely to play a more prominent role.

Table 3.2 The stages of social learning

	Questioning of the status quo	Fostering a new consensus	Consolidation through political reform
Defining characteristics	Realization that at least one taken for granted assumption on the functioning of the economy is not valid anymore bringing a specific feature of a complex social phenomenon to the fore	Consensus building on the implications for the future through a more structured process Emergence of an agenda that is structured by a specific understanding of the situation	Implementation of concrete policy proposals that are in line with the new consensus
Major drivers	Uncoordinated responses Mobilization of affected groups Media coverage	Reassessment of past developments and discussion of the implications for the future in working groups, by commanding scientific expertise etc.	Nature of the measures Institutional resources and veto points
Role of the institutional context	Limited, only very fundamental features matter	Intermediate, venues where an agreement is fostered are decisive	Relatively high, but mediated by the collective understanding of the situation

Source: Own elaboration.

The results thereby depend on the ways in which the new consensus interacts with the institutional resources of those defending it and the veto points in place (Immergut 1992), hindering or promoting policy change. While social learning mediates the effects of the formal institutions in place, it will usually not fully offset them. A new collectively shared understanding of what the situation is about has an enabling effect for actors whose position is rather weakly represented in the institutional configuration in place and it may constrain others from fully profiting from their institutional resources associated with power and access. Social learning can be more or less influential in shaping future developments, depending on how successful this final stage is.

3.5   From path dependencies to developmental paths

The following chapters analyse both how the global financial crisis led to the questioning of existing beliefs on banking that were widely shared and taken for granted in the years before and the lessons drawn from it for future developments. The analysis begins at the global level, studying the participation of French and German representatives in international banking reforms. It moves on to explore how the financial crisis was perceived domestically and the lessons drawn from it there. The crisis brought different aspects of banking to the fore, leading to opposed conclusions with respect to the future role of the banks in funding the economy. While France and Germany defended rather similar positions in the negotiations on international banking reforms, the understandings of the implications of the financial crisis drawn from it domestically differed considerably. As we will see, these differing understandings are insufficiently explained by materialist variables, such as power and access.

The lessons learnt have to be contextualized with respect to the features the crisis had brought to the fore in the light of specific developments within both economies in the years prior to it. The conclusions drawn from the crisis responded to specific taken for granted features that were questioned collectively and adapted in response to it.

One may wonder to what extent the lessons learnt in response to the global financial crisis are the natural or somehow objective lessons to emerge. In other words, did the developments in France and Germany up to the crisis inevitably lead to the conclusions that were drawn in response to it? As a matter of principle, the lessons learnt from a crisis and the reformatory steps initiated in response to it are not self-evident and objectively and without ambiguity assessable (e.g. Blyth 2002; Froud et al. 2012; Hay 1996, 1999; Widmaier et al. 2007). A telling empirical example of the fact that there is no direct link between crises and the nature, the direction, and the extent of policy change is the Fukushima nuclear accident, which led to a complete policy U-turn by the German government with the decision for a nuclear power phase-out, but not in other countries, including Japan.

The conclusions drawn from a crisis are those a significant coalition of actors can agree on and they tend to resonate with how a specific situation is understood in circles that transcend the policy-making community. The lessons learnt result from the sense-making or the rationalization by relevant actors of what they perceive is going on. When looking back, the conclusions drawn, or the lessons learnt, may well appear reasonable or even seem obvious. However, this does not mean that alternative reasonable interpretations could not have been conceivable ex ante.[4] At the same time, the chosen diachronic comparative approach, combining comparisons among separate units of analysis and within case analysis over time, allows us to see that the specific conclusions drawn from the crisis in France and Germany did not have the same chance of occurring in both countries after the crisis, nor were they likely to be seen randomly at other moments in time. In that sense there is an objective anchor, something inevitable in the circumstances that delimits what is compatible with the available evidence at hand.

When a taken for granted assumption is questioned collectively and a new consensus found on what the situation is about and how to deal with it, this is not the beginning of a new developmental trajectory from scratch. Rather, the understanding of the situation itself and the conclusions drawn from it for future developments are informed by how actors reassess and make sense of past developments. Future trajectories are not necessarily determined by previous developments and the institutions in place in a path-dependent way, but they are informed—to differing degrees—by what happened in the past. They are conditioned by the ways in which and the timing of when past developments are no longer considered as a valid and reliable depiction for the future. In that sense, one can speak of developmental paths.

In order to study moments of institutional change, it is necessary to recognize that the functioning of real-world institutions as effective governance arrangements builds both on informal shared assumptions of what the social world is like and on formal rules that influence human behaviour either because they are coercive and defection can be punished or because they are

---

[4] We will come back to this aspect in Chapter 8.

instrumental in achieving goals, as is the case with procedural rules (Djelic and Quack 2003b, 18; Keller 2014, 29 ff.). Studying institutional change requires analysing their interplay. Important moments of political reform are tied to the dynamics of stability and change in informal institutions and to the changes in their substance. Informal institutions shape processes of formal institutional change because they mediate the extent to which formal institutions can be deployed by strategic actors.

4

The Great Recession and international banking reforms

What implications did the global financial crisis have for the future of banking? A partial answer to this question lies in the conclusions drawn from it in regulatory terms in international fora. This chapter deals with how French and German representatives participated in the negotiations of what has become known as 'Basel III', and its adaptation and transposition into European law by a reform and an amendment of the Capital Requirements Directive (CRD). Basel III is the major reform piece on banking agreed upon internationally in the aftermath of the Great Recession. It is an overhaul of previous Basel II framework. Since it sets standards for risk management and limits to the activities banks may pursue, it affects banks in their everyday business.

Given that bank intermediation and the utilization of the bank balance in financing the economy by granting credit and holding it until maturity does not play the same role in so-called bank-based as compared to more market-based financial systems, it is particularly interesting to observe the extent to which representatives from France and Germany supported regulations that could potentially have a negative impact on classic bank intermediation. If representatives from countries with so-called bank-based financial systems, so the underlying assumption goes, care about bank intermediation in a specific way, we should see this in the negotiations on global banking reforms.

The first section gives a short overview of the origins and the propagation of the global financial crisis. In a next step, the internationally coordinated response to the crisis is presented. The focus thereby is on key elements of Basel III and CRR-CRDIV—bank capital, liquidity, and leverage—and how they potentially impact bank intermediation. The third section moves on to describe how the relevant policy communities in both France and Germany dealt with these issues—the priorities they had identified and the demands they articulated during the reform process. The chapter concludes by comparing French

Financial Crises and the Limits of Bank Reform: France and Germany's Ways Into and Out of the Great Recession.
Eileen Keller, Oxford University Press (2021). © Eileen Keller. DOI: 10.1093/oso/9780198870746.003.0004

and German priorities to those articulated by representatives from the United States and the United Kingdom and their traditionally more market-based financial systems.

The chapter shows that some of the priorities expressed by national banking regulators both in the ministries and the central banks were relatively similar to those advanced by banking sector representatives, an observation that can be attributed to structural characteristics of the respective domestic banking sector and the implications the reforms had in terms of adjustment costs and, consequently, for the competitiveness of the domestic financial sector. On the global level, where negotiations occur on a highly aggregated level, the major divide was between countries where traditional bank lending plays a major role and those where market-based forms of funding are more prominent. Representatives of intermediated financial systems do care about the regulatory effects on bank lending in a specific way.

4.1 From the crisis towards reforms

The Great Recession, which became the most encompassing financial crisis in the western world since the Great Depression, began as a crisis in the US-American housing markets in summer 2007 with the bursting of a bubble. Housing markets there saw a considerable boom in the period prior to the crisis, with house prices rising by an average 11 per cent per year between 2000 and 2005 (Mayer et al. 2008, 21). With rising prices, acquiring real estate was attractive and more and more Americans became homeowners. This trend was supported by political measures that aimed at diversifying the social structure of homeownership and was further fuelled by the expansive monetary policy of the Federal Reserve, whose low interest rates contributed to an increasing demand for real estate. Innovative financial techniques also supported the housing boom as—with hindsight only seemingly— sophisticated risk management techniques allowed the granting of ever riskier loans by the banks. Thanks to them and rising house prices, selling real estate to individuals with little equity capital and hardly any collateral had become a profitable business (Krugman 2009).

These high-risk loans, also called subprime loans because of their inferior quality, were transformed into highly complex financial products (structured asset-backed securities, ABS or collateralized debt obligations, CDOs) thanks to securitization techniques. These techniques, which were originally developed in the United States in the 1930s, allowed for the transformation of illiquid receivables, such as bank debt, into tradable financial products. For this purpose, the banks transferred a loan portfolio to a bankruptcy remote investment vehicle (Special Purpose Vehicles, SPVs or Conduits) and with it—that was the assumption—the associated default risk, passing from an originate to hold to an originate to distribute business model. De facto, banks avoided regulatory costs and increased their leverage by outsourcing some of their activities into structures that were subject to lower regulatory standards (Laeven and Valencia 2010), profiting from regulatory arbitrage (Brunnermeier 2009). With risks being transferred, incentives and internal risk management in financial organizations were massively distorted (Carmassi et al. 2009).

The SPVs pooled a portfolio of credit and—this was new—issued financial products with different tranches according to how they would be treated in the case of defaults in the underlying portfolio. Some of these tranches were consequently deemed riskier than others and even though the quality of the underlying portfolio was inferior, most of the tranches were rated a safe investment.[1] The vehicles drew on short-term wholesale funding, such as repurchasing agreements and asset-backed commercial papers (ABCPs). This sector, which became known as the shadow banking sector after the crisis, engaging in bank-like activities without being subjected to banking regulation, sold its financial products on to investors worldwide, including many banks in the United States and Europe, creating 'an opaque web of interconnected obligations' (Brunnermeier 2009, 98).

As the economist Herbert Stein put it, 'if something cannot go on forever, it will stop' (documented in Joint Economic Committee 1976, 262): From 2006 onwards, the housing market in the United States began to show signs of a reversal and a self-reinforcing downward spiral set in. Housing prices began to fall and as interest rates were rising, an increasing number of homeowners who held contracts with flexible interest rates defaulted on their debt. This, in turn, put further pressure on house prices. With house prices in free fall, the banks had to sell the real estate from defaulted homeowners at a loss and faced solvency problems themselves. Accordingly, the highly complex mortgage-backed securities began losing value from summer 2007 onwards and saw drastic downgradings by the rating agencies (Sabry and Okongwu 2009). The market imploded, as did the ABCP market, and the vehicles had to draw on the credit lines from the sponsoring banks, putting them under pressure.

---

[1] Thanks to the tranching, about 96% (!) of the tranches were rated AAA, and hence considered a safe investment even though the underlying portfolio only had a BBB rating (Sachverständigenrat 2007, 114).

Investors worldwide had to incur massive write-downs and reoriented their investments towards safe havens. According to estimations by the IMF, losses and write-downs amounted to 1.2 trillion US dollars in Europe and to 4.1 trillion worldwide (Dattels and Kodres 2009).

The crisis culminated with the shutdown of the US-American investment bank Lehman Brothers on 15 September 2008, which triggered a large scale crisis of confidence among financial institutions worldwide. The subprime crisis developed into an encompassing liquidity crisis. The interbank market, which plays an important role in short-term bank refinancing, dried up because the trust of the banks in the solvency of one another had disappeared, literally from one day to the next. The banks refused to lend to each other, even on a short-term basis, because everyone feared lending to a failing bank. In the years prior to the crisis, the interconnectedness among large financial institutions had increased, and many (investment) banks relied on short-term wholesale funding and (overnight) repurchasing agreements. Their maturity mismatch had increased accordingly, amplifying the contraction, once the crisis hit (Brunnermeier 2009; Hellwig 2008).

In order to contain the situation, the central banks intervened massively from mid 2007 onwards, lowering interest rates, easing access to central bank liquidity, and buying up assets. The US government and many governments in Europe set up huge public support schemes, including guarantees for fragile banks, equity participations, lending facilities, and fiscal stimulus packages for the real economy (Panetta et al. 2009; Woll 2014). On average, European governments granted support equalling 11 per cent of GDP to the financial sector (European Commission 2011c, 7). By far the largest share of the losses occurred in the United States (55 per cent), followed by the United Kingdom (12 per cent), Germany (9 per cent), Switzerland (7 per cent), and France (3 per cent) (IMF 2009, 14).

While the real economy suffered from a severe recession in the subsequent period—2009 was, until then, the only year since the beginning of the World Bank records in 1960 in which the world gross domestic product shrank—the encompassing rescue measures had the desired effect and the international financial system stabilized from autumn 2008 onwards. With the emergency measures in place and signs of a stabilization of the situation apparent, reflections on how to reform the international financial architecture intensified rapidly. With respect to the regulatory architecture of banking, a first set of regulatory measures introduced in July 2009, also known as Basel II.5, aimed at rectifying major shortcomings of the regulatory architecture in place concerning the risks to which banks were exposed when dealing with complex financial products. These included the capital requirements for the trading book, the prudential treatment of securitized products, and the framework for market risk (Basel Committee 2009).

Whereas these initial measures targeted specific regulatory deficiencies, the regulatory agenda that followed was much more encompassing and aimed at making the entire financial system more resilient in the case of financial shocks. It was, in other words, not just about correcting specific aspects of the regulatory architecture, but an attempt to reshape it more generally. With respect to banking, this led to the establishment of the Basel III framework. It modified the existing Basel II framework in important ways and is the reform initiative with the most immediate impact on the future economic role of the banks.

4.2 Genesis of Basel III and CRR-CRDIV

With the tremendous write-downs many banks incurred and the costs of the bailouts, an agreement emerged among governments worldwide that banking regulation—as financial sector regulation more generally—had to be revised. In November 2008—hence only few weeks after the breakdown of Lehman Brothers—the first ever G20 Summit of the heads of governments and states took place in Washington DC. The G20 Forum was set up to coordinate the global reform efforts. Part of the agreement among political leaders early on was to review the existing regulatory framework for bank risk and liquidity management. The banking sector reforms were part of a broader reform agenda, which was detailed in a 47-point action plan and refined and implemented successively over the subsequent G20 summits (G20 2008). Besides ending too-big-to-fail, making derivatives markets safer, and enhancing the resilience of the shadow banking sector, building more resilient banks was one of the four key areas of regulatory reform (Financial Stability Board 2018, 6).

By the second G20 Summit, which took place in London in April 2009, the political leaders had agreed on a set of elements that became the cornerstones of the future regulatory treatment of global banks. The details of these plans for reform were elaborated by the Basel Committee of Banking Supervision (Basel Committee or BCBS hereafter), the international forum of central bankers originally founded by the G10 countries in 1974 and joined by other states later on. The Basel Committee functions as a global standard setter in the realm of prudential banking regulation and comprises 28 member nowadays.

Among the key measures agreed upon on were additional capital buffers, higher capital minima, an enhanced capital definition, a non-risk-based measure to limit the build-up of leverage, the development of a framework for capital buffers, and better practices for the risk management of asset securitization (G20 2009, 2–3). At the subsequent summits, political leaders confirmed their commitment to the reforms repeatedly and welcomed the partial agreements that had been reached by the Basel Committee up to then. In November 2010, the heads of governments and states formally endorsed the 'landmark agreement reached in the Basel Committee on the new bank capital and liquidity framework' and announced that they would 'adopt and implement fully these standards within the agreed timeframe' (G20 2010, 7).

4.2.1 From political commitments to new standards

The reform procedure initiated by the G20 group altered the way the Basel Committee operated. Until then, the committee of central bank representatives and banking regulators operated autonomously and defined its working programme independently of direct political influence. With the crisis, political leaders took control and defined the reform priorities the Basel Committee was subsequently asked to work on (interview 2013103019D). Figure 4.1 gives a chronological overview of the Basel III and CRR-CRDIV reform processes.

In March 2009, the Basel Committee officially announced its endorsement of the bank capital reforms in line with the commitment expressed by political leaders at the London G20 Summit. A first draft reform proposal was elaborated by the end of the year and submitted to public consultation in December 2009. In July 2010, based on the feedback from the consultation process and the results of the quantitative impact assessment, the Group of Governors and Heads of Supervision (GHOS), the central oversight organ of the Basel Committee, published its agreement on major design elements and a list of modifications to the December 2009 consultation paper. The final calibration of the new instruments was announced for the second semester of the same year and elaborated during the subsequent committee meetings (Basel Committee 2010e). The final version of the original Basel III framework was published on 16 December 2010 (Basel Committee 2010a, 2010b).

The transposition in Brussels was realized through the third revision of the Capital Requirements Directive (CRD), the harmonized European legal framework for banking. The European Commission launched two public

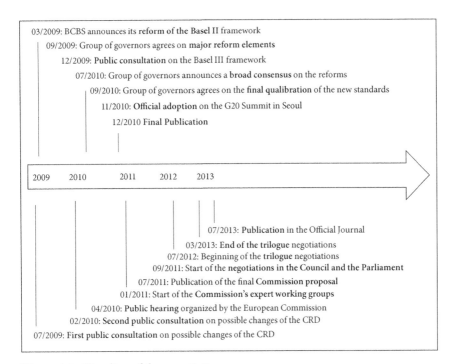

03/2009: BCBS announces its reform of the Basel II framework
  09/2009: Group of governors agrees on major reform elements
    12/2009: Public consultation on the Basel III framework
      07/2010: Group of governors announces a broad consensus on the reforms
        09/2010: Group of governors agrees on the final qualibration of the new standards
        11/2010: Official adoption on the G20 Summit in Seoul
        12/2010 Final Publication

2009   2010   2011   2012   2013

        07/2013: Publication in the Official Journal
      03/2013: End of the trilogue negotiations
      07/2012: Beginning of the trilogue negotiations
      09/2011: Start of the negotiations in the Council and the Parliament
    07/2011: Publication of the final Commission proposal
    01/2011: Start of the Commission's expert working groups
  04/2010: Public hearing organized by the European Commission
  02/2010: Second public consultation on possible changes of the CRD
07/2009: First public consultation on possible changes of the CRD

Figure 4.1 Timeline of the negotiation process
Source: Own elaboration based on press releases of the Basel Committee and the EU procedure files.

consultations on potential modifications to the CRD in July 2009 and February 2010.[2] In early 2011, the Commission started to gather informal working groups with experts from the competent national regulatory and supervisory agencies, in which the future contours of the banking regulation were discussed. The Commission published its final legislative proposal in July 2011.

The Commission's proposal for the revision of the Capital Requirements Directive included, for the first time, a *regulation* on capital requirements (capital requirements regulation, CRR). Contrary to a directive, its content would thus be directly applicable in all the (then) 28 member states without being transposed into national law. The introduction of a single rulebook marked a shift away from minimum towards maximum harmonization, reducing the scope for national discretion. The European Council and the

---

[2] In addition, two public consultations dealt with countercyclical buffers and certain types of counterparty credit risk in early 2011 (see documentation of the European Commission, http://ec.europa.eu/internal_market/bank/regcapital/legislation_in_force_de.htm, accessed on 17 March 2014).

European Parliament, prepared by technical working groups[3] and the Committee for Economic and Monetary Affairs (ECON), had internally agreed on their respective versions of the reform proposal by May 2012. The trilogue negotiations between the Commission, the Council, and the Parliament started in July of the same year and lasted, at ten months, unexpectedly long.

The final agreement on the European reform proposal was achieved in March 2013. The application of the new rules had to be postponed by a year compared to the original timeline. The reform package was adopted by the European Parliament on 16 April and by a large majority in the Council on 27 May. The final publication of the third revision of the Capital Requirements Directive (CRDIV, Directive 2013/36/EU) and the newly introduced Capital Requirements Regulation (CRR, Regulation (EU) No 575/2013) was on 17 July 2013. Some aspects of Basel III as well as some of the adjustments made in 2016 and 2017 (Basel Committee 2017, also known as Basel IV) were implemented with the CRR2-CRDV reform package in 2019.

4.2.2 Important reform elements

The financial crisis had led to the recognition that the regulatory regime was globally insufficient. Thus the approach to regulatory reform in response to it was broad and tackled various aspects of banking in such a way that the reforms were likely to have an impact on the everyday business of even those banks not directly involved in the build-up and the propagation of the crisis. Both Basel III and CRR-CRDIV are encompassing reform packages that cannot be presented in detail here. The following description will therefore be restricted to three core elements: stricter capital requirements, the introduction, for the first time, of harmonized standards for liquidity, and a non-risk-based leverage ratio regarding the banks' balance sheet volume as a complement to the Basel II risk-weighted approach.

Part of the consensus among politicians and regulators was that the pre-crisis capital requirements were not sufficient.[4] Regulatory capital requirements

---

[3] The work in the Council is realized by technical working groups. They are composed of representatives of the Finance Ministries from the member states, who are accompanied by technical advisers from the competent national regulatory and supervisory authorities. Remaining contentious issues are negotiated by the permanent representatives in Brussels (Coreper II; interview 2013070317).

[4] The following description is based on the Basel III framework. Divergences in Europe will be discussed subsequently. As banking regulation quickly becomes quite technical, further details on the reforms are provided in the footnotes.

define the loss absorption capacities of a bank both on a going concern basis (losses that occur in relation to the day-to-day business without threatening the bank's existence) and in the case of a bankruptcy (Deutsche Bundesbank 2011, 7). If the capital level of a bank falls below the minimal regulatory requirements, it has to face sanctions by the supervisor, which may lead to the withdrawal of the bank licence as last resort. Two elements were at the core of the reform: An overall increase of the required capital levels and a more stringent and more restrictive capital definition. The calculation and the calibration of the capital requirements for credit risk, by contrast, were, apart from minor adjustments, initially not modified.[5]

Regarding the amount of capital, the new rules increased its overall level from 8 per cent to 10.5 per cent. This new minimum capital ratio includes a capital conservation buffer that can be used up in times of financial distress under certain conditions.[6] The capital levels banks have to hold may, however, reach higher levels due to the phase-in of an anti-cyclical buffer of up to 2.5 per cent, and additional capital surcharges for global and domestic systemically important banks (so-called G-SIBs and D-SIBs). Substantively, the Basel Committee defined as core tier 1 capital, the most restrictive category of equity capital, shares and retained earnings only. For financial institutions that were not listed on a stock exchange and, hence, did not dispose of equity capital in the form of shares, a catalogue of 14 criteria was defined in order to guarantee an equivalent loss absorption quality. The role of further equity capital instruments was restricted, its structure simplified, and more assets had to be deducted (Deutsche Bundesbank 2011, 9–13).

The second major element was the introduction of a binding liquidity ratio. Liquidity requirements complement the capital requirements by making prescriptions regarding the composition of the assets- and the liabilities side of a bank balance. Two quantitative measures were introduced to that end: The short-term Liquidity Coverage Ratio (LCR) and the longer-term Net Stable Funding Ratio (NSFR). The LCR is based on an estimation of the liquidity of bank assets and the stability or volatility of a bank's liabilities.

---

[5] Basel III modified the correlation coefficient in the IRB approach for exposures to big financial institutions. Basel II.5 modified the risk weights for certain assets of the trading book (interview 2013103019D). Additional modifications followed in December 2017, adjusting some risk weights and their granularity (Basel Committee 2017).

[6] The level of core equity tier 1 capital (CET1) was raised from 2% to 4.5% of risk-weighted assets. The importance of the lower quality capital components, additional tier 1 and 2, was lowered from 2% to 1.5% and from 4% to 2% respectively. A bank can use the 2.5% capital conservation buffer under certain circumstances to absorb losses. However, the lower the capital conservation buffer is, the more restricted is the distribution of profits. Banks thus have an incentive not to fall below the buffer (also see Deutsche Bundesbank 2011, 8 ff.).

The ratio requires that a bank's stock of so-called high-quality liquid assets (HQLA), which are easily convertible into cash, is superior to the net outflow of funding sources in a scenario of increased financial stress (Basel Committee 2013). The ratio is supposed to guarantee that a bank can survive a one month period of restricted access to financial resources without public or central bank support because it holds a sufficient stock of liquid financial assets it can easily sell off to meet its payment obligations (also see Deutsche Bundesbank 2011, 30–2).[7] The NSFR complements the LCR, covering a longer time horizon and focusing on stocks instead of the in- and outflows of funds. The NSFR aims at limiting a bank's engagement in term transformation by restricting the maturity spread between a bank's assets and liabilities. The ratio requires that the volume of long-term financial sources available is superior to the long-term financial sources needed over a period of one year.[8]

The third main element of the new Basel agreement is the leverage ratio which limits the on- and off-balance volumes of a bank as a percentage of its equity capital on a non-risk-weighted basis. According to the proposed calibration, the ratio of core (tier 1) capital to all assets may not fall below 3 per cent. The ratio puts an absolute limit to an ever-increasing leverage of financial institutions (Deutsche Bundesbank 2011, 28–9). The final specification and calibration of both, the liquidity ratios and the leverage ratio were not determined by the Basel III framework itself. Given the fact that both measures had not existed as global standards before, the central bank representatives included review clauses and agreed on subjecting the final calibration to further investigation and an observation period. Final adjustments of the approach to credit risk, and the measurement of the leverage ratio were published by the Governors and Heads of Supervision in December 2017 (Basel Committee 2017).[9]

---

[7] The calculation of the LCR is based on assumptions of how a bank's assets and liabilities will be affected by a period of financial stress. Regulatory prescriptions define the degree of liquidity of different categories of bank assets and the degree of stability of bank liabilities and potential outflows in a period of financial stress. Among the highly liquid assets are cash, central bank deposits and highly liquid debt titles of central banks and states (level 1 assets) and, to a minor extent, other assets, such as corporate debt titles, covered bonds, RMBS (level 2 assets) (Basel Committee 2013, Annex 1).

[8] The NSFR is based on a classification of assets according to their need for long-term funding and of liabilities in terms of their long-term commitment character. Among the stable sources of funding are equity capital (100%) and retail deposits (80–90%), and, to a lesser extent, wholesale funding by non-financial corporations, development banks, and central banks (50%). Among the assets which require long-term funding are unencumbered listed equity securities (50%), loans (50–100%), and debt securities with a rating below A- (100%) (Basel Committee 2010b, 46–7).

[9] The LCR was supposed to be introduced in 2015, but it was postponed. In January 2013, the GHOS finalized the LCR, modified certain dispositions regarding its calculation, and agreed on a gradual phase-in up to 2019 (Basel Committee 2013). Further details on the NSFR were published in October 2014; it has been operative since 2018. Regarding the leverage ratio, the banks started

The three reform elements—more and better equity capital and new measures for liquidity and leverage—share several important commonalities. First, all three resulted from the re-politicization of banking regulation in the aftermath of the crisis. Rather than being exclusively the result of technocratic consensus building among regulatory and supervisory elites, they were in the first place proposed and endorsed by the political leaders of the G20 countries, who had committed themselves to strengthening the resilience of the banking sector. Therefore, the elements must be considered as political choices and not as purely technical ones—a fact often used as a reproach against them during the reform process.

Secondly, the three elements transport important insights from the crisis on the shortages of the pre-crisis regulatory architecture into regulatory and supervisory practice. The reform of the capital requirements addresses quantitatively insufficient pre-crisis levels of capital endowments and qualitatively their composition (the elements that are taken into account when the regulatory capital is calculated). In addition, the capital buffers add a macroprudential component to the existing microprudential approach to banking regulation. The introduction of binding liquidity standards in addition to the capital requirements reflects the recognition that the pre-crisis regulatory regime had focused too exclusively on the solvency of financial institutions. Prior to the crisis, regulators and supervisors had largely assumed that financial institutions would not face severe liquidity problems as long as they were solvent, holding sufficient loss absorbing capital—an assumption that the crisis had strikingly proved wrong (interview 2013103019, Deutsche Bundesbank 2011, 30). Finally, the introduction of a leverage ratio recognizes the limits of a risk-based approach to banking regulation and the capacities of both supervisors and financial institutions to assess financial risks correctly. Accordingly, the leverage ratio sets an absolute limit to the overall indebtedness of banks, irrespectively of the risk profile.

Thirdly, the three elements have implications for the economic functions banks can—or are likely to—fulfil as financial intermediaries. Depending on how strict the new standards are, the attractiveness of bank credit relative to other forms of funding can be questioned to a greater or lesser extent, because there is 'a trade-off between the extent and degree of regulation on banks, to make them safer, and their capacity to intermediate between lenders and

reporting on the ratio to their supervisor in 2013. The initial schedule foresaw the publication of the ratio in 2015 and its introduction as a binding pillar 1 measure in 2018 (Basel Committee 2010c). A revised measurement and a leverage ratio buffer for G-SIBs was introduced in December 2017 and will be implemented by 2022 (Basel Committee 2017).

borrowers, in particular their ability to generate credit flows on acceptable terms to potential borrowers' (Goodhart 2010, 175; also Brunella et al. 2018b). Even if regulatory changes result in complex adjustment processes depending on how various economic actors respond to the new incentives, regulatory reforms can have effects that go beyond the regulatory prescription as such, due to regulatory arbitrage and shifts in the relative cost of different bank activities and alternative sources of funding they may trigger. Regarding the elements of interest here, this may be the case in several ways.

With respect to bank capital, an increase in the overall capital requirements and a more restrictive definition of what counts as loss absorbing capital has, all things being equal, an impact on both the costliness of a bank credit in terms of equity capital and the global volume of credit a bank can attribute with a given capital base. This does not necessarily mean that bank credit will be costlier for the debtor because it is possible that the adjustment is made at the expense of the bank's margins, especially when competition within a certain market segment is high (interview 20130926D). While it is not entirely clear how strong the link between capital levels and capital costs is, because higher equity levels might lead to lower risk premia (e.g. vbw 2012, 19–21), there could be constraints to capital increases even if the link was weak because of an unfavourable market environment or because not all banks are joint-stock companies.

The liquidity requirements in turn may have two effects: On the one hand, they restrict the banks' capacities to engage in maturity transformation and, hence, transform their short-term liabilities (e.g. bank sight deposits) into long-term assets (e.g. middle and long-term credit), the mechanism which has been central to the development of modern banking. Long-term credit could consequently become scarcer and more expensive (Griffith-Jones et al. 2009, 19 ff.). On the other hand, given the specific definition of which assets are considered to be liquid or volatile, banks are incentivized to engage in credit-substitution businesses, for example by investing in debt titles rather than issuing credit (e.g. DSGV 2013).

Finally, the leverage ratio puts another overall limit to a bank's activities, in addition to the capital requirements. The leverage ratio thereby is particularly penalizing for the traditional, so-called originate-to-hold bank business model, and low-risk—and hence low capital consuming—bank activities (BMF 2010). A bank that engages in this form of banking issues credit and holds it on balance until the term of the contract. In contrast, when a bank issues a credit and sells at least parts of the credit risk (or the claim itself) to an investor (originate to distribute), as it was increasingly the case in the years prior to the crisis, bank lending contributes much less to an increase of the bank's balance sheet volume. The ratio might thus ultimately contribute to an increase in the use of the securitization techniques that had contributed to the financial crisis in the first place, at the expense of traditional bank lending.

The impact study conducted by the Basel Committee in parallel to the elaboration of the new standards suggested that all post-crisis modifications of the capital requirements taken together, including the so-called Basel 2.5 agreement on trading book activities, would lead to a decrease of the current capital ratio from 11 per cent (Basel II calculation) to 5.7 per cent according to the stricter capital definition of the new Basel II.5 and III standards for the big banks, having a tier 1 capital volume above 3 billion Euros, and from 10.7 per cent to 7.8 per cent for smaller banks. The additional capital volume to be built up in order to meet the new 7 per cent core tier 1 capital ratio (CET 1) was estimated to be 577 billion Euros for the big and 25 billion Euros for the smaller banks (Basel Committee 2010d, 8, 10).

In order to meet the liquidity ratios, the banks would need an additional 1.73 trillion Euros of liquid assets for the LCR and 2.89 trillion Euros of stable funding resources for the NSFR (Basel Committee 2010d, 17 ff.). According to tests based on a preliminary definition of the leverage ratio, it amounted to 2.8 per cent for the big and to 3.8 per cent for the smaller banks; overall, 42 per cent of all banks would have to reduce their balance sheet in order to meet the new 3 per cent ratio (Basel Committee 2010d, 14–15).[10] Even though some experts recommended much higher capital levels and a much simpler definition (e.g. Admati and Hellwig 2013), the new requirements did imply considerable adjustment costs for many banks. To what extent did regulators from France and Germany endorse and push for the reforms in order to make the banks more resilient?

4.3   Defining reform priorities

The decision-making process in both Basel and Brussels is strongly marked by its bargaining character. International negotiations usually imply conflicts of interest even if all participants share the conviction that a collectively shared solution is preferable to a situation without shared standards. The typical outcomes of negotiations are compromises. All participants have to

---

[10] The leverage ratio is defined as the ratio of capital (numerator) to assets (denominator). Hence, the higher the leverage, the lower the leverage ratio.

make concessions, but usually obtain some recognition of their major concerns or priorities, depending on their negotiation strategy and the power resources at their disposal (e.g. Abbott and Snidal 1998; Hirschman 1970; Keohane 1984; Krasner 1983; Moravcsik 1991; Scharpf 1997). The logic of negotiations usually implies that no party sees all of its policy preferences realized in the final agreement. Participating in international and European negotiations consequently requires prioritizing among one's policy preferences and singling out key issues to make sure that some recognition is achieved on one's most pressing issues.

In the following subsections, the focus is on the policy preferences and priorities French and German representatives expressed during the reform process. Did the French and the Germans agree on measures that could potentially constrain bank lending? Or, inversely, were they particularly rigid in making sure that the banks, which are important for the domestic economy, would be more resilient in the future? The financial industry's lobbying efforts suitably illustrate the crucial nature of what was at stake for the banks: One representative of the banking sector counted 49 meetings of her federation with the European Commission's bureaucracy, 50 meetings with members of the European Council, and 60 meetings with members of the European Parliament during the CRR-CRDIV negotiations alone (interview 2013052401).

The policy preferences defended during the negotiations can be considered as an indicator of how supportive representatives from both countries were of classic bank intermediation and how willing they were to defend the domestic financing model where banks and bank lending play a prominent role. The following discussion shows that the key issues advanced by French and German representatives can be attributed to structural characteristics of the domestic banking sector and the distributional consequences the reforms implied in terms of (relative) adjustment costs. If one extends the analysis to the broader coalitions which opposed each other during global banking reform negotiations, one can see that both the French and the German representatives defended bank lending in a similar way and were much more cautious regarding the potential impact of the reforms on classic bank intermediation than, for instance, representatives of the United States or the United Kingdom.

4.3.1 Germany: Protecting bank diversity

A major concern for Germany with respect to Basel III was to make sure that the specificities of the German banking model based on the three-pillar structure with its diversified banking landscape would not come under pressure. The cooperative and the savings bank sector were very active in emphasizing that they were different from other banks. They insisted that they best represented the German long-term funding culture, that they had maintained long-established, deep regional roots, and that they were crucial partners for the real economy, for smaller and middle-sized enterprises in particular. In addition, representatives from both banking groups did not tire of emphasizing that they were not directly involved in the build-up and the propagation of the financial crisis and that their lending behaviour had a stabilizing effect during the crisis.

The preferred solution of the savings and the cooperative banking sector was to be excluded from the rules of Basel III and to apply the new rules to the transnationally active, big financial institutions only. Representatives from both banking sectors argued that Basel III only addressed the problems of the big banks, which were active in market-related activities and that the reform did not concern the smaller banks that were above all involved in classic bank lending and relationship banking. This stands in contrast to their positioning on Basel II, where they had lobbied actively to be included in the scope of application of the new rules.[11] As one banking representative explained:

> At that time, there was a longer discussion...and it was a conscious decision to lobby for the fact that Basel II would be applicable to all [credit] institutions. The focus of Basel III is different. It's a child of the financial crisis and it deals more with bank liabilities than with bank assets....That's the difference, because neither the savings nor the cooperative banks, as they are all small financial institutions, were involved in or responsible for the crisis. That's why it [Basel III] does not fit all banks, whether big or small, international or regional, in the same way as it was true for Basel II, that's the difference between the two regulatory regimes.   (Interview 2013101412D)[12]

This demand was not endorsed politically by any relevant party because it was not deemed a politically feasible solution (interview 2013120526D). At the same time, taking the specificities of the cooperative and the savings banks into account was consensual among all major political parties. As an exclusion from the scope of Basel III was not feasible, representatives from the banking

---

[11] The purpose of the Basel Committee is to harmonize key regulatory prescriptions for transnationally active banks. Within Europe, the decision was made to apply the Basel rules to all EU banks, irrespective of their size.

[12] All quotations from the interviews are own translations.

sector, but also the corporate sector, lobbied for the use of a directive rather than a regulation regarding its implementation at the European level in order to leave some room for domestic adjustments. The demand was taken up by the then Social Democratic opposition party SPD in a resolution but rejected by the governing coalition (Deutscher Bundestag 2012, interview 2013120526D).

A second issue of immediate concern in the context of bank diversity, for both the regulators and the banks, were the bank capital requirements, both in quantitative and qualitative terms. Given the fact that the Basel Committee defined bank capital in the form of common shares (plus retained earnings, share premia, and disclosed reserves) as the capital form with the highest loss absorption capacity (Basel Committee 2010a, 12 ff.), the new capital definition was particularly disadvantageous from a German perspective because many banks were simply not constituted in the form of joint-stock companies and many capital instruments that were of frequent use in Germany under Basel II did not meet the new criteria. This concerned the so-called silent participations (*stille Einlagen*) for banks in public ownership and uncalled liabilities (*Haftsummenzuschlag*) for cooperative banks. An analysis by the consultancy firm BCG had indeed shown that the German banks belonged to the group of banks that was the most strongly affected by the new capital requirements in the sample of banks analysed (Dayal et al. 2011, 14).

Given this competitive disadvantage, German representatives, together with representatives from Japan, whose banks were also strongly affected by the new capital definition, were very active in making sure that the Basel text would include a formulation, at least in a footnote, that would allow for the use of alternative capital instruments for non-joint-stock banks (Basel Committee 2010a, fn. 12) so that the issue could be taken up during the negotiations in Brussels without derogating from the Basel text (interview 2013101319D). Germany's preferred solution was a substance over form approach, hence, a capital definition that was neutral with respect to the legal form of the bank. German representatives also sought to obtain the maintenance of some of the specific German capital components, but the suggested less stringent capital definition was refused by the other members of the Basel Committee. In order to express the dissatisfaction with the outcome, Germany was the only country that did not formally endorse the Committee's agreement from July 2010 on major design elements. Because of its concerns, Germany had 'reserved its position until the decisions on calibration and phase-in arrangements [were] finalized in September' (Basel Committee 2010c, 1, fn. 1). These concerns were, according to a source cited by Reuters, mainly due to outstanding decisions on the capital definition and, hence, the additional need for bank capital (quoted in Aussannaire 2010).

4.3.2 France: Fighting for bancassurance

From the French perspective, the startling observation for both government officials and banking sector representatives was that even though the French banks had weathered the crisis, with few exceptions, relatively well, the regulatory reforms had quite a strong impact on the domestic banking sector, which is dominated by large financial conglomerates in the form of *bancassurance*, consisting of banking and insurance business within a financial conglomerate. The two measures that were particularly disadvantageous from a French perspective were the capital deductions within financial conglomerates, which were perceived as a threat to the model of bancassurance and the liquidity ratios.

Compared to other European banks, French banks hold relatively few deposits on their balance. This is due to the attractiveness of life-insurance contracts as a savings scheme, which are balanced by the insurers' subsidiaries. In addition, a significant fraction of the deposits collected by the French banks in the form of savings books (Livret A, Livret Bleu and Livret de développement durable) is centralized at the CDC, a public bank, and serves predefined social purposes. Because of this, French banks issue more credit in terms of total volumes than they have deposits on their balance and the liquidity rules would have a particularly constraining effect on them.[13] According to an estimation by McKinsey, the French banking groups had the highest funding gap in Europe under the new liquidity ratio, amounting to 433 billion Euros because they relied heavily on short-term refunding (Gerken et al. 2013, 11–13).

Mediating the effects of the liquidity rules was the main priority for both French regulators and bank lobbyists and they defended their position 'very, very fiercely' during the negotiations (interview 2013062715F). In their joint contribution to the second consultation of the European Commission on the CRDIV, the Finance and Economic Ministry, the French central bank, and the supervisory authority argued that it would be better to renounce on

---

[13] The ratio of non-securitized loans to deposits amounted to 128% in France compared to 90% in Germany and 68% in the United Kingdom. Compared to the ratio in other European countries, however, the French ratio is not outstandingly high (298% in Denmark, 193% in Spain, 137% in Switzerland) (Daruvala et al. 2012, 46).

standardized liquidity ratios altogether. Instead, the banks should be allowed to use internal methodologies for liquidity measurement. In addition to that, the French authorities suggested a very broad definition of eligible assets, including liquid equity and debt titles of non-financial corporations and financial institutions in addition to the assets eligible for central bank refinancing (Minefi et al. 2010, 3–4).

The French, together with other partners, including the European Central Bank (ECB), achieved some recognition of their demands. In January 2013, the Basel Committee modified its definition of the LCR, extending the eligibility criteria for the highly quality liquid assets (HQLA) and requalibrating certain in- and outflow assumptions.[14] In addition, the calendar for the implementation of the liquidity rules was postponed. The inclusion of certain assets that were eligible for refinancing operations with the central bank was left to national discretion (Basel Committee 2013, Annex II); a general recognition of central bank eligibility was, however, not achieved (Guyony and Garrouste 2013).[15]

At the European level, the issue was reconsidered, and some deviations from the Basel text were taken into consideration early on. In its consultative document from February 2010, the European Commission had, long before the Basel Committee decided to modify its definition of the LCR, considered the inclusion of corporate securities, covered bonds, and certain central bank receivables in the calculation of the LCR (European Commission 2010, 69–70). The final calibration within the EU was based on the results of an observation period and implemented by a delegated Commission act. The CRR text emphasizes that the final ratio should be similar to the Basel definition while taking 'Union and national specificities' into account (CRR, point 101 of the introduction).

---

[14] According to the compromise from January 2013, HQLA include certain corporate debt securities with at least a BBB rating, certain unencumbered equities and residential mortgage-backed securities with at least an AA rating, certain haircuts and up to a maximum amount of 15% of all HQLAs (Basel Committee 2013, Annex II).

[15] The then French central banker and chair of the Basel working group on liquidity at that time Sylvie Matherat (who became chief regulatory officer at Deutsche Bank) explained in an interview that the decision not to define all assets admitted to central bank refinancing as liquid was taken because '[t]he members of the committee didn't want to anticipate on the central banks' decision in terms of liquidity provision'. Having opted for such a solution would have implied, 'to consider the actual situation where the ECB refinances bank activities infinitely as perennial' (cited in Guyony and Garrouste 2013, own translation).

4.4 Domestic priorities and the
banks vs. markets divide

Beyond these priorities, which are closely linked to the specific set-up of the domestic banking sector, it is worthwhile emphasizing that both French and German representatives took similar stances on many issues during the negotiations, both in Basel and Brussels. Regulators from the central banks, the regulatory agencies, and the finance ministries had endorsed the task of stabilizing the financial sector and did not question, for instance, the need for an overall increase of capital levels and a simplification of the capital components. At the same time, they were attentive to the potential effects of these measures and closely monitored whether, with which transition phases, and with what consequences for bank lending the domestic banking sector would be able to adjust to the new rules. As one banking regulator summarized:

> We have always counterchecked if our banks would be capable of meeting the qualitative and quantitative capital requirements in a reasonable time horizon. We were concerned that if the capital requirements were too restrictive, this would have negative consequences for the banks' lending capacities.   (Interview 2013103019)

French representatives supported German demands on adequate capital rules for non-joint-stock banks as cooperative banks also play an important role in the French banking market. In addition to that, special capital rules on the treatment of insurance subsidiaries, which became known as the Danish compromise, were particularly important for the French banks. Inversely, Germany was among the group of countries that asked for a more inclusive and less conservative definition of the liquidity ratio, including corporate and covered bonds (BMF 2010, 2–3). With respect to the NSFR, the German Ministry of Finance emphasized that its calibration might 'be overly restrictive in terms of "traditional banking business" such as retail lending compared to investment banking' (BMF 2010, 4). Representatives from both countries also emphasized that further empirical evidence on the effects should be collected and details on the calibration be defined before binding ratios were introduced. Differences in the positions French and German regulators defended related to specific aspects, such as the importance of the central bank eligibility criterion or the inclusion of ABS in the LCR, which was advanced by both the ECB and the Banque de France, but refused by the Deutsche Bundesbank (Tachdjian 2012).

With respect to the leverage ratio, representatives from both countries were reluctant regarding the introduction of a uniform ratio that was insensitive to the specificities of different bank business models. They also pointed to the difficulties associated with the measure, for instance regarding differences in accounting rules. In their official response to the European Commission consultation, the team of the German Ministry of Finance noted in bold letters that they 'principally d[id] oppose the introduction of a binding leverage ratio' and that no modification of the suggested ratio whatsoever would make them overcome their principled opposition (BMF 2010, 13). Representatives from both countries also expressed the preference that the ratio would not become a binding pillar I measure[16] and be calculated in different ways depending on the bank business model (Minefi et al. 2010; Landrot 2012, interview 2013103018D).

Fairly similar positions were not only true for regulators from France and Germany; a comparable pattern also holds for the positions held by the state authorities and the domestic banking industry. Overall, the positions of regulators and banking industry representatives on capital requirements, the liquidity and the leverage ratios shared significant overlaps. Differences were more an issue of degrees, meaning that domestic regulators and bank lobbyists did not contradict one another on key issues (also see the position papers of the banking federations FBF 2010; Zentraler Kreditausschuss 2010).

Overall, during global and European negotiations on the future of banking, the main divide on capital, liquidity, and leverage was indeed between Anglo-Saxon and (some) continental European countries both in Basel and in Brussels. France and Germany were among the countries that preferred the implementation of less constraining standards and they had to face the strict opposition of the United States and the United Kingdom. One government official, who was present during the negotiations, emphasized that the characteristics of intermediated and disintermediated countries mattered in shaping policy preferences:

> An argument that we indeed tried to put forward was: Attention, some economies are heavily intermediated and others are disintermediated and the impact [of the reforms] is not systematically the same. The fact that all economies are not the same must indeed be taken into account.
>
> (Interview 2013070317)

---

[16]   Basel II introduced a regulatory architecture composed of three pillars. Pillar I comprises the harmonized substantive regulatory prescriptions, such as capital requirements. Pillar II defines requirements for the bank-internal supervisory and risk management process. Pillar III refers to disclosure requirements, which are designed to enhance market discipline (also see Basel Committee 2006).

Great Britain and other countries reacted harshly to the efforts by France, Germany, and other more intermediated economies, to obtain more favourable rules for their banks (James 2016). After a first internal draft of the European Commission's proposal had become public via a leak in May 2011 (Autret 2011), the British Chancellor of the Exchequer George Osborne, joined by his colleagues from Bulgaria, Estonia, Lithuania, Slovakia, Spain, and Sweden, which together formed a blocking minority, complained in an open letter to the Commissioners Michel Barnier (Internal Market) and Olli Rehn (Economic and Monetary Affairs) about the deviations from the Basel text regarding capital and liquidity levels, transition agreements, and the use of the Financial Conglomerates Directive on deductions of holdings in insurance companies (Djankov et al. 2011).

Differing preferences regarding the strictness of the future regulatory standards also crystallized on the issue of capital levels. The issue was amongst the most contentious ones during the negotiations in the European Council, with Germany, France, Italy, and others pitted against the United Kingdom, Sweden, and others. The 'key outstanding issue' (European Council 2012, 2), blocking an agreement on a general approach within the Council until May 2012 was the transposition of the Basel minimal as *maximal* capital requirements under the full harmonization approach of the single rulebook, which hindered individual countries from going beyond the Basel capital requirements via so-called gold-plating. The original proposal of the Commission had not foreseen any room for discretion on capital endowments by the national authorities. The Commission proposal was supported by both the French (Minefi et al. 2010, 27) and the German negotiators, albeit in the latter case with the qualification that '[b]efore the option of gold plating w[ould] be deleted it ha[d] to be assessed whether the current rules adequately address existing risks in all cases' (BMF 2010, 24).

All in all, consensus building proved to be particularly difficult both in Basel and Brussels. In the Basel Committee, negotiations were blocked to the extent that subgroups had to be built to discuss thorny issues separately in order to overcome deadlocks in the negotiation process. These subgroups were composed of members of the GHOS, who are usually not involved in the negotiation process (interview 2013103019D). In Brussels, the trilogue negotiations lasted relatively long and their expected completion was postponed several times. The European Parliament alone discussed around 2,000 amendments to the Commission text.[17]

---

[17] See procedure files of the CRR and CRD on the homepage of the legislative observatory: http://www.europarl.europa.eu/portal/en, accessed 9 April 2014.

Despite these efforts, not all issues were successfully settled by the end of the negotiation process. The United Kingdom dismissed the final European compromise and declared that it could not support the reform package because it was concerned 'that the legislation m[ight] not be compliant with the Basel 3 agreement for internationally active banks in certain significant areas'. The government also emphasized that the caps on executive pay, which met with the fierce resistance of the City, '[would] be damaging to financial stability and the soundness of affected credit institutions' (European Council 2013, 2–3). In the European Parliament, 84 per cent of the deputies supported the final compromise. Among the votes against the reform package, almost half of them (17 out of 40) came from British deputies.[18]

Negotiating the future of banking was a contentious process, both at the global and the European level. The negotiations saw countries with tendentially market-based financial systems in opposition to those where classic bank intermediation plays a more prominent role. At the global level, France and Germany defended the future of banking in relatively similar ways with priorities that were closely related to the specificities of the domestic banking sector (similarly Howarth and Quaglia 2013, 333). Regulators were sensitive to the implications of international rules for the domestic banks, in terms of adjustment costs, despite the benefits international agreements have for financial stability (Quaglia and Spendzharova 2017). Negotiations about global banking regulations have always been, as Ethan Kapstein (1989) long ago pointed out, inextricably linked to issues of competition and competitiveness. They bring a specific pattern of preference definition to the fore that does not necessarily reflect domestic debates on the very same topic—and this even holds for the negotiations in the aftermath of a financial crisis as consequential as the Great Recession.

That the setting of international negotiations had a strong impact on the reforms initiated in response to the financial crisis is also confirmed by Mügge and Stellinga on other aspects of post-crisis regulatory reforms. Based on the analysis of the positions advanced by the US-American, the British, the French, and the German governments in four policy areas—accounting standards, derivatives trading, credit ratings agencies, and banking rules— they conclude that 'governments have been staunch defenders of their national firms' competitive interests in regulatory reforms' and that it 'has

---

[18] See homepage of Vote Watch Europe: vote in the Council: http://www.votewatch.eu/en/regulation-of-the-european-parliament-and-of-the-council-on-prudential-requirements-for-the-credit-i.html, vote in the Parliament: http://www.votewatch.eu/en/prudential-requirements-for-credit-institutions-and-investment-firms-draft-legislative-resolution-vo.html, accessed 23 March 2014.

been the relative impact, compared to foreign competitors, that counted in reform positions' (Mügge and Stellinga 2010, 321).

In international negotiations, national representatives tend to act as 'economic patriots', and a definition of interests, 'different from the one that determines domestic politics comes to the fore' (Mayntz 2012b, 23). The comparison of costs and benefits among countries plays a prominent role. The specific settings in which international negotiations take place therefore provide a partial answer as to why institutional change was less radical than widely expected. If international negotiations are different from domestic politics, what did influence the policy responses there? As we move from the highly aggregated level of global negotiations to the domestic debates that took place in France and Germany the similarities fade and a different picture emerges.

5

The French and the German financial crisis

Political responses to the Great Recession were elaborated in different settings. As we move from the international banking reforms to the domestic debates about the future of banking, the nature and the focus of the debate change. Whereas regulatory concerns about financial stability and the relative adjustment costs different countries had to bear predominated at the global level, broader considerations concerning the role of the banks in financing the economy and the impact of the reforms on access to financial sources and, consequently, economic growth began to play a more prominent role. They were paired with more specific reflections about the strengths, weaknesses, and pitfalls of the domestic financial sector and the banks in particular. This chapter deals with how the domestic policy communities, key stakeholders, and the broader public experienced the crisis, interpreted its consequences, and debated the need for reform.

Broadly speaking, the financial crisis was primarily understood as a crisis of bank intermediation and bank lending in France. In contrast, in Germany, even though more banks had run into severe difficulties, the crisis was above all perceived as a crisis of financial innovation, Anglo-Saxon finance, and the failure of individual banks' business models, not as one of banking per se. As the predominant understanding of the situation differed, so accordingly did the suggestions on how to resolve it. Whereas the French concluded that the time for alternatives to classic bank intermediation had come, key German actors focused on supporting traditional bank lending. From a rather similar situation at the beginning of the financial crisis, the interpretations of the crisis and the reform priorities that emerged in response to it were remarkably different. The following sections discuss the specificities of the domestic context for banking reform compared to the set-up of international negotiations, they outline how both French and German banks were affected by the crisis, and present the main lessons drawn from it with respect to the future role of the banks in both financial systems.

Financial Crises and the Limits of Bank Reform: France and Germany's Ways Into and Out of the Great Recession.
Eileen Keller, Oxford University Press (2021). © Eileen Keller. DOI: 10.1093/oso/9780198870746.003.0005

5.1   Moving from the international to the domestic arena

The domestic context for banking reform differs from the global arena in several ways. While competitive concerns and the relative adjustment costs among territorially separate entities matter in international negotiations, this is much less the case with domestic reforms. In the latter case, the winners and losers of a reform are all within the same territory and the government is accountable to all of them. The costs and benefits are thus endogenous to the scope of government responsibility. Even if governments have to take the effects of their policies on the domestic financial industry relative to foreign competitors and marketplaces into account, the pattern of losing or winning relative to an exogenous third party is more circumscribed.

In addition to the institutional specificity of an intergovernmental bargaining logic, the composition of the policy-making community is different. While access to the Basel committee is relatively restricted, the domestic context is more easily accessible. Negotiations in Basel take place in remote club-like settings among banking regulators and central bankers (Tsingou 2015). Usually, only the banking federations and the big transnationally active banks are involved in the consultation procedures when regulatory reforms are launched, and they often have privileged access to the regulators. Beyond this, the array of actors directly involved is limited. Smaller banks, representatives of the non-financial sector, and civil society organizations find it difficult to be heard. To some extent, this also holds for the European level, even though the institutional set-up has more in common with the domestic level regarding the potential for politization and the involvement of the parliament. At the domestic level, the parliament is involved, the weight of the technocrats from the competent regulatory and supervisory agencies is lower than in the Basel Committee and politicians tend to have a stronger say. The non-financial sector and representatives from civil society are heard more easily and the voice of economic policy-makers has more weight.

The composition of the relevant policy-making community is also likely to have an impact on the goals of financial sector reforms. While the aim of fostering financial stability tends to predominate in fora where regulators and supervisors play a key role since this is what they are responsible for, other legitimate policy goals, such as promoting economic growth or restoring social justice, are more likely to play a role in contexts with a more diverse set of actors. One can thus expect that the arguments and observations that mattered at the domestic level are different from those that predominated in the highly technical debates about banking reforms in the Basel Committee.

Finally, as we move from the global to the domestic level, the frames of reference tend to change. Global level banking reforms must make abstractions from the various local contexts in which banks operate, focusing on the activities of the large transnationally active banks and the stabilization of the global financial system. In contrast, at the national level, debates tend to focus on the domestic financial sector: How did the crisis affect the domestic banks? Was there a bubble? Had the banks embraced sophisticated securitization techniques or invested in complex financial products in the years prior to the crisis? Did the banks secure the real economy's access to financial resources during the crisis and how did the bank lending relationship evolve?

The attentive reader will not be surprised that the lessons drawn from the crisis domestically and the measures implemented in response to it were different from those discussed in the Basel Committee. As we move from the aggregated levels of international and European negotiations to the domestic arena, the picture of similarities fades as the negotiation logic is different, the composition of the policy community broader, and the frames of reference disparate. The lessons drawn from the crisis domestically were closely linked to the development of the national financial sector and the domestic banks' behaviour in the years prior to and during the financial crisis.

5.2 The unfolding of the crisis in both countries

Both France and Germany were considerably affected by the financial crisis, with parts of the German banking sector more strongly. Given the losses individual financial institutions had to bear and the generalized crisis of confidence among financial institutions from September 2008 onwards, the French and the German governments intervened, as did governments in many western countries, with encompassing rescue plans to complement the accommodating monetary policies implemented by the central banks from mid-2007 onwards. In France, the rescue measures were primarily based on the Plan de soutien au financement de l'économie, which was intended to support the funding of the economy, as its name indicates. In Germany, the measures were laid out in the financial markets stabilization law (Finanzmarktstabilisierungsgesetz) and complementary acts of legislation. In both countries, they included state guarantees, recapitalization measures, and in the case of Germany, asset purchases and the option to establish bad banks (see also Panetta et al. 2009).

Among the large French banking groups, Crédit Agricole, Société Générale, and BNP Paribas incurred considerable write-downs from summer 2007 onwards, but these did not immediately threaten their solvency because they were balanced by encompassing retail banking activities (Hardie and Howarth 2009, 1023; Howarth 2013). The closing of three investment vehicles by BNP Paribas in August 2007 was one of the early signs of disruption in the interbank market. After the crash of Lehman Brothers, the French government intervened to save the investment bank Natixis, the joint venture of the then still separate banking groups Caisse d'Epargne and Banque Populaire. The two groups were merged as a consequence of the crisis in July 2009 and the French state participated in the capital of the new group. In addition, the French, Belgian, and Luxemburg governments organized the bailout of the Franco-Belgian bank Dexia, a financier of local governments, providing guarantees and recapitalization measures which amounted 150 and 6.4 billion Euros respectively. Both banks had got into difficulties through their activities on the subprime market, but also due to a high maturity mismatch, especially in the case of Dexia.

Besides these individual bailouts, the large French banks profited from recapitalization measures and eased refinancing conditions. In autumn 2008, a state investment society (Société de Prise de Participation de l'Etat, SPPE), was set up to take (minor) equity participations in the large French banks. The aim was to increase their regulatory (tier 1) capital by half a percentage point in order to boost their solvency. In addition, the banks profited from better refinancing conditions thanks to a financing society, which was jointly owned by the large banks and the state (Société de financement de l'économie française, SFEF), raising funds on the markets backed with a state guarantee. These measures alleviated the financing constraints that came with the freezing of the interbank market and the capital flight of investors towards safer investments (Banque de France 2010, 56–80). They made the French banking sector more resilient during the crisis and contributed to the fact that the French banks weathered the crisis relatively well. Overall, the initial phase of the crisis was characterized by two individual bailouts that were negotiated within a rather short period of time, and the set-up of a safety net in which all major banking groups were obliged to participate irrespective of their affectedness by the subprime meltdown.

In Germany, the depth of exposure of parts of the banking sector to the subprime crisis came for many as a shock. The financial sector was considered to be lacking in innovation, to have prudent financial regulation, and the banks were not expected to be prone to crisis (Handke and Zimmermann 2012, 119). Despite this, the estimated amount of losses and write-downs by the banks as a result of the crisis amounted to about 60 billion Euros, more than twice the amount of losses accumulated by the French banks (Bloomberg list, cited in Sinn 2009, 189 ff.). Among the German banks, the large commercial banks and several Landesbanken, wholesale banks that are at least in part owned by regional governments, incurred severe losses through their activities in the subprime market, but also because of bad investment decisions in other areas and unsustainable business models more generally (see also Hüfner 2010).

After the breakdown of Lehman Brothers, the German government set up an encompassing rescue scheme. In total, nine banks asked for public guarantees, amongst which were several Landesbanken and private commercial banks. Four banks—Aareal Bank, Commerzbank, Hypo Real Estate (HRE), and WestLB—profited from state equity participation. In addition, the financial markets stabilization fund (SoFFin) bought assets from Portigon (formerly WestLB). Bad banks were implemented for the toxic assets of HRE and WestLB (FMSA 2016). The Commerzbank was partially, HRE almost completely nationalized in 2009, a step that was rejected as too interventionist by parts of the political community. Compared to France, the process of bailing out and stabilizing the banking sector was a lengthy one that required intervention on multiple occasions.

Overall, both the French and the German banking sectors were considerably affected by the crisis. The governments of both countries made huge efforts to contain the crisis, committing up to 30 per cent (Germany) and 20 per cent (France) of the domestic GDP to rescue the banks (Panetta et al. 2009, 12).[1] However, the importance of the measures taken cannot be reduced to the emergency liquidity and the guarantees actually provided to individual financial institutions, since the measures made sure that per se solvent banks did not suffer from the liquidity crisis on the interbank market. Thus, the banking sectors as a whole profited from the stabilizing effects of the public support schemes, leading to the restoration of mutual trust and the normalization of the situation, whether they were directly affected by the subprime crisis or not.

Relatively speaking, the German banking sector was more severely affected than the French one. This is also reflected by the actual amounts of state aid

---

[1] The figures include the announced size of the rescue packages and the standalone actions.

that were requested under the respective rescue programmes: Whereas the recapitalization measures and guarantees amounted to roughly 20 and 80 billion Euros respectively in France (Cour des comptes 2013, 158), they amounted to 30 and 170 billion Euros in Germany, without even taking the cost of the other measures (asset purchases and bad banks) into account (FMSA 2016). While the French bank bailout had a positive effect on the state budget (Cour des comptes 2013; ECB 2015)—the fees and premiums paid by the banks in return for state support were superior to the costs of individual bailouts—the German bank bailout left the taxpayer with a net loss of an estimated 59 billion Euros.[2] The bailout of HRE alone amounted to 20 billion Euros and the final bill may even be higher because of open commitments (Gammelin 2018). In the light of the support programmes, the risks, and the actual costs the taxpayers had to bear because of the banks, what were the implications for their future role?

5.3 Diagnosing the crisis

The French and the German responses to the financial were not restricted to the implementation of emergency aid for the domestic banking sector. With the first shock of the crisis 'digested' and the rescue measures in place, broader discussions on the implications of the crisis developed. In this process, interpreting the crisis and understanding the situation more precisely took predominance. What were the causes of the crisis and which lessons could be drawn from it for the future? The following sections deal with how the crisis came to be understood in a specific way in both countries. The turns the debates took were different and diverged in ways one would hardly expect, given the degrees of affectedness by the crisis and the extent to which banks from both countries were engaged in the US-American subprime sector. Whereas the financial crisis developed into a generalized crisis of banking in the perception of the broader public in France, the problems of the German banks were largely perceived as being linked to the failures of individual banks' business profiles that were active on financial markets.

---

[2] However, problems reappeared with the European sovereign debt crisis in 2011, leading to the winding up of Dexia. When taking related losses into account, the bill of the French bailout is much less favourable.

5.3.1   France: A crisis of banking

Even though the French banks weathered the subprime crisis comparatively well, it did not shield them from finding themselves in a veritable crisis of banking in the general perception. Satisfaction with the banks fell to its lowest during the crisis, especially among small business owners, and many bankers realized too late the extent to which a generalized feeling of distrust in and dissatisfaction with the banks would lay the ground for subsequent government measures. Something had changed in the way the behaviour of the French banks was widely perceived. In the perception of many entrepreneurs, France had entered an acute financing crisis.

At the core of the French banking crisis was the perception of the banks' lending behaviour. In the face of the public support the French banks had received, any credit that was refused to a small business, whose credit-worthiness had worsened during the economic slowdown, was judged unfair and unacceptable. In this first largely uncontrolled phase, portrayals of angry entrepreneurs, whom the bank had refused a credit or reduced a credit line, kept circulating through the press and further fuelled the anger. The newly introduced—deemed highly successful—system for credit mediation, which intervened when bank lending had become conflictual between a bank and a customer, backfired, since it put the focus on the difficulties in the bank lending relationships.[3]

The situational dynamic further escalated as the individual instances of credit refusal gradually led to the much more encompassing claim of the imminence of a credit crunch, hence a situation in which the banks do not attribute new credit at normal market conditions, refusing to lend, even though the financial situation of the borrowers conforms to the usual standards. From the borrowers' perspective, the bank rejects a demand for credit for reasons that are not tied to their financial situation. Several prominent representatives of the French corporate sector, such as the President of the Group of the sectoral industrial federations (GFI), and the general secretary of the employer association of small and medium-sized enterprises (SMEs) (CGPME), fuelled the debate in late 2011, publicly expressing their concerns about the availability of bank credit (Piliu 2011).

While the banking sector maintained close ties and a smooth working relations with the French government throughout the crisis (Jabko and

---

[3] See also Chapter 6 on this aspect.

Massoc 2012; Woll 2014, 125), the rhetoric in public by many politicians was harsh and further contributed to the perception of a banking crisis. President Sarkozy himself repeatedly emphasized the need to moralize capitalism in the light of the excesses of the financial sector. This discourse was fuelled by the bonuses many banks paid, despite the support schemes. It also fell on fertile grounds in the light of the fraudulent practices of the French trader Jérôme Kerviel, who fragilized the French bank Société Générale with a 5 billion Euro loss in January 2008 (Jabko 2012). Many politicians responded to the feeling of unfairness by criticizing the banks.

One of the implications of public support for the banks was that they were deemed morally obliged to support bank lending. The businessman René Ricol, a good friend of Nicolas Sarkozy and the intellectual father of the system for credit mediation, for instance, argued that the banks faced a 'moment of truth' because the whole country was looking at them and that he would not hesitate to 'denounce to the President all those bankers who refuse to nourish the French economy with fresh money' (cited in Bordet 2008, 59; own translation). Roughly one year later, the then economic and finance minister Christine Lagarde wrote an open letter to the CEOs of the main French banks asking for additional efforts to support economic growth by increasing their lending volumes (Michel 2009). In a similar vein, François Hollande, in his election campaign, blamed bank lending rather than a cost problem or the need for structural reforms as the reason why French businesses were less competitive than foreign firms (Hanke 2013).

The pressure put on the banks by the political authorities remained high and the public discourse on bank lending and the banks' behaviour remained harsh. 'Condemning the bankers who didn't issue enough credit and were malicious' had become, as one bank manager emphasized, 'the predominant political posture both on the right and the left' (interview 2013072431F). In a similar vein, a French official confirmed that an 'anti-banker-mood' was widespread in public opinion (interview 2013061406F). The climate had worsened through a largely uncontrolled development of events and public statements, which, with hindsight, did more harm than good, resonating with a generalized feeling of dissatisfaction with the banks.

The banks, on their part, complained about the way in which they were treated in the media and by many politicians in public. 'We were wondering whether we would be obliged to leave the meeting in handcuffs. We felt like the citizens of Calais', said the director of one the big French banking groups after a meeting with President Sarkozy (Les Echos 2008; own translation). One may be sceptical about the accuracy of the historical comparison with the group of citizens from Calais who volunteered to be sacrificed in order to spare the population. What the banker probably wanted to express was the feeling that the banks were put on a public trial and 'sacrificed' for the greater good. During the interviews, bankers complained repeatedly about the unfair way in which they felt they had been treated since the crisis.

In response to the reproaches made and in order to improve their image, the banks launched a massive communication campaign, underscoring their lending capacities and demonstrating their commitment to accompany the real economy. The French banking federation (FBF) issued dozens of press releases, documenting the progress in actual lending volumes and highlighting that the French banks were committed to bank lending, supporting the domestic economy. From the banks' perspective, the *problématique* was that they wanted to issue credit, but could not find borrowers. As one banker explained:

> These days, the problem is that we do not have this demand [for credit]. For years, the demand exceeded our capacities, so it was quite easy to meet our [lending] targets. For several years now the situation has been puzzling. To calm the market, our communication strategy was to explain that we would commit ourselves to issue 7 billion of new credit in order to signal to the entrepreneurs: 'We want to accompany you, come and meet us!'...In the newspapers, you could often read that the banks wouldn't lend any more....We wanted to communicate to the market that it's not true.
>
> (Interview 2013071626F)

Representatives from the business sector responded that the reverse was true, namely that the businesses did not go and see the bankers anymore because they would not get the credit. As one business representative remarked:

> When we ask the bankers, they tell us: 'I would like to issue more credit, but I don't have the clients for it.' When we see the owners of small businesses, they tell us: 'we won't go and see the bankers because they will just tell us: "No!"' (Interview 2013112936F)

In the years following the peak of the crisis, it was impossible to find common ground for mutual understanding between the banks and the business sector on the banks' lending behaviour. The financial crisis had developed into a severe financing crisis for the French banks, even though they had weathered the initial phase of the financial crisis comparatively well.

5.3.2   Germany: A financial markets crisis

Even though the German banking sector was more severely affected, the crisis did not lead to a generalized feeling of dissatisfaction with the banks. In late 2008, German businesses were, as was the case in France, concerned with the availability of bank credit and the German government also decided to nominate a credit mediator. However, the situation normalized, and the crisis only had a modest impact on the satisfaction with the availability of bank credit. Anecdotal evidence on the difficulties individual businesses had in obtaining bank credit, which, of course, also existed, did not become the object of broader public and media attention. The financial crisis did not develop into a generalized crisis for German banking that questioned their role as financial intermediaries.

Overall, three elements shaped the perception of the crisis in Germany: Firstly, the reasons that led to the destabilization of each of the failing banks were different, the reason why the crisis was above all associated with individual business models and not with banking per se. Secondly, the crisis was primarily understood as an imported one that was associated with Anglo-Saxon innovative finance and risky activities abroad. Finally, the good performance of the savings and the cooperative banks throughout the crisis, which contributed to the fact that the idiosyncratic configuration of the banking system—universal banking organized in three pillars—was seen as an advantage rather than a root cause of the crisis.

The lengthy chain of failure of German banks began with the IKB Industriebank in July 2007 when the bank announced losses that threatened its existence. The failure of the IKB, which was re-established after the war as a private self-help financial institution for the industrial sector, resulted from its activities in the American subprime sector with the freezing of the asset-backed commercial paper market. With hindsight, the IKB Industriebank became the first bank worldwide that needed to be bailed out because of the subprime crisis, holding a poor-quality credit asset portfolio (Forbes et al. 2015). Only two weeks later, Sachsen LB, the Landesbank of Saxony, faced equally threatening liquidity problems through the activities of its Irish subsidiary in the American mortgage market, leading to the resignation of Saxony's finance minister. The bank was merged with LBBW, the regional bank of Baden-Württemberg, in 2008.

Additional aid packages for the IKB followed in autumn 2007 and spring 2008. In early 2008, massive losses by WestLB and Bayern LB, the

Landesbanken of the regions North Rhine-Westphalia and Bavaria, were made public, leading to the resignation of the Bavarian finance minister in autumn 2008. Discussions on a bailout for Hypo Real Estate (HRE), one of the largest European financiers of commercial real estate founded in 2003, began in September 2008, leading to a lengthy and costly process of winding up the bank (e.g. Buder et al. 2011). The HRE was the first bank in German post-war history that was nationalized. Guarantees for and equity participations in the Commerzbank, Germany's second largest commercial bank, and other banks also followed on several occasions up to autumn 2009. Peer Steinbrück (2010, 194) remembered this period as the one of the 'regulatory weekends' when a solution had to be found over the course of the weekend before financial markets opened on Monday morning in Asia. During that period, Angela Merkel is reported to have wondered which bank would announce additional losses on that day when waking up in the morning.

Despite the plethora of failures, the crisis did not question bank intermediation as such, as the causes behind the failure of each bank were different. In the case of HRE, it was the illiquidity of the Irish subsidiary Depfa (acquired in October 2007), a German public-sector financier, which had moved to Ireland because of lighter touch regulation, that destabilized the bank. With the freezing of the money markets, Depfa could not roll-over its short-term debt, given an increasing maturity mismatch and a lack of bank deposits (Hellwig 2018, 31). In the case of the Commerzbank, the acquisition of the Dresdener Bank contributed to the difficulties. IKB, Sachsen LB, WestLB, and others in turn had sponsored their own off-balance vehicles.

As far as the Landesbanken were concerned, which bore 43 per cent of the losses accumulated by German banks until May 2008 (Sachverständigenrat 2008, 138), the difficulties were attributed to the special situation in which they were, with the phase-out of the state guarantees judged incompatible with European competition law in 2001. The agreement found with the European Commission included a transition phase up to 2015. Between 2001 and 2005, the beginning of the phase-out, the Landesbanken took up a maximum of low-cost money thanks to the state guarantee and they looked for attractive placements, buying assets abroad (Hüfner 2010; Sachverständigenrat 2008, 139 f.) with some of them '[g]ambling for survival' (Hellwig 2018, 19). The Landesbanken contributed significantly to the global demand of ABS products and were able to fund large conduits because of the still existing state guarantees (Acharya and Schnabl 2009).

Even though all Landesbanken had to deal with the end of the state guarantees, the degree of affectedness of the 11 Landesbanken that existed at the beginning of the crisis and the reasons behind the fragilization of those that needed support were not the same. While several Landesbanken, including BayernLB, Sachsen LB, and WestLB, suffered from severe losses that were directly related to the subprime crisis, leading to billions of Euros of write-downs, unsustainable business models that preceded the crisis also contributed to it. In the case of banks from the northern regions, HSH Nordbank and NordLB in particular, their financial difficulties mainly resulted from bad loans in the shipping business.

In the general perception, the crisis was an imported one due to financial innovation, asset securitization in particular, that had developed in the Anglo-Saxon context. In his government declaration to the German Parliament from September 2008, shortly after the collapse of Lehman Brothers, the then finance minister Peer Steinbrück highlighted the extent to which the crisis was due to Anglo-Saxon laissez-faire capitalism. Despite the considerable risks German banks had accumulated, he emphasized the stabilizing role of the three-pillar structure and praised the merits of the savings and the cooperative banks as reliable partners for smaller businesses. The three-pillar structure and the universal bank model were seen as an advantage rather than a root cause of the crisis:

> The fact that Germany did not face a credit crunch—and I really want to emphasize this—is primarily due to the savings banks... This largest crisis in decades shows how well the universal banking system with its three pillars... fits our economic model of the social market economy. It is much more robust than the Anglo-American separate banking system, with its exaggerated focus on profits.... The comparatively broad range of business activities has shown its merits during the crisis.
>
> (Steinbrück 2008; own translation)

While one can understand that Steinbrück wanted to avoid adding fuel to the fire, since his words could provoke market reactions, his interpretation was similar to others who diagnosed the crisis in terms of their proximate causes—financial innovation and risky individual business decisions abroad. The metaphor of Germany being torn into the financial crisis like a boat in a maelstrom, and that the shockwaves triggered by the US-American subprime crisis reached German financial markets, suggested that the country was a victim of a crisis, and that uncontrollable natural forces were at work. The metaphor was used by Axel Weber, President of the Bundesbank at that time, on several occasions (e.g. Weber 2009).[4] In a similar vein, the law and the fund that were implemented to stabilize the failing banks bore the stabilization of financial markets rather than the banks in their name.

Finally, that the German banking system was seen as an advantage rather than a root cause of the crisis is also due to the savings and cooperative banks, which were not directly affected by the crisis. Their business model remained rooted in a traditional banking model, based on the collection of savings and the lending to households and the local economy. They even increased their lending volumes, despite the economic downturn that strongly affected Germany with its high export orientation (Hardie and Howarth 2013a). Both banking groups exploited this in their communication, highlighting repeatedly that they were different from the large commercial banks. Whereas the French banks were perceived as a relatively homogeneous block, all offering a broad range of financial services and profiting from the public support schemes, the affectedness of the different German banking groups was not the same and the problem did not become one of banking per se.

Overall, the relevant policy community was highly supportive of bank inter-mediation based on the existing three-pillar system. The threats the crisis revealed with respect to bank failure were not considered as a problem of financial intermediation per se or the specificities of the set-up of the domestic financial sector. The coalition treaty of the grand coalition from December 2013, for example, stated that the specific German three-pillar model needed to be maintained (CDU et al. 2013, 8) and that the coalition would be active in making sure that: 'the classic financing modes of the German Mittelstand by the savings, the cooperative and the commercial banks as well as development and guarantee banks w[ould] persist' (CDU et al. 2013, 16, own translation).

5.4 Lessons learnt

While the initial reactions to the crisis were driven by an uncontrollable situational dynamic, discussions about the implications for the future took place in a more structured way, allowing consensus building and the

---

[4] 'Deutschland ist in den Sog der globalen Finanzkrise geraten. Die von den USA ausgehenden Schockwellen haben den deutschen Finanzmarkt im Sommer 2007 nahezu unverzüglich erreicht' (e.g. Weber 2009).

emergence of a coherent reform agenda. These debates resonated with the initial crisis perceptions. In both countries, the relevant policy-making communities of politicians, regulators, representatives of the employer federations, and the financial sector associations were collectively mobilized on debating the conclusions to be drawn from the crisis and the reforms needed. Discussion and working groups were set up and various reports analysed the crisis and made suggestions for reform. Very often, the same people or at least representatives of the same organizations participated in several of these working groups. In these circles, key issues and shared assumptions emerged that became the focus of the subsequent reform debates. They contributed to the clustering of the debate around a specific interpretation of the crisis and the emergence of a corresponding reform agenda. Whereas key stakeholders in France discussed the possibilities of becoming more independent from the banks by strengthening alternatives to bank intermediation, the focus in Germany was on the possibilities for strengthening classic bank intermediation.

5.4.1   France: Time for alternatives has come

In the light of the dissatisfaction with the banks' behaviour and the potential impact of the international banking reforms, several professional organizations, both from the real economy and the financial sector, set up working groups, which debated the issue and published reports with suggestions for reform, in addition to the reports commissioned by the government. The High-level Committee of the Parisian marketplace (HCP) created in 2007 played an important role in gathering the relevant members of the financial community. It was hosted by the Trésor, the key unit for economic forecasting and decision-making attached to the Finance and Economic Ministry, and Paris Europlace, the lobbying organization of the French marketplace. The HCP had been used for concerted actions between the public and the private sector on several occasions before.

These working groups contributed to the clustering of the debate around the need to strengthen alternatives to bank lending. Reports diagnosing the lessons to be learnt from the crisis and making suggestions for reform along these lines were issued by the business federations and the financial sector. They were also elaborated on the request of and by key ministries from spring 2009 onwards (Table 5.1). As one financial sector representative explained:

Table 5.1 Reports and position papers on financial disintermediation in France

From the business sector	- A report by the Paris Chamber of Commerce on alternative financial sources for SMEs, September 2009 (Hautefeuille and Doulazmi 2009)
	- A report on access to funding by the Conference of Industry, February 2010 (Rudant and Genain 2010)
	- A report by the CGPME on suggestions for corporate finance, March 2011 (CGPME 2011)
	- A report on a small business act by Medef, June 2011 (Lanxade 2011)
	- A report on the future of long-term financial sources for unlisted enterprises by the Paris Chamber of Commerce, October 2011 (André-Leruste 2011)
	- A position paper on corporate finance by the French Association of corporate accountants, October 2012 (AFTE 2012)
From/for the public sector	- A report on SME financing (Chertok et al. 2009) and the funding of the economy, given the new regulatory environment (Couppey-Soubeyran et al. 2012) by the Council for Economic Analysis in March 2009 and in December 2012
	- A report on equity funding for SMEs by a French deputy (Forissier 2009), March 2009
	- Two reports elaborated on the Minefi's demand on SME financing by the financial markets in summer 2009 (confidential, unpublished) and July 2011 (Rameix and Giami 2011)
	- Reports on the role of life-insurance and the state in financing the economy by the French General Accounting Office in January and July 2012 (Cour des comptes 2012a, 2012b)
	- A report on the allocation of private savings by two Socialist deputies, April 2013 (Berger and Lefebvre 2013)
	- A framework document on crowdfunding by AMF and ACP (2013), May 2013
From the financial sector	- A report on improving financial market access for smaller enterprises by Nyse Euronext and the CDC, July 2009 (Giami and Lefèvre 2009)
	- Two reports on corporate finance, the funding of the economy, and sustainable economic growth by Paris Europlace in March 2012 and February 2013 (Paris Europlace 2012, 2013)
	- A report by a consultative committee of NYSE Euronext on the creation of a stock exchange for smaller businesses, July 2012 (NYSE Euronext 2012)
	- A joint working document of AFG, AMAFI, Medef, Europlace, and PME Finance on creating a savings plan for SME shares, July 2013 (AFG et al. 2013)
	- A working document by AMAFI on the funding of medium-sized enterprises by debt obligations, September 2013 (AMAFI 2013)

Source: Own compilation.

We tried to respect the Basel III criteria as much as possible regarding the financing of the economy. In France, based on that observation, we wondered: 'How will things develop?' That's why we set up that working group and we started to reflect on the issue. Our starting point was: How can we improve the funding of SMEs because they are the most fragile and they will suffer the most from the situation. From the SMEs we came to corporate finance and from there we moved on towards the funding of the economy. (Interview 2013061208F)

Several of the reports concluded that the financing model of the economy needed to be reformed. A report elaborated by a working group under the auspices of Paris Europlace argued that the pre-crisis financing equilibrium had come to an end and that France, but also other European countries, were facing a transition phase towards a new financing equilibrium, whose contours were not yet clearly discernible (Paris Europlace 2013, 91–6). In a similar vein, a report by the Paris chamber of commerce stated that '[t]he financial crisis ha[d] turned corporate funding upside down, especially for SMEs, by profoundly and permanently affecting the capacity of the banking system to fulfil its economic function' (Hautefeuille and Doulazmi 2009, 9; own translation). A report by the French General Accounting Office argued that the pre-crisis financing model, based on ever higher amounts of debt, had come to an end and that France had to pass from a debt economy to an equity economy and one of higher self-financing capacities of the state (Cour des comptes 2012a, 260). Finally, a report commissioned by the then finance and economic minister François Baroin concluded that:

All in all, there is a good reason to assume that there is a strong tendency in favour of a partial disintermediation of corporate funding and a stronger role of financial markets in responding to the financial needs of medium-sized and intermediate enterprises both in terms of equity and debt. Not to be prepared to respond to this development with a sufficient dynamism of the Parisian marketplace would be a mistake, which could have a negative impact on both economic growth and the attractiveness of the financial market. (Rameix and Giami 2011, 26; own translation)

In the aftermath of the crisis, the general perception of the future role of bank lending changed. The main conclusion drawn from the crisis by key actors from the public, the corporate, and the financial sector was that the financing model of the economy had to be reformed and that alternative sources of funding—that is alternatives to classic bank credit—should be strengthened. Proposals included the strengthening of financial disintermediation, namely the move from intermediated forms of funding, especially bank credit, towards direct forms of funding on financial markets but also forms of non-bank intermediation. This is, for instance, the case with the capital provided by institutional investors, such as pension funds or insurance companies, in the form of private placements.

From an analytic point of view, the positioning of the corporate sector is particularly interesting. To the (limited) extent that different financing sources are functional equivalents, a shift from one to the other can be more easily identified as learning. This is because it is less immediately entangled with a firm's fundamental interests, as is the case with market operators and (institutional) investors, which both have a particular interest in strengthening alternatives to bank intermediation, irrespective of social learning. As a representative of the business sector explained, a reform of the financing model by strengthening alternative sources of funding was inevitable. In his view, this was the natural lesson to be drawn from the crisis, a description of what the financial world looked like after the crash, resonating with the lived experience of many French entrepreneurs:

> The issue is not whether or not we support it [further disintermediation], that's how we see the development of the financial sector. We are moving right now towards a new world, which is more disintermediated....A grow-ing awareness has developed that the banks cannot play the role they used to in the future. This is true for various reasons, prudential, strategic, and eco-nomic ones. We make sure that this consciousness is widely diffused among the French public....Our starting point was the following: There was a real financing crisis because the banks had serious problems due to the subprime crisis. Several factors contributed to the fact that the banks were too fragile to support SME lending. So we thought: 'we need to find alternative sources of funding for those enterprises which are mainly financed by banks. How can we reduce their bank dependence?'   (Interview 2013112936F)

Many other business sector representatives argued similarly. One indicated that his federation had 'tried to push quite a lot for further disintermediation even though [they] knew that only a certain category of businesses would be concerned by it' (interview 2013112735F). Another added that they also had 'to find alternative sources of funding for crafts enterprises, such as crowd funding' (interview 2013112937F). And yet another diagnosed that a broad spectrum of alternatives to classic bank credit would emerge:

> We will see the development of a bunch of new intermediaries, organisms for alternative sources of funding in order to remedy for SME's needs to finance investments. Oséo [the French state development bank, predecessor of the Bpi] developed offers in this context. In addition, there are all these investment and guarantee funds, which are supposed to be an alternative for a banking sector which does not fulfil its primary duty, which is the funding of the local economy.   (Interview 2013052802F)

Representatives of smaller businesses and the crafts sector, for which alternatives to bank credit are usually not easily available, were more modest in their claims and emphasized that the issue was not to reform finance per se, but to add new complements and alternatives to the existing model (CGPME 2011, 13). In addition to crowd funding, some reports included suggestions for reform that were supportive of bank lending, such as additional public guarantees, or better availability of credit-insurance (e.g. AFTE 2012; CGPME 2011; Soularue et al. 2010).[5]

The demands for disintermediated sources of funding were also supported by the government. One official argued that working on alternative sources of funding was necessary, because it was unclear whether a credit crunch would materialize or not:

> We supported all those connected measures because we didn't stop worrying about a decrease of bank credit. The bankers were the first to tell us: 'We will be more constrained than in the past due to the new rules.' So we tried to anticipate on that development.   (Interview 2013070420F)

Another public sector representative added, when interrogated on the issue, that it was 'true' that 'the direct role of institutional investors in financing [the economy] w[ould] increase' (interview 2013072432F). Yet another government official stated that: 'We feel that we are in a transition phase with a

---

[5] In addition, the Loi Brunel formalized certain aspects of bank lending, legally prescribing a minimum delay of 60 days in case a bank cancels a credit and imposing further transparency obligations on banks, insurers, and credit-insurers (Loi du 19 octobre 2009).

developing innovation. We try to orientate it in a way that it is most beneficial for the business sector' (interview 2013071023F).

Even the French financial markets regulator, whose main task had traditionally been the guaranteeing of the efficient functioning of the market and investor protection, defined the funding of the economy as one of its three strategic main axes. In its strategy paper, the authority underlined that '[t]he financing modes of enterprises w[ould] see a readjustment between bank credit and the market due to the development of the prudential norms' (AMF 2013, 33; own translation).

The banks, on their side, seemed to share the diagnosis of a new financing equilibrium, at least to some extent. Since the crisis had revealed the risks associated with big banks, whose failure threatened the stability of the entire financial system, a readjustment towards a more decentralized, less intermediated financial system was desirable. As one bank representative highlighted:

> I oversimplify, but what happened is that we revealed that because every-thing shows up on our balance sheet, we had become very big and we were heavily indebted towards the market and the insurers and when there was a problem, the whole planet would destabilize. So the regulator told us: 'Reduce your size!'... But then what to do? That means that the chain between the investor, the financial market, and the real economy does not systematically pass through our house. That's what is happening at the moment. We say: 'That is fine for us.... There are still plenty of occasions where we will be useful – typically insurers don't finance SMEs.
>
> (Interview 2013061811F)

While this banker was rather optimistic regarding the implications of these changes, most banks responded by highlighting that they had the capacities and were willing to lend to the real economy. The demand for alternative, disintermediated sources of funding was not pushed by the banking sector itself. As one banker put it:

> A lot is going on at the moment in order to prepare for the businesses' need to diversify their sources of funding.... Actually, we say: 'We can issue credit, we will do it, no problem!' But our clients push us a lot towards developing a disintermediated financing offer so that they have a more stable funding source for their growth. Bank credit can be gone from one day to the other.
>
> (Interview 2013072431F)

Of course, banks can also profit from financial disintermediation, to the extent that they are active in market-related activities, such as the underwriting business. The measures discussed in the French case, however, were disadvantageous from the banks' perspective and not actively promoted by them.[6]

With the crisis and the questioning of the up to then valid assumptions on the conditions for bank lending and the future role of bank credit, key actors of the French policy community, including state representatives, politicians, representatives from the financial sector, and employer federations agreed on the diagnosis that the financing model needed to be adapted. That the new world was inevitably less bank-dependent and that steps that supported these developments were necessary became the main lesson drawn from the crisis with respect to the future economic role of the banks. Reducing bank dependence by strengthening alternatives to bank credit had become a widely recognized social fact.

5.4.2   Germany: The revival of originate to hold

The French diagnosis, namely that time for alternatives to bank intermediation had come, was anything but shared in Germany. The interviews for the book, mainly conducted in Berlin, Frankfurt, and Stuttgart, showed that the issue was not relevant for a sufficient number of key actors to make it on to the political agenda. When consulted on the issue, many German corporate sector representatives indicated that it was simply not a priority for them, as bank credit was abundantly available and cheap. Some stated that, in principle, it would be good to see some diversification in order to be somewhat less dependent on bank credit. Nevertheless, this did not lead to the suggestions for reform made in France. When questioned on the issue, one government official explained that there were no plans to strengthen financial disintermediation. Additional support programmes would only be implemented if a real need for them were to materialize in the light of the new prudential rules for the banks:

> We consider bank credit as the most important external source of financing here. And I think this will be true for quite some time. There is nothing wrong with that as long as everyone is happy—and it's evident that it functions quite well.   (Interview 201312324D)

---

[6] See Chapter 7 for details.

Rather than reforming proactively before knowing for sure what the impact of the regulatory reforms, Basel III in particular, on bank lending would be, some respondents suggested that it would be wiser to wait. The experience of the financial crisis and the prudential reforms that had been initiated in response to it did not question the role of financial intermediation per se. As one representative of the finance industry put it:

> It is important to see first what the impact of Basel III on financing the economy will really be. There are divergent interpretations on the issue. Our impression is that long term financing will be scarce due to the capital requirements and the need for alternative long-term financing sources will increase. Insurers might contribute to that. But it is important to see first how that really develops.   (Interview 2014012332D)

A business sector representative added:

> The availability of bank credit is not a problem at all at the moment. Hence, alternatives are less appealing than ever. There were times when we philosophized about ABS-financing and organized workshops on the issue. We have a working group on SME financing here...and the last time we met, there was not a single corporate financing issue on our agenda.
>
> (Interview 2013102917D)

Reforming corporate finance was not a pressing issue for representatives from the corporate sector, politicians, government officials, and the banks. When explicitly questioned on whether there was any debate on corporate finance reform in Germany, a member of the German Bundestag confirmed that this was not even an issue behind closed doors:

> I get bashed when I say in panel discussions...that my imagination is broader than to assume that businesses absolutely need to be financed by classic bank credit. That's very difficult....There is hardly any debate on Germany as a marketplace from an industrial politics perspective....Strengthening Frankfurt as a marketplace is not even on a hidden political agenda, really.   (Interview 2013121629D)

A representative of the corporate sector confirmed that there was no such debate, highlighting that 'the impression that I got is that our enterprises are not very open-minded regarding new forms of funding' (interview 2013120323D).

Even those who were more sceptical about the effects of international banking reforms with respect to the future availability of long-term funding by the banks did not see any need for acting immediately.

While supporting financial disintermediation and alternatives to bank intermediation was not an issue for key actors in Germany, it would be a mistake to conclude that the Germans were collectively less concerned with the implications of the financial crisis and international banking reforms. The Germans were just as mobilized as the French on reducing the uncertainty on the availability of financial resources in the future, but the preferred solution was different. At the centre of the German debate were means that would support classic bank intermediation rather than looking for alternatives.

In order to limit the potential impact of the international banking reforms, key actors in Germany discussed regulatory measures that were supportive of traditional bank lending. Similar to the reform proposals elaborated in France on strengthening alternative sources of funding, a debate developed in Germany on the ways in which classic bank intermediation as it was practised by the savings and the cooperative banks could best be strengthened. Many employer organizations produced reports on how the potential impact of the banking reforms could be limited (Table 5.2). As in France, a clustering of the debate around a specific understanding of the situation can be observed. Given the insights of the crisis in the risks of innovative market-based banking, the focus was on strengthening those aspects of the German banking system that had nothing to do with the global financial crisis—traditional bank lending by the savings and the cooperative banks.

The demand to protect bank lending from the effects of the regulatory reforms emerged in the circles of the savings and the cooperative banks in close cooperation with business representatives. The AG Mittelstand, a working group composed of representatives of both banking groups' federations (but not the private sector banks) and several business federations was crucial in diffusing the information. Arguments about the unfair treatment of credit risk compared to market-related bank activities began circulating in Germany. Given that classic bank intermediation had nothing to do with the origin and the propagation of the financial crisis, it had to be strengthened by special rules for SME lending, so the argument went. It was taken up by all central employer federations of the corporate sector in their publications and became an integral part of their communication strategy.

Both the banks and the business sector were particularly attentive to the development of the reforms and they followed the reform process closely, especially the one in Brussels. As one representative from the corporate sector explained when asked on how he had been involved in the banking reforms:

> Basically from the very beginning. As soon as something is published in Brussels, it's on my desk.... And then I have to scan: Does it have an impact on us or not?... Before they really start working on the issue, we turn up at their offices and say: 'With these decisions of the Basel Committee, please, keep in mind that etc.' (Interview 2013101814D)

The German employer federations, together with the banks, were concerned about the impact of the new regulatory standards on bank lending and they were mobilized on the issue early on. In September 2009, when the Basel Committee had just agreed on the very rough cornerstones of the reform, the AG Mittelstand published a joint appeal warning about the impact of the reforms on continental Europe's successful financing model—as they emphasized. They demanded that the banks should not be constrained in their lending activities and that the preferential treatment of SME credit under Basel II be maintained (AG Mittelstand 2009).[7]

The issue was also taken up by the Mittelstandsbeirat, an advisory board to the Ministry for Economic Affairs on SME issues. The board was founded in 1956 at the behest of Chancellor Adenauer and is composed of individual entrepreneurs and experts on SME issues, but not the business federations.[8] In February 2011, the board issued a resolution on Basel III, warning that the reform package could de-incentivize bank lending, long-term funding in particular. The board recommended alleviating the potential negative effects of the Basel III higher capital requirements on SME lending by making credit less costly in terms of equity capital (BMWi Mittelstandsbeirat 2011).[9]

In a similar vein, a joint resolution of all parties in the German Parliament (Bundestag) except for the leftist party, asked the government to pay attention to the impact of the reforms on the real economy and the threat of a credit crunch when defending German interests in international and European negotiations (Deutscher Bundestag 2010, 1). A resolution of the Social Democratic parliamentary group explicitly asked for a more favourable

---

[7] Basel II introduced favourable regulatory prescriptions for SME lending, applying the lower risk weight for retail borrowers to SME credit up to a certain threshold.

[8] Also see BMWi homepage: http://bmwi.de/DE/Ministerium/beiraete,did=161990.html, accessed on 14 March 2014.

[9] See Chapter 7 for details.

Table 5.2 Reports and position papers on bank lending in Germany

From the corporate sector	- A position paper on banking regulation and a study on the impact of Basel III on the German Mittelstand by the Association of Medium-sized Enterprises in June 2010 and August 2011 respectively (BVMW 2010, 2011) - A position paper on the transposition of Basel III into European law by the German federal chamber of industry and commerce, April 2011 (DIHK 2011) - A report on the impact of regulatory reforms on bank lending in Germany commissioned by the association of family-owned enterprises, August 2011 (Die Familienunternehmer 2011) - A position paper of the German federation of the skilled crafts sector on Basel III, May 2011(ZDH 2011) - A joint position paper of the AG Mittelstand on Basel III and on corporate finance, November 2011 (AG Mittelstand 2011) - A study on the impact of Basel III on corporate finance by the Bavarian trade association, January 2012 (vbw 2012)
From/for the public sector	- A report of the advisory committee of the Ministry for Economic Affairs on banking regulation after the financial crisis in 2010 (BMWi Wissenschaftlicher Beirat 2010) - A resolution by the advisory board of the Ministry for Economic Affairs for SME issues on Basel III, February 2011(BMWi Mittelstandsbeirat 2011) - A resolution by the Social Democratic parliamentary group on stabilizing the financial sector and strengthening the real economy, March 2012 (Deutscher Bundestag 2012)
From the banking sector	- A publication of the banking federation BdB together with the German chamber of industry and commerce on the consequences of Basel III for the Mittelstand in Oktober 2011(BdB and DIHK 2011); a revised second edition followed in 2013
Other	- A study on Basel III and Mittelstand financing by the Friedrich Ebert Foundation in 2011, the political foundation of the Social Democratic party (Angelkort and Stuwe 2011)

Source: Own compilation.

regulatory treatment of SME credit risk (Deutscher Bundestag 2012, 3). The Bundestag organized several public hearings on the issue with experts from the regulatory oversight bodies, academia, and the banking sector. The scope of these hearings was much broader than what the Bundestag actually had to decide on and shows the extent to which the policy community was mobilized on the issue.

The forming of a broad coalition was not limited to the national level. The chamber of industry and commerce of the region Mainfranken in north-west Bavaria, for example, explored the impact of Basel III for the companies in the region (Genders 2013). In a similar vein, the chamber for industry and commerce and the chamber for the skilled crafts of the Land Baden-Württemberg, together with the regional savings banks federation and the federation of the cooperative sector, issued a joint resolution on Basel III (BWHT et al. 2012). The topic was also endorsed by the working group of the ministries for economic affairs of the 16 German federal states (Länderarbeitskreis), which created a subgroup on Basel III and its impact on the economy. The committee invited representatives from the Bundestag and the Basel Committee in order to obtain up to date information on the state of the reform. These meetings were used to express the concerns on the potential negative effects of the banking reforms for the economy (interview 2013103018D).

5.5   The reform coalitions compared

Both the French and the German policy communities were highly mobilized on discussing the implications of the financial crisis for their banking sectors. However, the conclusions drawn from the financial meltdown were remarkably different. While reducing bank dependency by strengthening alternative sources of financing became the main lesson drawn from the crisis in France, the main conclusion drawn from it in Germany was the strengthening of classic bank intermediation by supporting bank lending.

In both countries, broad coalitions emerged that supported a set of reform proposals that was in line with one specific understanding of the financial crisis and its implications. The respective interpretation that gained predominance was supported by a broad coalition of actors, including representatives from the financial sector, the real economy, and the public sphere. These coalitions lobbied actively for the consolidation of the respective insights and proposed various political measures to this end. In both countries, coherent reform agendas emerged as clusters of different reform proposals that were bound together by one specific understanding of the implications of the crisis.

In France, strengthening alternatives to bank credit included both strengthening financial disintermediation and non-bank intermediation, especially by insurers. The demand for disintermediated sources of funding was endorsed by the corporate sector—by Middlenext, Medef, and the Parisian chamber of commerce in particular—and parts of the finance industry, especially Europlace and the federation of the insurance sector (FFSA). On the administrative side, the demand was supported by the Trésor and it was endorsed politically by the minister for economics and finance. The French banks lacked broader political support in the debates that followed once the rescue packages were in place.

On the other side of the Rhine, bank intermediation was not as controversially discussed. The diagnosis that banks were not reliable funding partners and that enterprises needed to diversify their financial sources was not widely shared. The reactions to the crisis focused on the merits of traditional bank lending, given the risky financial practices that had destabilized several German banks during the financial meltdown. The collective preference towards which many actors converged in the face of the crisis and the uncertainty regarding the banks' future lending capacities was on limiting the impact of the regulatory reforms. The collective dynamic by which large parts of the policy community were mobilized included the banking federations (BVR, DSGV, BdB, VÖB), the employer associations (BDI, ZDH, DIHK), the Ministry for Economic Affairs, and many parliamentarians.

While political attention gravitated around these two differing interpretations of the crisis and corresponding reform measures, they were by no means uncontested, neither in France nor in Germany. In both countries, parts of the policy community were more sceptical with respect to the appropriateness of the conclusions drawn. In France, some observers highlighted the structurally high bank dependency of the French SMEs and the little experience French insurers had in evaluating credit risk. In a similar vein, the Bundesbank, the supervisory agency (BaFin), and the Ministry of Finance—the authorities which are primarily responsible for banking regulation and financial stability—remained sceptical with respect to the appropriateness of the reform proposals. In both countries, a specific interpretation of the crisis defined the contours of the public debates, defining the range of policy instruments that were discussed as remedies.

6

Social learning in response to the crisis

Why were the perceptions of the crisis and the conclusions drawn from it in France and Germany different? Was it because the immediate material effects of the crisis with respect to bank lending were indeed fundamentally different? The observations made in the previous chapter would hardly be surprising if the financial crisis had led to a credit crunch in France, while parts of the German banking sector increased their lending volumes. In this case, the obvious response by any reasonable French business owner would have been to look for alternatives.

The following sections show that the availability of bank credit during the crisis was rather similar, despite the strong criticism of the French banks. Taken together, the available evidence suggests that access to bank credit was at best slightly more restricted in France than in Germany. In total, only a small fraction of micro-enterprises, newly created businesses, and enterprises with a deteriorated financial situation faced severe financing constraints. Econometric analyses confirm that the threat of a credit crunch did not materialize, either in France or in Germany. The banks' lending behaviour during the crisis and differences in the immediate material effects of the financial crisis are thus insufficient in accounting for the differences observed.

In order to understand why the crisis engendered differing responses regarding the future role of the banks, it is necessary to broaden the scope of our attention from the immediate aftermath of the crisis to the dynamics in the years prior to it and the collective reassessment that occurred with the crash. The French and the German collective experiences of the crisis were different because they triggered differing processes of social learning regarding the functioning and the future development of the domestic financial sector. While this process concerned the conditions and the availability of bank lending in France, it was linked to the risks and the potential of financial innovation and new forms of market-based banking in Germany. In the light of different pre-crisis dynamics regarding bank lending and the timing of financial sector reforms, specific insights came to the fore and informed the subsequent reforms.

Financial Crises and the Limits of Bank Reform: France and Germany's Ways Into and Out of the Great Recession.
Eileen Keller, Oxford University Press (2021). © Eileen Keller. DOI: 10.1093/oso/9780198870746.003.0006

6.1   Was the crisis different?

While the affectedness of the French and German banks by the crisis was, contrary to the developments in other countries not directly linked to their lending behaviour to the domestic economy, it still had an impact on the business sectors' access to financial resources, bank credit in particular. Given the uncertainty the crisis had fuelled regarding the banks' own financial situation, potential write-downs, hampered access to liquidity, and the economic slowdown, the banks became more reluctant to make new loan commitments and many of them tightened their lending standards. Despite these factors, the situation stabilized rather rapidly thanks to the supportive measures implemented by both the central banks and the governments.

6.1.1   Government support to bank lending

In the light of the uncertainties many banks faced, the French and the German governments both feared a credit crunch, a situation in which credit is not available for customers at normal market conditions. Attention to the effects of the crisis on bank lending was consequently high. The supportive measures for the financial sector, including the accommodating unconventional monetary policies by the European Central Bank, the capital participation schemes, the special lending facilities, and the guarantee schemes adopted by many western governments were designed to stabilize the banks' lending capacities.

Additional measures targeted bank lending directly: In October 2008, Nicolas Sarkozy decided on a 22 billion Euro support programme for bank credit to SMEs and to increase support by the state bank Oséo by two billion Euros.[1] In addition, Sarkozy introduced a system for credit mediation, a commitment that was subsequently formalized by an *accord de place* between the Finance and Economic Ministry, the French Central Bank and the French Banking Association in July 2009. Under this scheme, enterprises that faced difficulties in obtaining a bank loan could ask for an external evaluation of the bank's loan refusal by the competent credit mediator, located at one of the 105 regional branches of the French central bank (Liebert 2009; Minefi 2009). The mediation cooperated closely with the

---

[1] The banks were allowed to keep more of the savings they collected via so-called regulated savings schemes on their balance instead of transferring them to the public bank CDC (see also Chapter 4).

French development bank Oséo (now Bpi). At the peak of the crisis, Oséo supported bank lending with guarantees of up to 90 per cent of the requested credit volume and intervened in 70 per cent of all cases that were dealt with by the credit mediation, either with guarantees or by lending directly (interview 2013071828F). Between 2008 and mid-2013, 40,000 cases were handled by the credit mediation. Out of these, over 17,000 cases were handled successfully (Prost 2013), leaving some 20,000 cases whose financial situation was not sustainable.

In Germany, similar support schemes were introduced. In October 2008, the grand coalition government introduced the 115 billion Euro Deutschlandsfonds, a 'safety net' for the real economy. The programme included a 40 billion Euro credit programme for the real economy and a guarantee programme (75 billion Euros). The Deutschlandfonds was managed by the German development bank KfW. As in France, public guarantee banks took over up to 90 per cent of the credit risk and the KfW released the banks from their liability of up to 90 per cent for investment credit to SMEs (also see BMWi 2009, 2010, 9–14). Following the French example, the then minister for economic affairs, Rainer Brüderle, also decided to introduce a credit mediator in December 2009. In March 2010, Hans-Joachim Metternich, the managing director of the Investitions- und Strukturbank Rheinland-Pfalz, a regional development bank, was nominated. Compared to France, however, the tool was introduced on a much smaller scale without an area-wide implementation and Metternich was only supposed to deal with cases where the credit volume was higher than 25,000 Euros and the annual turnover below 500 million Euros (Neukirchen 2012).

In Germany, over 29,000 enterprises asked for public support between October 2008 and December 2010. A total of 8.7 billion Euros of public support were granted in the form of additional credit by the KfW and an additional 5.3 billion Euros were secured by the guarantee banks (Krüger 2011). Contrary to France, the credit mediator was little involved in this procedure. Only 1,260 cases were handled by the mediation. Out of these, the bank had refused a credit prior to the beginning of the mediation only in some 300 cases; the mediation was successful in 97 of these (Bender 2011). While the importance of credit mediation was clearly not the same in France and Germany, and business default somewhat higher in France, public support in the form of guarantees played a considerable role in both countries at the peak of the crisis. How did access to bank credit develop, given these supportive measures?

6.1.2   Bank lending during the crisis

The combined effect of the accommodating monetary policies, the rescue programmes, and the stimulus packages was that the situation stabilized shortly after the peak of the crisis. Thanks to the supportive measures, interest rates began to fall and credit volumes fairly quickly returned to positive growth rates, despite the economic recession that set in. Figure 6.1 displays the average interest rates paid by the non-financial sector in France, Germany, and the Euro area as a whole. The business sectors' borrowing costs began to rise when first signs of a reversal appeared in the markets—well before the magnitudes of the crisis became fully visible. Interest rates rose steadily from mid-2006 onwards and peaked after the collapse of Lehman Brothers in autumn 2008, with average interest rates between 5 per cent and 6 per cent. Shortly thereafter, they decreased strongly, even falling below pre-crisis levels from the first quarter of 2009 onwards. Compared to the dynamic triggered by the collapse of Lehman Brothers, the Eurozone crisis had a less significant impact on bank lending in terms of interest rate increases.

Overall, the interest rate increase was somewhat stronger in France, as interest rate levels used to be lower than in Germany in the pre-crisis period,

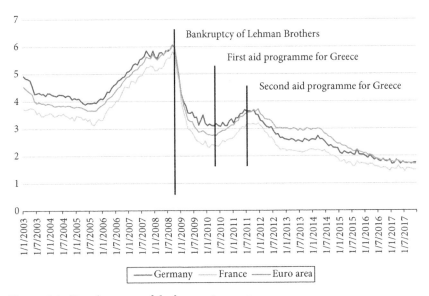

Figure 6.1   Development of the borrowing costs

Source: Own elaboration based on ECB data. The graph displays the composite borrowing cost indicator for non-financial corporations. It is a weighted average of the short- and long-term interest rates (percentages per annum) to the business sector for new loan commitments.

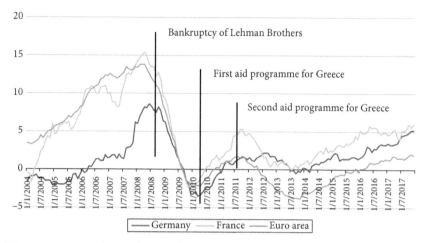

Figure 6.2   Annual growth rate of credit

Source: Own elaboration based on ECB data. The graph shows the annual growth rate of loans to domestic non-financial corporations, all maturities and currencies combined.

but they dropped even lower from autumn 2008 onwards. The development of the cost of bank credit in terms of interest rates paid was thus even more favourable in France than in Germany. Interest rate levels consequently cannot account for the observed differences in the satisfaction with bank lending during the crisis.

Figure 6.2 shows how the volumes of the newly issued credit developed over the same period. Right after the peak of the crisis, the credit growth rates converged towards a similar pattern in France, Germany, and the Euro area: They fell abruptly and became negative from September 2009 onwards, outstanding credit volumes were thus shrinking. Yet again, developments in France were not unambiguously worse than in Germany. While the contraction was more pronounced in France because the demand in the years prior to the crisis was higher, credit to the non-financial sector was back to increasing credit volumes by July 2010. In Germany, this was only the case by the end of February 2011. In addition, the French growth rates increased more strongly than in Germany and the rest of the Euro area for most of the post-crisis period. The French banks thus provided faster growing credit volumes to the real economy than the banking sectors in many other European countries did.

While the growth rates during the crisis are hardly compatible with the claim of an encompassing credit crunch, the graph does show one significant difference between France and Germany, which concerns the developments prior to the crisis: Whereas credit volumes were shrinking between 2004 and

2006 in Germany (negative growth rates), they were strongly increasing in France and the Euro area as a whole over the same period. It was only from early 2007 onwards that they began to follow a similar pattern. The difference in the development of credit growth pre-crisis compared to post-crisis was thus clearly more pronounced in France than in Germany. This pattern is important, and we will come back to it in the second part of the chapter.

Overall, credit was available to both French and German businesses during the crisis at roughly similar conditions. The absence of a credit crunch is also confirmed by studies on the development of the supply of and the demand for credit. Economic analyses show that decreasing lending volumes were scarcely caused by restrictions on the supply side, hence the banks' offer of credit. Rather, they were the result of the slowing down of demand for new credit, given the uncertain and unfavourable macroeconomic context (on France, see Cabannes et al. 2013; Guinouard et al. 2013; Kremp and Piot 2014; Kremp and Sevestre 2013; on Germany: Deutsche Bundesbank 2009, 2015b; Rottmann and Wollmershäuser 2013). Kremp and Sevestre (2013, 3757; emphasis added), for instance, conclude:

> French SMEs do not appear to have been strongly affected by credit rationing since 2008. *This result goes against the common view that SMEs suffered from a strong credit restriction during the crisis* but is perfectly in line with the results of several surveys about the access to finance of SMEs recently conducted in France.

The lower growth rates were thus not caused by a contraction of the supply of credit by the banks, but by a lower demand for new credit—per se not a surprising development during a recession. Neither in France nor in Germany did the crisis lead to a situation where bank lending was severely hampered on a large scale. Despite the impression of an acute financing crisis, the French banks did not cut off the domestic economy from new credit.

That the French banks were willing to lend and surprised by the reproaches made by many business sector representatives during the crisis is also confirmed by the fact the banks themselves had proposed increasing their lending volumes in return for the government support they received during the crisis. When the French government set up the support package for the banking sector, the big French banks agreed to comply with credit targets, namely, to increase credit volumes at an annual rate of 3 to 4 per cent. The commitment to maintain the lending targets was renewed in March 2010 (Le Monde.fr 2010). Part of the agreement was that the banks submit their lending volumes on the targeted borrower groups on a monthly basis. If the targets were not met, the banks had to explain why this was the case (interviews 2013060707F and 2013072020F).

Indeed, the proposition to increase bank lending by 3 to 4 per cent came from the banks themselves (Jabko and Massoc 2012, 574). This was the increase they expected they could realize, given the market environment at that time. As one banker explained:

> We had to give figures for credit to the economy, our commitment for credit to the economy; I was warned at 8pm on a Saturday night…X called and told me, 'I have been summoned, with members of the FBF [the French banking federation], to a meeting at 10am at Bercy [the Ministry of Finance]. We absolutely must give them a forecast: what level of credit can we commit to for 2009?'…I called my colleagues, business partners, we all looked at our data, we called around…In three hours, we had arrived at 3 to 4%.
>
> (Cited in Jabko and Massoc 2012, 574)

The calculation thereby was that a commitment to lending volumes was less of a burden than, for instance, a limit on executive pay as a counterpart for public support. At the early stage of the crisis, the banks expected that lending levels would increase. With hindsight, it became clear that they strongly overestimated the increases that could be realized.

The immediate effects of the crisis on bank lending were thus rather similar in both countries. Many French and German banks reacted to the uncertainties at the peak of the crisis by tightening their lending standards. Political decision-makers feared a credit crunch and adopted additional measures in order to support bank lending, leading to a stabilization of the situation from 2009 onwards. The feared credit crunch did not materialize. Interest rates paid by non-financial corporations fell even below the pre-crisis rates and loan volumes continued to increase after a short phase of contraction, especially in France. The conclusions drawn from the crisis can, in other words, not be imputed to a change in the underlying material conditions of bank lending.

6.2   Reassessing past developments

In order to understand why the French and the Germans drew different conclusions from the crisis despite aggregate-level similarities, one has to examine the developments within both countries in the years prior to the crisis and how they were reassessed. Divergent pre-crisis dynamics regarding the development of bank lending and the timing of financial market reforms have influenced the collective experience of the crisis and the terms of the debates in a non-trivial way. In France, the business sector had become more bank-dependent in the years prior to the crisis. At the same time, only minor adjustments regarding the development of the domestic financial sector had taken place in that period. In Germany, an inverse dynamic was decisive: In the years prior to the crisis, German enterprises reduced their bank dependence, albeit coming from high levels. At the same time, the pre-crisis period was characterized by increased efforts to make the banking sector more competitive and to catch up with financial market reforms that had already taken place in many other western countries by that time.

6.2.1   France: The limits of bank intermediation

In France, no major efforts to strengthen financial markets were made in the years prior to the crisis. Developing market access for small and medium-sized enterprises (SMEs)—one of the priorities that emerged in response to the Great Recession—was not on the political agenda in the pre-crisis years. In 2005, Alternext, a market segment for smaller businesses, was introduced at the French stock exchange, but without major involvement of state authorities. That reforming corporate finance was not a priority in France in those years was also confirmed by archival research conducted at the Franco-German Institute (dfi) in Ludwigsburg in December 2013. The institute has a press cuttings archive of articles from the French and the German press on a wide range of issues. The very thin file on corporate finance related issues in France from that period confirms that reforming or easing access to financial sources was, contrary to the post-crisis period, not an issue at that time.

Major adjustments regarding both the banking sector and the financial market environment were realized during the 1980s, when the French government liberalized the domestic financial sector (Chapter 2). The reformatory efforts back then even included the establishment of a legal framework for asset securitization—the financial technique that was essential to the build-up of the subprime crisis. In 1988, a mechanism for securitization under French law was introduced and the French appeared to be far ahead of the developments elsewhere in continental Europe at that time (Nési 2005, 70). At the same time, the French regulatory set-up remained restrictive.

Originally, only credit institutions and the state bank CDC could issue securitized products and only bank loans with a maturity of over two years could be securitized (Birouk and Cassan 2012, 100 f.).

As a consequence, the French market for securitization had difficulties developing because it was perceived as too constraining by many market actors (Béal 1997, 116). Asset securitization was not a major activity of the French banks. Even though the framework for securitization was somewhat liberalized on several occasions,[2] the treatment of securitization by the French supervisors and domestic accounting norms was more restrictive than in other European jurisdictions and the importance of securitization remained more modest (interview 2013052903F; Thiemann 2018).

While the financial crisis did thus not have major implications regarding the generalized perception of previous financial sector reforms and innovative financial techniques, it did so with respect to bank lending. Overall, the years prior to the crisis were characterized by growing credit volumes. Between 2004 and September 2008, the annual growth rate of loans to non-financial corporations amounted to an average 8 per cent. By the second quarter of 2008, it had reached 15 per cent (Figure 6.2). In the perception of many French entrepreneurs, credit was abundantly available and relatively cheap. The banks had eased their lending standards and the bank dependence of the non-financial sector, smaller businesses in particular, increased (also see Gabrielli 2007). In the light of this pre-crisis dynamic, the financial crisis with the tightening of the lending standards provoked a collective awakening. Widely shared pre-crisis assumptions on the availability of and the conditions for bank lending were no longer deemed valid by a considerable share of French business leaders, leading to a public outcry.

Reconstructing what exactly happened at the peak of the crisis with respect to bank lending is difficult, since competing interpretations and contradictive statements exist. Publicly available information that goes beyond anecdotal evidence is limited because the issue touches upon sensitive bank-internal procedures and client-related information. Instruments that allow for a more concise understanding of the development of the bank lending relationship have only been implemented in response to the crisis, precisely because of the uncertainties generated by it. This is true for the Survey on the Access to Finance of Enterprises (SAFE), which was introduced by the European

---

[2] The Loi du 4 janvier 1993 and the Décret du 6 octobre 1997 allowed for a broader collateral, abolished certain obligations, and allowed certain non-bank actors to securitize (Béal 1997, 114–16). The Loi de sécurité financière de 2003 and a decree in 2004 flexibilized the legal framework in order to allow for a more diversified use; in addition, synthetic securitizations were introduced (Nési 2005).

Central Bank (ECB) in 2012. In addition, the French central bank and the state development bank introduced their own surveys that have been regularly conducted among French enterprises since then.

The available evidence suggests that the banks readjusted their approach to risk governance. Several of the big French banking groups reduced the scope of autonomous lending decisions by their branches and centralized decision-making in the Parisian or regional headquarters in order to have tighter control over the lending policy. This probably contributed to the delays in the communication of lending decisions business representatives complained about. Banks also asked, at least in some cases, for additional guarantees and collateral and they charged higher credit costs in some cases (interviews 2013060707F, 2013070922F). As one bank manager explained when asked about whether the bank's appraisal of the creditworthiness had changed, and bank lending conditions become stricter:

> No, they haven't become stricter. They were readjusted compared to the spe-
> cial period 2003–2007, the period where everyone could become lever-
> aged.... There was a debt bubble, a leverage bubble where all, the states, the
> regions, the enterprises, were allowed to hold a higher level of indebtedness
> compared to the century before. This tendency has been reversed.... Certain
> businesses might have the feeling that we lend less, effectively, if their point
> of reference is the period 2003-2008, then yes, we are more conservative
> than we have been. By contrast, compared to the period before, during the
> 1990s, then no, we haven't changed our criteria.
> (Interview 2013061811F; similarly: interview 2013072432F)

A study by the French central bank shows that the French banks have indeed become more risk-sensitive when pricing credit. While the general interest rate level fell under the effects of the ECB's accommodating monetary policies, the interest rate spread between the financially soundest enterprises compared to those reflecting higher default risks increased (Avouyi-Dovi et al. 2016). Even though there was no large-scale problem of the availability of and access to bank credit, a specific clientele of the French banks—businesses with a deteriorated financial situation, micro-enterprises, and newly created businesses—encountered difficulties when applying for new credit lines or higher bank overdrafts (Kremp and Piot 2014, 97).

Collectively, what happened on the client side was that many entrepreneurs were shocked by the abrupt reversal of the bank lending conditions. The message many entrepreneurs understood was that the banks would not lend any more. They felt abandoned by the banks and turned away from them. A significant number of enterprises reacted to the experience of the crisis and the perceived reluctance of the banks in making new loan commitments by increasing their liquidity reserves and postponing investment decisions (also see Cayssials and Servant 2011). In doing so, they contributed to the prolongation of the recession. As one representative from the corporate sector explained:

> The enterprises, especially smaller and medium-sized ones, reacted by an adjustment of their financial structures and this adjustment was made at the expense of investment decisions. And there was probably also an element of self-censorship in the [low] demand for credit directed towards the banks, especially on the investment side. We think that a certain number of the SMEs preferred holding cash, given the low foreseeability of their order books. They directed parts of their funds towards short term funding, reducing, by this, their demand for investment loans.   (Interview 2013112735F)

The degree to which bank lending had become the object of contention and contrasting views is nicely illustrated by the conclusion of a report on the access of micro-enterprises to financing sources—the banks' potentially most fragile clientele. It was elaborated by the then national credit mediator Gérard Rameix on the demand of economic minister Christine Lagarde (Rameix 2011). The report, whose team undoubtedly had access to the best statistical sources and to all relevant experts on the issue in the public administration, the corporate, and the banking sector, concluded that the 'opposition of the points of view...ma[de] a clear-cut conclusion difficult' on the issue of bank lending. The report describes that, at one extreme, representatives from the corporate sector emphasized that 'the micro-enterprises which want[ed] to renew their bank debt [were] confronted with an ever increasing animosity by the banks'. The banks on their side claimed that they were 'put in the dock without any reason' and 'contest[ed], sometimes in a radical way, criticisms based on marginal cases' (Rameix 2011, 5, 35–6, all translations are own).

The fact that the crisis came as such a shock to many businesses was explicitly put in the context of the specific historical development of the French financial sector and the abundance of cheap credit by some actors. As one French expert on corporate lending emphasized:

> There is one thing that one should not forget: France is one of the few countries—and this still holds nowadays—where debt, credit is abundantly

available.... When the quantitative credit restrictions were lifted [in the 1980s], credit was extremely abundant, the banks lent a lot and at very low cost. The French culture is one of low margins and liquidity is abundant. So what happened? The entrepreneurs all relied on highly leveraged business models with little equity capital and a lot of credit. That's what made them extremely vulnerable.[3] ... That's about to change: What happened in 2008 was that the impact of *Basel III accelerated the philosophical change of tendency in corporate financing*.   (Interview 2013070419F; emphasis added)

The dominant perception in the pre-crisis years was that bank credit was abundantly available and at low cost; the relatively lax pre-crisis standards were taken for granted. French enterprises had no incentive to reduce their bank dependence. Their awareness of the banks' perspective on bank lending and lending criteria was low and stricter lending standards in response to the crisis came as a shock. The financial crisis provoked a collective awakening, both for the banks and the French enterprises, and the pre-crisis assumptions on the availability of and the conditions for bank lending were no longer deemed valid. In the light of these changes, strengthening alternatives to classic bank credit became the lesson drawn from the crisis. It was widely assumed that the banks would no longer play their former role in funding the economy and the time for partial financial disintermediation and non-bank intermediation had come.

6.2.2 Germany: The limits of market-based banking

The conclusions drawn from the financial crisis in Germany were different because the developments in the years preceding the crisis with respect to bank lending and the timing of financial sector reforms were different.

---

[3] From an economic point of view, the main difference between French and German smaller businesses did not lie in their respective indebtedness, but in their cash flows. Even though comparative data needs to be treated with caution because of differences in national accounting standards, balancing rules, and the methodological treatment of the data (Rivaud-Danset et al. 2001, 9–12), comparative evidence from the European BACH database suggests that the French enterprises were, on average, not more indebted towards the banks than their German counterparts and tended to hold higher levels of equity capital (Cayssials and Kremp 2010; Companies Observatory 2012). The main problem was their low profitability and, related to this, difficulties generating the surpluses or cash flows that would allow credit to be paid back (interviews 2013061812F, 2013070922F, 2013052903F, 2013070419F, 2013062113F). Given higher surpluses, German banks allow for higher debt levels. Higher surpluses increased their internal financing capacities and lowered their dependence on external sources of funding (also see Brunella et al. 2018a; Cayssials et al. 2008; Companies Observatory 2012; Deeg and Braun 2020).

Lending volumes had stagnated there for quite some time and only began growing moderately shortly before the crisis. The collective questioning of the conditions for bank lending and the availability of bank credit, which arose in France with the financial crisis and the potential effects of Basel III, had occurred in Germany roughly a decade earlier. In the context of increased difficulties in the banking sector in the late 1990s and the development of new tools for the management of credit risk, which appeared on the horizon with the elaboration of Basel II from 1998 onwards, the banks began to adapt their lending practices.

Considered from a historical perspective, German businesses, especially smaller ones, used to hold fairly high levels of bank debt—considerably more than their French counterparts. A joint study by the French and the German central banks based on the harmonized balance sheet data of 24,000 businesses from the manufacturing sector documents a significantly higher degree of bank debt for (West) German enterprises compared to their French equivalents for the period between 1987 and 1995 (Sauvé and Scheuer 1999). According to the study, the median of bank debt relative to balance sheet totals amounted 18.9 per cent in Germany compared to 10.0 per cent in France (Deutsche Bundesbank 1999, 34).

Between 1987 and 1995, French enterprises decreased their external debt and increased their own funds from an average 26 per cent in 1987 to 37 percent in 1995. This was primarily a result of tax incentives in favour of retained earnings. In Germany, the fraction of equity capital remained constant at a lower level in that period. In 1995, the median as a percentage of balance sheet totals for equity capital amounted to 15.7 per cent. The greatest difference was found in the smallest category of enterprises with less than 20 employees. Their median equity capital ratio was roughly a third of what French business of the same size held: 10.1 per cent compared to 30.1 per cent (Deutsche Bundesbank 1999, 33–4; Friderichs et al. 1999, 34). Smaller German businesses were thus highly bank dependent. The fact that the German banks tolerated relatively high debt levels, in smaller businesses in particular,[4] was attributed to both the favourable treatment of creditors by the German bankruptcy code and the close Hausbank relations (Deutsche Bundesbank 1999, 35).

This changed in the late 1990s with increased risks in the German banking sector. Many banks, especially from the cooperative and the savings bank

---

[4] One specificity of corporate funding in Germany up to the late 1990s was a bifurcated pattern regarding the financial structure of smaller and larger enterprises with the former holding higher levels of bank debt and less equity capital (Deutsche Bundesbank 1999, 35).

sector, faced considerable difficulties which were, at least in part, due to insufficient risk management (BAKred 1998, 59; 2000, 48). Many banks realized that they had to improve and modernize risk management, developing and implementing tools that were more sensitive to the individual creditworthiness of the borrower. In the light of these developments, all German banking groups announced the implementation of more risk-sensitive techniques even before they became legally binding as a part of Basel II. The banks put considerable pressure on their business clients, especially the smaller ones, asking them to increase their equity capital levels if they wanted to avoid difficulties in obtaining bank credit in the future (interview 2013092303D). The enterprises began to realize that the conditions for bank lending were about to change—as did French businesses in response to the crisis.

Data from the corporate finance survey, which is regularly conducted by the KfW in cooperation with several German employer federations, documents that corporate finance was in 'troubled waters' and that financing problems of the Mittelstand had increased at the turn of the millennium (Plattner 2002, 1, own translation). In 2002, 45 per cent of the participants indicated that obtaining a bank credit had become more difficult. This was primarily attributed to higher transparency standards and additional guarantees (Plattner 2002, 10, 13). Fifty-five per cent of the respondents signalled that they intended to increase their equity ratio, primarily by retaining earnings (Plattner 2002, 49).

In the perception of many German entrepreneurs, the Basel II reforms were a real threat. The realization that previous assumptions on the availability of bank credit and the conditions for bank lending were no longer valid had dawned on most business owners by then. Seventy-four per cent of the respondents to the KfW survey indicated that they expected a more disadvantageous access to financial resources under Basel II (Plattner 2001, 37). The reforms did thus not leave the supposedly close Hausbank relationships unchanged: Both interpersonal trust and reputation began to play a lesser role in the banks' lending decisions with increasing sensitivity to profitability indicators and the use of formalized credit ratings (Bluhm and Martens 2008).

The difficulties many banks, especially smaller cooperative and savings banks, faced in that period and their decision to implement new tools for risk government altered the business sector's assumptions on the availability and the conditions of bank lending. The SMEs reacted to these developments by a professionalization of accounting, a proactive transparency strategy, and a rise of the equity capital ratio, which fulfilled a signal function (Bluhm and Martens 2008, 44). The employer federations intervened to support the transition, sensitizing the enterprises with respect to the banks' lending criteria and offering training on credit negotiations with their bank(s) (interview 2013101814D). Between 1997 and 2004, the equity capital ratio increased by 150 per cent for SMEs with an annual turnover of up to 50 million Euros. The increase resulted from the reinvestment of benefits and a readjustment of the assets that were balanced as belonging to the enterprises relative to those that were treated as the private property of the firm owner (Deutsche Bundesbank 2007, 59–60). De facto, German businesses reduced their bank dependence, a dynamic that was spurred by the high profits the export-led growth model had generated in the early 2000s (Deeg and Braun 2020).

With these adjustments widely realized prior to the crisis, the German business sector and the bank lending relationship weathered the crisis fairly well. As one German banking analyst observed:

> It is interesting to see that smaller enterprises haven't been complaining during the crisis in Germany, at least not more than the larger ones. That was still a very different story 10 to 15 years ago. ... At that time, around the year 2001, the complaint was that the smaller ones were cut off from credit and that only the larger ones had access. That has clearly changed, apparently already before the crisis.   (Interview 2013092303D)

As a consequence, the global financial crisis and stricter lending standards did not provoke a collective awakening with respect to the availability of bank lending because most German businesses had by then already realized that it can become scarcer and that the credit attribution is risk-sensitive.

While changing assumptions on bank lending were essential to understanding the response to the Great Recession in France, the same applies to financial sector reforms and the risks associated with market-based banking in Germany. In the years prior to the crisis, efforts to strengthen the competitiveness of the German financial sector and to catch up with developments elsewhere were ongoing. The German financial system was considered to be 'undergoing fundamental change towards a stronger market orientation', which was desirable because of efficiency gains (Sachverständigenrat 2005, 455; own translation). It was expected that the German financial system would become more similar to Anglo-Saxon finance because of the international integration of financial markets, that the Hausbank relations were about to change and that classic bank lending would play a lesser role, being at least partially substituted by alternative sources of funding (e.g. Sachverständigenrat 2004, 353). The German Council of Economic Experts, which advises the government on economic policy, encouraged political decision-makers to 'continue the course of liberalization and modernization of the German financial marketplace quickly in order to use the potential of new financing instruments' (Sachverständigenrat 2005, 493; own translation).

In 2003, the Initiative Finanzstandort Deutschland was founded, seeking to promote the German marketplace. Besides banks from the three banking groups, the banking federations and the insurances association, it included the Bundesbank, the German Ministry of Finance, and the German development bank (KfW). The large US-American (investment) banks—Goldman Sachs, Citigroup, JPMorgan, Lehman Brothers, and Merrill Lynch—and the Swiss giant UBS were associated members. It is likely that this was one of the channels through which German banks accessed the US subprime market in the first place (Dill 2011).[5] In short, a 'widely shared political consensus [had] emerged that saw the deregulation of the financial sector as a factor of competitiveness, source of economic growth and employment...' (Röper 2017, 378).

The focus on financial liberalization also led to increased pressure on the persistence of the three-pillar structure of the banking sector. The limits to takeovers between the groups were increasingly seen as a problem for bank profitability and allocational efficiency as the German banks were, on average, considerably less profitable than the banking sectors in many other European countries and their situation had worsened. This was especially true for the large German commercial banks. While their return on equity was negative in 2003 (-13 per cent), the savings banks were profitable (+11 per cent), benefiting from their solid anchorage in retail banking (Sachverständigenrat 2004, 357–8). The pillar structure was seen as a potential root cause of their fragility, besides increased competition resulting from financial integration, questionable business decisions—a disinvestment from retail banking in particular—the cost of bank restructuring, and write-downs (Sachverständigenrat 2004, 357).

The Bundesbank was known to be open to the idea of a privatization of the savings banks, which had been realized in many other European countries at that time. Its then President Ernst Welteke, for instance, said publicly that his institution would not consider the pillar structure 'sacrosanct' if

---

[5] Martin Hellwig (2018, 19) reports that the German Landesbanken were called 'stuffies' by international investment bankers 'because you could always stuff them with things you wanted to sell'.

market-driven processes would lead to change (cited in Braun et al. 2004). In 1996 already, William Coleman (Coleman 1996, 146; emphasis added) concluded that '[t]he idea of a public or state role in the banking system to promote a general or common interest [wa]s *no longer taken for granted*' in Germany. In 2004, the city council of Stralsund (Mecklenburg-Western Pomerania) decided formally to examine if they could put the local savings bank on sale, but the move was pre-empted by a change of the regional savings bank law.

The German Council of Economic experts studied the effects of bank consolidation and the role of a public banking sector on the availability of bank credit, finding that the evidence from other European countries was inconclusive and that harm should not inevitably be expected. They also discussed the legal possibilities of opening the capital of the savings banks to private investors under the existing regional savings banks laws (Sachverständigenrat 2004). The discussion was also fuelled by a paper of the International Monetary Fund, which recommended the privatization of the savings banks in order to boost competitiveness (Brunner et al. 2004). What the private banks had long wanted, was finally being more widely considered, even though the public banks had their advocates, too.

More specifically, from the early 2000s onwards, asset securitization was increasingly seen as a means to modernizing the German banking sector. Many hopes were put in the securitization of bank assets with respect to financial stability, bank profitability, and the availability of bank credit. Transforming bank assets into tradable financial products promised to diversify risks, increase the profitability of the banking sector, potentially improve the availability of bank credit, and offer smaller businesses an indirect access to the capital markets, since many of them refrained from raising capital on the markets directly.

The idea that resonated with several German banks at that time, especially the Landesbanken and the large private sector banks, was that synthetic securitizations, where parts of the default risk are transferred from the banks to investors by credit derivatives, would lead to a reduction of the required regulatory equity capital the banks would have to hold against the underlying credit risk. Consequently, the banks could issue new and, overall, more credit with a given volume of capital. The ideal end point some German observers had in mind at that time was a bank business model, where credit portfolios would not remain on balance, but be actively managed by the bank. The bank lending business would tie up 'much less equity capital, none at all in the marginal case'. Rather than holding loans until maturity, the bank would become a 'credit broker and use its balance only as an interim storage facility' (Ranné 2005, 57; own translation).

In 2000, the KfW introduced PROMISE, short for Programme for Mittelstand Loan Securitization, a programme under which it took over SME credit risk from issuing banks by a credit default swap before selling the claims to investors. The KfW thereby intervened as a catalyst, spurring the development of the securitization market by reducing the initially high transaction costs, which would sink the more transactions were made. The chosen set-up, which involved the KfW, allowed profiting from a regulatory arbitrage opportunity under Basel I.[6] In return, the banks were contractually obliged to issue pre-defined new amounts of SME credit. The KfW was also involved in the creation of the True Sale International GmbH (TSI) in 2004, a joint initiative of 12 German banks, which pooled their resources in order to create and promote a framework for true sale securitizations under German law.[7] In comparison, this form of public support in order to boost the development of a market for securitization had never existed in France (interview 2031052903F). Overall, regulators took a benign stance on its regulatory treatment, contributing to the engagement of German banks in this segment (Acharya and Schnabl 2009, 23; Hellwig 2018, 39; Thiemann 2018). New forms of market-based banking had found their way into the German banking system.

With the devastating effects of the crisis on several German banks that were massively invested in the subprime sector, trying to build up expertise in order to reach the critical size necessary to become an important actor in that market, the limits of that strategy became manifestly visible. Social learning in response to the crisis revealed the weaknesses of the originate to distribute model, as it was increasingly practised prior to the crisis in parts of the German banking sector. With respect to the implications of the crisis for the German financial system, the German Council of Economic Experts

---

[6] Basel I, which was effective until 2007, allowed a choice either between the default risk of the holder of a loan portfolio or the default risk of the portfolio itself. Since the KfW is owned by the German state, it has the best credit rating and the relief of required regulatory capital was higher compared to when a privately owned bank would have held the very same portfolio. Through the transfer of the credit risk to the KfW with its triple A rating, the originator did not have to hold equity against the default risk of the portfolio anymore. This practice came to an end in 2007 (interview 2013110120D; see also Krämer-Eis et al. 2001 and Ranné 2005).

[7] True sale securitizations differ from synthetic securitizations in that the loan claim (and not only the associated credit risk) is transferred to a new legal entity. Whereas a credit claim remains on the balance of a bank in the case of a synthetic securitization, true sale securitizations lead to a balance sheet contraction. The latter are primarily motivated by the need to diversify the funding side of the bank, creating a source of bank refinancing which is, contrary to bonds, independent from the creditworthiness of the bank (Ranné 2005, 45; interview 2013052903F).

back-paddled on the pace and the merits of the financial sector reforms it had recommended prior to the crisis arguing that:

> As a matter of principle, the high instability of securitization and, by that, of credit intermediation by the market, whose appearance was highly unexpected to most observers, shows that economic policy should be very cautious, when reforming financial systems.
>
> (Sachverständigenrat 2008, 150; own translation)

While the Council advised against 'returning to the old world of pure bank intermediation', renouncing on asset securitization altogether, it highlighted that it would be decisive for financial stability to have a sufficient number of banks, whose main business was in traditional bank lending and that the decentral structure of the German banking sector with the savings, cooperative, regional as well as foreign banks was a stabilizing factor during the crisis. From an economic policy perspective, there were no 'immediate reasons to fundamentally question these structures', except for the sector of the Landesbanken, which needed profound reforms (Sachverständigenrat 2008, 150–1).

In 2015, the Bundesbank concluded that the financial crisis had ended the period of expansion of the larger banks, which had focused on capital markets and investment banking, largely funded by the markets rather than deposits. Earning drops, changes in financial markets, and regulatory reforms led to a reduction of proprietary trading, a refocusing on core businesses, and the substitution of financial markets-based resources by deposits, 'partially reversing those developments from the period prior to the crisis' (Deutsche Bundesbank 2015a, 33; own translation). The assumption of the future development of the German financial sector towards a market-based banking model and the potential of asset securitization relative to the associated risks saw a readjustment with the crisis. The traditional bank lending model that had been questioned as outdated and inefficient prior to the crisis re-emerged in new splendour.

6.3 Developmental paths compared

The previous sections traced the divergent developmental paths with respect to bank lending and financial sector reforms in France and Germany.

Understanding why the French and the Germans responded differently to the financial crisis, requires considering what had happened in the decade prior to it. The divergent dynamics with respect to bank lending are also confirmed by survey data. Both the French banks and the French business sector reacted particularly strongly to the financial crisis which can be seen as an indicator for social learning. Figure 6.3 displays the development of the credit standards for bank lending to the business sector in France, Germany, and the Euro area as a whole. The graph displays the net percentages, that is the difference between the percentage of banks that tightened minus those that eased their credit standards. This indicator is commonly used to understand how the banks' lending policy develops. As the graph shows, the years prior to the crisis were characterized by relatively stable standards. The aggregate net variations regarding the banks' lending criteria from one observation period to the next were limited. For Germany, a slight tendency towards loosening the standards (net easing, negative values) can be observed from 2006 onwards, following the period of tightening in the years before.

Banks everywhere began to tighten their standards from summer 2007 onwards. In autumn 2008, at the peak of the crisis, over 60 per cent of the participating Euro-area banks indicated that they had tightened their credit standards over the past three months—by far the strongest tightening effect

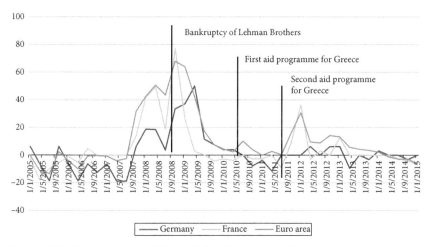

Figure 6.3 Development of the banks' lending standards

Source: Own elaboration based on the ECB Bank Lending Survey. Development of the banks' credit standards towards their business clients (all enterprises) backward looking over the last three months in terms of net percentages, i.e. the frequency of banks that tightened minus those that eased or reversed.

ever recorded.[8] The banks responded to the uncertainties of the crisis by becoming more prudent when making new loan commitments. At the same time, the banks' standards stabilized rather quickly around a more balanced pattern (values close to zero) thanks to the measures implemented by governments. In the second half of 2011, a second, albeit more moderate peak emerged in France and the Euro area as a whole—but apparently not in Germany—fuelled by the Greek sovereign debt crisis. Since then, the standards have remained relatively stable, albeit at a stricter level than in the pre-crisis period.

As the graph shows, the French banks reacted to the crisis with an abrupt reappraisal of their lending standards from mid-2007 onwards. At least 80 per cent of the banks indicated in autumn 2008 that they had tightened their credit standards over the past three months. The tightening was somewhat more pronounced than in the Euro-area as a whole and clearly more than in Germany, where only about half of the participating banks indicated that they had modified their lending standards.[9] At the same time, the French banks stabilized their conditions relatively quickly after their strong initial reaction, faster than the Euro-area banking sectors on average. Half a year after the peak of the crisis, only a small majority of banks were tightening their standards compared to those that had begun easing them.

That many French businesses on their side reacted strongly to the banks' reversal of lending conditions is confirmed by survey data on the expectations of the future availability of bank lending. With some delay to the initial tightening by the French banks, French businesses lowered their expectations drastically (Figure 6.4). From September 2010 onwards, French enterprises were extremely pessimistic about the future availability of bank lending. Over 30 per cent (net percentages) of them expected that access to bank credit and bank overdrafts would worsen over the next six months. Their appraisal was much more pessimistic than in Spain and Italy, even though there was a stronger bank-driven restriction of the supply of credit there. The reaction of

---

[8] The net percentages correspond to the difference between the banks that tightened their standards minus those that loosened their standards. The absolute number of banks that loosened or tightened their standards depends, however, on the size of the middle category (neither nor) of the scale of five. Unfortunately, this information is not made public by the central banks and no further information was provided to the author upon request. The absolute number of banks that tightened their standards is thus at least the amount of net percentages, but can be (considerably) higher, the smaller the middle category is.

[9] That fewer German banks tightened their standards during the crisis is probably also since many had done so in the early 2000s already. In 2002, almost 60% of the banks (net percentages) indicated a tightening (Sachverständigenrat 2004, 364). The (net) loosening only began in 2005. The French standards were thus most probably not stricter than the German ones.

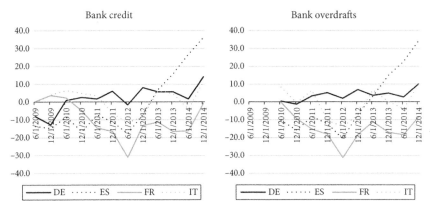

Figure 6.4   Business expectations on the availability of bank credit

Source: Own elaboration based on ECB SAFE data. The graphs show the net percentage points of the share of SMEs that expects an improvement regarding the availability of bank credit/bank overdrafts over the next three months minus those that expect a deterioration.

the French entrepreneurs goes, in other words, beyond what one could expect when considering the material conditions only.

At the same time, it can be shown that the French banks underestimated how the business sector would respond to the tightening of their lending standards. In the second half of 2008, the French banks considerably overestimated the development of the demand for credit compared to the volumes they actually attributed, when looking back on the same period. It was only from 2009 onwards that their expectations mirrored the real developments (Lacroix and Montoronès 2009, 24). The banks had thus underestimated how many entrepreneurs would respond to the changes in their credit distribution policy. The strong reaction by both the banks and the non-financial sector can be seen as an indicator for social learning, leading to reactions that cannot satisfactorily be explained by shifts in the underlying material conditions alone.[10]

In a similar vein, one can show the extent to which the developments in France and Germany were different in the years prior to the crisis regarding widely shared expectations on access to bank credit among business owners. According to the results of a Flash Eurobarometer on SME access to finance from 2005, German enterprises were judging their access to bank loans the most difficult in Europe (Figure 6.5). Only 14 per cent of the German respondents indicated that access was very or fairly easy compared to 46 per cent in the EU-15 on average. Forty per cent felt that access to bank credit was

---

[10]   Also see Chapter 8 on this aspect.

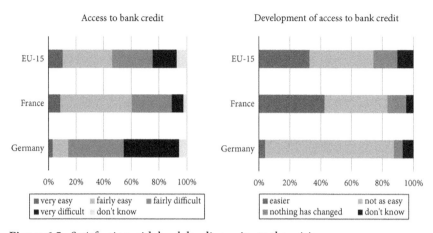

Figure 6.5   Satisfaction with bank lending prior to the crisis

Source: Own elaboration based on the Flash Eurobarometer 174 SME Access to Finance from September 2005. On the left: Responses to the question 'Would you say that today, access to loans granted by banks is very easy, fairly easy, fairly difficult or very difficult?' On the right: 'Would you say that compared to a few years ago it is easier or not as easy to obtain a bank loan?'

very difficult compared to 8 per cent in France and 17 per cent in the EU-15. As these numbers show, bank lending does not work inherently better in Germany than anywhere else.

In addition, 84 per cent of the German SMEs indicated that access to bank credit had become more difficult over the past years. Only 4 per cent observed an improvement. Ninety-five per cent of the respondents—more than in any other participating country—indicated that the banks did not want to take risks in lending to SMEs—the same reproaches that appeared in France in response to the financial crisis. The German respondents even came last when asked whether they felt that their banker understood the specificities of the sector and activity, despite the presumably close Hausbank relations: 57 per cent in Germany compared to 65 per cent in the EU-15 on average. Arguably, a majority in Germany still expressed satisfaction with the banks in this regard, but this was a lower share than in any other country at that time.

In France, the share of firms that was satisfied with its access to bank loans amounted to 60 per cent. When asked to compare their access to bank credit to the situation a couple of years earlier, bank lending conditions were largely perceived as stable or, at least, not having changed unequivocally: While 42 per cent of the French participants observed a deterioration of their access to bank credit, almost exactly the same amount, 41 per cent, reported an improvement. Regarding the risk-averseness of the banks, 63 per cent confirmed that this was the case with respect to SME lending compared to 71 per cent on average. Seventy-two per cent felt that their banker understood their business profile. Nothing of the mutual incomprehension that was frequently described in France during the crisis was thus present in the years before.

Contrary to Germany, where collective learning on the conditions and the availability of bank credit was fuelled by Basel II, this recognition only reached many smaller French business owners after the crisis. When questioned retrospectively on Basel II, two business sector representatives from different employer federations confirmed that the Basel II reforms had not been an issue for the French business sector at that time, but that this had changed with the crisis and Basel III:

> The enterprises do not know what Basel II is about, it means nothing to them. They just see their banker and they see that every second or third time, they are told: 'No'. But they don't go further and try to understand why, on what criteria, they were told: 'No'.   (Interview 2013112936F)

> The discussions on banking regulation have reached a broader public with the crisis and the discussions on Basel III. So, in the end, they [the enterprises] didn't ask too much about Basel II because it was considered an issue, which only concerned the banks.   (Interview 2013112735F)

Since equity capital levels were higher and financial ratios improving over the 1990s and early 2000s (Cayssials et al. 2007), there was no need to adjust lending practices drastically. This contributed to the fact that Basel II was not an issue for most French enterprises. It was only with the financial crisis and Basel III that the majority of the French small and micro-enterprises became aware of the banks' risk management techniques and their impact on bank lending conditions—an awareness that had emerged in Germany roughly a decade earlier.

Two reasons may have contributed to the fact that social learning in the context of Basel II happened in a smoother way in Germany and did not lead to the escalation observed in France. On the one hand, the timing was more favourable. While the French learning occurred in a situation of acute economic distress, the overall macroeconomic environment was more favourable when the German adjustment process took place. In France, many entrepreneurs had the impression that access to financial resources was literally gone from one day to the next. The lending criteria were tightened at a moment in which the financial situation of many enterprises worsened due to the economic slowdown. In Germany, the adjustment process was realized over a longer period of several years and, consequently, the enterprises had more time to adjust. The banks announced that they were about to adapt their lending standards and that their customers would have to hold higher equity levels in order to obtain bank credit in the future.

On the other hand, the German employer federations were actively managing the transition and supported their members. The representatives of the craft sector maintained close working ties to the banking associations, in particular of the cooperative and the savings banks. In addition, the regional chambers of industry and trade, and of the crafts sector played an important supportive role in helping their members prepare meetings with their banks, offering to step in as a form of mediator in the case of difficulties (interview 2013101814D). The German employer federations thus fulfilled a somewhat similar function to the French system of credit mediation introduced during the crisis, intervening when a bank lending relationship had become conflictual.

7

Consolidating the lessons learnt

The French and the Germans were collectively mobilized on learning the lessons of the crisis, but they did do so through defining differing priorities. Tracing priorities is not enough if we are interested in the effects they actually have on the future development of financial sectors. The following sections analyse the measures that have been initiated in response to the crisis, focusing on the extent to which the institutional dispositions in place have hindered or spurred this process. If successful, this formalization process stabilizes the lessons learnt, since it adds a formalized component to it. As the following sections show, the success of this process ended with the limits of state influence and the limits of voluntary self-interested cooperation by various market actors in France. In Germany, the bank lending coalition profited from the institutional dispositions in place, despite opposition, and even found support outside the country, since the measures fell under European legal competence.

7.1 France: Alternatives to bank lending

The French focus on strengthening alternatives to bank credit comprised two dimensions. One targeted the demand side—investors willing and, from a regulatory point of view, allowed to buy these products. It was achieved by strengthening the role of investors, insurance companies in particular, in financing the economy. The other targeted the supply side—hence the conditions for issuing debt and equity. It was realized by a series of measures and initiatives, easing smaller businesses' access to financial markets.

7.1.1 Ending the bank monopoly and counting on investors

Any initiative that aims at strengthening market-based forms of funding has to consider potential investors who are interested in buying the newly issued

Financial Crises and the Limits of Bank Reform: France and Germany's Ways Into and Out of the Great Recession.
Eileen Keller, Oxford University Press (2021). © Eileen Keller. DOI: 10.1093/oso/9780198870746.003.0007

financial products—and from a regulatory point of view allowed to do so. Part of the consensus in France, therefore, was that both individual and institutional investors should, given their financial volumes, play a more prominent role in financing the economy. In order to strengthen the demand for products offered on public markets or arranged in (semi-)private settings, the French authorities modified the investment prescriptions for insurers, changed the taxation of domestic savings schemes, and (co-)invested directly in smaller businesses.

The most important reform initiatives in this context targeted insurers. Insurers' primary economic role is to protect individuals or organizations against certain risks by providing a monetary indemnification. The funds collected by insurers are, of course, not accumulated in a bank account, but actively managed in such a way that they match the insurers' liabilities towards the policy holders. Insurance contracts usually have relatively long time spans. Compared to the resources other financial intermediaries have on the liability side of their balance, those of insurers are characterized by a fairly high degree of stability. They are, for instance, more stable than bank deposits on average.

Like banks, insurers are tightly regulated in Europe, notably by the Solvency regime, which makes investment prescriptions and defines capital requirements amongst other things. Investment prescriptions are based on quota up to which insurers may invest in different asset classes and with what degree of diversification. Overall, because of these regulatory prescriptions, insurers in Europe have strongly invested in titles considered liquid and low-risk, notably state bonds (28 per cent), corporate bonds (36 per cent), and, to a minor extent, equity of large corporations (15 per cent) (Insurance Europe and Oliver Wyman 2013, 19, status as of end 2011).

In 2011, the French state bank CDC together with the French insurers' federation FFSA, supported by the Trésor, launched a first initiative by setting up a collective fund scheme whose funds were invested in the equity of smaller listed businesses. These funds, called Nova 1 and Nova 2, were supposed to provoke a capital shock, bringing new capital to financial markets for small and medium-sized enterprises (SMEs) (CDC 2012, 2; own translation). The aim thereby was to improve the image of financial markets as a reliable source of funding for the corporate sector and to highlight the return of institutional investors to that market segment (CDC 2012).

A second, and further reaching initiative aimed at modifying the investment prescriptions for insurers so that they could invest more easily in the less liquid securities issued by smaller businesses. This initiative was part of a concerted action between the state and the insurance sector in order to bring fresh capital to smaller unlisted enterprises. As one participant of the initiative summarized:

> The context is, let's put it this way, the general concern of the Trésor is to invest in smaller and medium-sized enterprises; previously, the Trésor's focus was on private equity. But the general context also is the need to diversify our assets a bit more towards corporate loans in the context of the sovereign debt crisis and bubbles on the corporate bond market. So this was also brought forward by the insurers themselves in a nonnegligible way, supported by the CDC. It's not a commitment, it's more a loosening [of the regulatory prescriptions] as part of a concerted action.
>
> (Interview 2013062714F)

In August 2013, a reform of the insurance code allowed insurers to invest up to 5 per cent of their balance sheet in more illiquid assets, in addition to the existing 10 per cent ratio (*ratio poubelle*). Under this new scheme, insurers could do so either by lending directly to unlisted enterprises or by investing in special funds, which in turn invest in unlisted debt obligations of smaller enterprises (Décret du 2 août 2013). For this latter purpose, the decree introduced the *fonds de prêts à l'économie* (FPE), special investment vehicles in the legal form of *fonds commun de titrisation* (FCT). FCTs are neither listed, traded nor rated, but they have to fulfil certain criteria as specified by the insurances law. FPEs can invest in the unlisted debt of smaller businesses from all sectors and all member states of the EU, including the debt of public corporations. Organizations that are exclusively active in financial activities are, however, excluded. The maturity of the debt needs to be superior to two years. The funds have to be single-tranched, managed by accredited asset managers, and submitted to regular internal as well as external evaluations (FFSA 2013; Pince et al. 2013). Several of the French insurers established cooperative agreements with banks in order to profit from this opportunity. Axa, for instance, cooperated with Société Générale and Crédit Agricole for the French market and with Commerzbank for the German market (Carlat 2013). In practice, these alliances function as co-investments: The involved bank manages the creditor relationship and usually retains part of the loan volume on its balance; the remaining volume goes to the insurer by the mechanism of a private placement (Royer 2012).

While this part of the reform avoided direct competition with the banks, since the FPEs invest in debt titles issued by the banks, the second part, which allowed for direct lending to unlisted companies, increased competition. The strict French banking monopoly had, apart from minor exceptions, restricted this activity to the banks. In order to grant unsecured credit to unlisted enterprises under the new framework, insurers needed the approval of the supervisory agency ACPR for a credit programme, which controlled the organizational capabilities of the concerned insurer in managing and analysing the credit risk according to the criteria established by the Arrêté du 9 décembre 2013 (interview 2013062714F). In 2013, the Novo fund was launched by the CDC and FFSA based on the new investment opportunities the French insurers now had. The aim was to invest up to one billion Euros in debt obligations of 30 to 40 smaller enterprises. Eighteen insurers agreed to contribute to the fund besides the CDC and a pension fund of the public sector (Erafp). Individual tickets amounted to at least 10 and up to 50 million per enterprise with a time span of five years (Garabedian 2013).

Further reform initiatives targeted individual investors and aimed at reforming the fiscal regime of the domestic savings schemes for investments in shares (*plan d'épargne en actions*, PEA) and in life-insurance contracts. The idea behind these initiatives was to channel the abundant domestic savings— France, like Germany, is one of the European countries with a high private savings rate—towards the real economy by aligning the taxation of the savings schemes more rigorously on the degree of risk taking and the factual length of the commitment.

Fiscal incentives for popular savings schemes have played an important role in the post-war era in France and they have had a strong allocative impact on private wealth management. Life-insurance contracts have been a particularly popular savings scheme since the 1980s, amounting to roughly 1,450 billion Euros (Berger and Lefebvre 2013, 19). Besides a favourable fiscal regime, one of its specificities are the *contrats en Euro*. These contracts guarantee the invested capital, primes are distributed annually, and the savings can be withdrawn at any time. In other words, life-insurance was a very safe and liquid form of investment and, as a consequence, heavily invested in liquid assets, such as debt obligations and monetary funds (Berger and Lefebvre 2013).

Since the crisis, the tax regimes of life-insurance and other regulated savings schemes had been increasingly criticized for the fact that they discouraged risk taking and long-term investments into the real economy, the reason why the abundantly available domestic savings were directed too little towards the funding of the real economy (see for example Cour des comptes 2012b). In October 2012, Prime Minister Ayrault asked the Socialist deputies Karine Berger and Dominique Lefebvre to write a report on how domestic savings could contribute more directly to the funding of the economy. The deputies suggested redirecting 15 to 25 billion Euros per year towards the French economy. The idea was to cut the tax advantage above a certain threshold unless the saver would either assume higher risks (*contrats en unités de compte*) or invest in a new life-insurance contract, which was introduced with the reform (*contrats Euro-Croissance*). Under this latter regime, the capital is only guaranteed if the contract is held until the end of the term (Berger and Lefebvre 2013), a measure that increased the stability of insurers' liabilities and gave them more leeway for long-term investments.

In addition, President François Hollande announced a special savings plan for SME shares in 2012. The idea was to introduce a new savings scheme for investments (directly or via funds) in the equity of smaller enterprises. The Loi du 29 décembre 2013 de finances pour 2014 lifted the general threshold of the preferential tax treatment for equity investments from 132,000 to 150,000 Euros. In addition, the law introduced a new savings scheme profiting from tax benefits for investments of up to 75,000 Euros in shares of SMEs or funds that are mainly invested (75 per cent or more) in securities issued by SMEs (Roulhac 2013c).

All these reforms were implemented smoothly. The business sector warmly welcomed the initiatives, even though the tax advantages could obviously have been even more generous. The large insurance companies, on their side, were the big winners of the reforms and appreciated this opportunity to play a more active role in lending. Until then, the French regulations on insurers' investments in illiquid assets had been relatively restrictive and only allowed for investments in the debt of listed corporations or debt that was guaranteed by a bank or a mortgage. Investments in unlisted corporations were only allowed indirectly and in a very restricted way via subscriptions to investment funds (FCPR and FCT) that were listed and traded on a recognized market (Pince et al. 2013).

Thanks to the combination of regulatory reforms and public subsidies, the big French insurance companies gained new investment opportunities and finally became active in a market segment that had been restricted to the banks until then, ending the banking monopoly. Overall, the reform put the insurance industry in the position to contribute with up to an additional 90 billion Euros to the funding of smaller enterprises. Given the decreasing returns on safe state bonds and the low interest environment, they appreciated the opportunity to diversify their investments and to invest in assets with a higher yield-risk ratio (interview 2013062714F).

The life-insurance reform, in contrast, was double-edged. On the one hand, the new contracts reduced the share of contracts with guaranteed returns and potentially increased the number of contracts that were held until maturity. This lowered the risks associated with guaranteed returns and gave insurers more stability on the liabilities side, protecting them from a massive outflow of sources in the case of an increase in interest rates on deposit-based savings schemes. On the other hand, the challenge was to make sure that the fiscal advantage of the life-insurance contracts would not be destabilized by the reform and lose its attractiveness compared to other savings products.

The biggest losers of the reform were the banks, which lost ground to the insurers. The banks asked for the introduction of a savings product that could compete with the popular life-insurance contracts, re-equilibrating the savings managed by banks and insurance companies, given the constraining effect of the Basel III liquidity rations (interviews 2013062714F, 2013072329F). This demand was, however, not taken up politically. The banks lacked support for measures that aimed at easing their liquidity constraint. Critical voices, highlighting the lack of experience insurers had in handling the credit risk, only had a modest impact on the debate:

> [The fact that insurers are allowed to invest up to 5 per cent of their assets in loans to the real economy] is not necessarily a good idea. The role that we would prefer playing is to relaunch the securitization of bank loans. As a matter of principle, in order to issue credit, you need the teams [which are competent in assessing credit risk]. These are in the banks and not in the insurance companies. So it would be better to reassure the banks in their role and help them surmount the Basel III hurdle, rather than trying to make us issue loans. We are not bankers!   (Interview 2014071125F)

Up to then, French insurers had invested little in in-house expertise on the evaluation of credit risk. In previous years, the tendency had been to delegate and outsource investment decisions to asset managers. In response to the reforms, some of the big insurers began to think about pooling resources in order to build up internal credit evaluation competences (interviews 2013061812F and 2013071125F). Rather than supporting bank lending, the French priority was on strengthening non-bank financial intermediation.

7.1.2   Easing market access for SMEs

Besides these efforts to strengthen the investor side, the French government intervened to ease smaller and middle-sized businesses' access to financial markets. It did so by working on an improvement of the market infrastructure for SMEs and supporting the issuing process with several measures. When considering market access for smaller businesses, this obviously concerns a fairly small subgroup of enterprises, mainly consisting of larger medium-sized enterprises with a sound development record, having achieved a certain reputation in their market segment and younger enterprises with a particular high growth potential (also called start-ups).

Access to financial markets for this type of businesses had existed both in France and in Germany prior to the crisis, but this was almost exclusively true for equity capital. Stock exchanges usually offer several listing segments. These differ in their respective transparency standards, minimal market capitalization requirements, and accounting rules. Special market segments for start-ups with a high growth potential emerged in France with the Nouveau Marché in 1996 and with the Neue Markt in Germany one year later. Both were shut down with the new economy crash at the turn of the millennium.

In 2005, new market segments for smaller businesses re-emerged in both countries. In France, a stock market reform divided the regulated market segments of the French market operator Euronext[1] into three compartments (A, B, and C) and introduced Alternext[2] as a regulated open market segment with lower listing requirements for smaller, high-performance enterprises (Rameix and Giami 2011, 12). In Germany, similar segments were introduced at several of the regional stock exchanges. Compared to Great Britain, however, where the Alternative Investment Market had emerged a decade earlier, the number of listed enterprises and the capital actually raised remained modest, both in France and Germany.

As a matter of principle, the functioning of the SME market segments is similar to the prime segments, such as the French CAC 40 or the German DAX. Enterprises issue shares or debt titles, which are bought by investors and traded on the secondary market, albeit to a much more limited extent. Alternext and its equivalents are, however, not *regulated* markets in the sense of the relevant EU directive (Markets in Financial Instruments Directive, MiFID), and hence, are not covered by European regulation. Compared to the classic *open* market (market segments established by private exchange law

---

[1] Euronext was created in 2000 as a merger of the Bourse de Paris with the stock exchanges of Amsterdam, Brussels, and Lisbon. It is the first transnational stock exchange (Rameix and Giami 2011, 11). In 2007, New York Stock Exchange (NYSE) and Euronext were merged. In 2013, IntercontinentalExchange (ICE) bought NYSE Euronext and separated Euronext from NYSE.

[2] Alternext was renamed Euronext Growth in July 2017.

agreements with the lowest level of investor protection), however, access to these market segments is conditioned by the respect of certain minimum standards regarding size, market capitalization, and transparency standards (see also Banque de France 2014).

The establishment of Alternext was not a success story and dissatisfaction with it preceded the crisis. The market segment was not very dynamic, and the amounts of capital raised by initial public offerings (IPOs) were modest, having dropped from 474 million Euros in its peak year in 2006 to 47 million Euros in 2008. This was much less than the capital provided by private equity investors to that market segment. The liquidity of the market in terms of daily trading volumes had also decreased (Giami and Lefèvre 2009, 22). Despite these deficiencies, it was only in the aftermath of the financial crisis, with the shared agreement on the need to strengthen financial disintermediation, that reanimating financial market segments for smaller businesses gained momentum and made it on to the political agenda.

The connection between the lessons learnt from the crisis and the need to improve market access was made explicit on several occasions during the interviews and it was omnipresent in press articles on the issue. A government official argued, for instance, that: 'Even though this concerns only a small minority of businesses, we tried to work on SME market access in order to attenuate for a possible decrease of bank credit' (interview 2013070420F). This is also confirmed by Euronext in one of its documents, where the company described the rationale behind the reforms:

> Precisely because of the crisis, many actors and reports called the political decision makers' attention to the need of establishing a more appropriate regulatory framework, regulatory practices which correspond better to the economic model of smaller and medium-sized enterprises and a reformed stock exchange tool.   (NYSE Euronext 2012, 3; own translation)

The issue was taken up and actively supported by the then economic and finance minister Christine Lagarde. One government official explained: 'For two or three years, the issue really was: What can we do in order to ease, to revitalize the SME segment, especially for the larger medium-sized enterprises?' (interview 2013070420F). Minor regulatory changes in 2009 and 2010 loosened certain listing prescriptions and constraints related to the listing and transfers between different market segments (Loi du 19 octobre 2009, Loi du 22 octobre 2010). The government also advocated for a Small Business Act and a special treatment of SME issues during the negotiations on the revision of the

European transparency and the prospectus directive and it submitted a pro-posal for a special prospectus for smaller and middle-sized enterprises to the European Commission (Lagarde 2009).

In the context of the fears of a credit crunch and the perceived need to develop alternative sources of funding, the credit mediator, together with the president of the French market regulator AMF, the directors of the public bank CDC and Euronext were commissioned to formulate a confidential report for Lagarde by October 2009. Their task was to explore the possibilities of how market access for smaller enterprises could be improved. The authors agreed on a catalogue of 15 measures which aimed at doubling the number of firms listed on Alternext in the subsequent 18 months (Lagarde 2009; also Banque de France 2012; Rameix and Giami 2011, 13). This aim was, however, not achieved. As a reaction to the failure of this joint initiative, an observatory on financing enterprises by the market was created in March 2010. Besides promoting market-based forms of funding, its function was to closely monitor the situation and to publish yearly reports.

Euronext remained reluctant in launching institutional reforms. The company was sharply criticized for showing a lack of commitment to the joint strategy and heavily attacked for having introduced a very disadvantageous tariffication for SME transactions without having consulted issuers. In addition, issuers reproached Euronext for the fact that the SME market segments were not a strategic and profitable activity for it. After the takeover in 2007, NYSE reduced the staff and the financial resources committed to smaller issuers and shut down the regional representations outside Paris (Rameix and Giami 2011, 34–5, interview 2013060606F). The major obstacle to improving SME market access was thus the market operator itself. As one industry representative put it, resonating with what several others had expressed similarly:

> Our problem is the market operator which, and this is to some extent the logical consequence of MiFID, reacted to the lifting of barriers to competition by fighting for the market segments, where its market share was threatened the most, that is the big corporations, at the expense of those segments with less competitive pressure, hence smaller businesses. As a consequence, the regional stock-exchange ecosystem deteriorated significantly.
>
> (Interview 2013112735F)

Given the failure of these early initiatives, economic and finance minister François Baroin, who succeeded Lagarde when she was nominated managing director of the International Monetary Fund (IMF), asked for a second in-depth report on the problems of listed SMEs in July 2011. Besides reform suggestions that dealt with the difficulties structurally inherent to SME market access, including market size, liquidity, cost, and transparency requirements, a strong emphasis of the report was on improving the market infrastructure (also see Rameix and Giami 2011).

Compared to previous initiatives, the atmosphere had become markedly tenser by that time and Euronext was openly threatened with the implementation of a competing platform. If the stock exchange operator was not willing to cooperate, the government would withdraw its confidence and support the establishment of a new market operator, a demand that was supported by several corporate sector representatives (interviews 2013060606F, 2013061812F). The official mission letter by Baroin stipulated that this possibility should be explored as the relations with Euronext had become manifestly conflictual (cited in Rameix and Giami 2011). Rameix and Giami report that they had been in touch with potential alternative market operators, an option that was presented as a way to put pressure on Euronext, a means of last resort if the market operator refused to cooperate (also see Rameix and Giami 2011, 37).

Substantially, the preferred solution of the rapporteurs was to transfer the SME market segment to a separate legal entity, whose capital should be opened to external strategic domestic investors with an outspoken interest in developing SME financial markets (Rameix and Giami 2011, 35–7). Euronext, on its side, developed its own reform proposal. In July 2012, Euronext's strategic orientation committee, an advisory committee to the senior executives with representatives from the issuer, the intermediaries', and the investors' side presented the idea of a Bourse de l'Entreprise as a merger of Euronext's listing compartments B, C, and Alternext, establishing a separate subsidiary (NYSE Euronext 2012).

Neither of the two reform proposals was, however, realized. All NYSE Euronext did was to improve the existing framework by creating EnterNext in May 2013. EnterNext is not a new trading platform, but a subsidiary with its own 18 million Euro budget, its own staff, a board of directors, and a stronger presence in the regions. EnterNext centralizes the services dedicated to enterprises with a listing inferior to one billion Euros. The listings themselves remained unchanged, however, on the compartments B and C or on Alternext (Roulhac 2013a). Euronext also introduced Initial Bond Offer (IBO) at its Paris marketplace in July 2012, a procedure for issuing bonds with requirements similar to those of an initial public offering (IPO). Yet, here again, success was limited. IBO was not very dynamic: only three enterprises used the format to issue bonds in the first year; out of these, only one was previously not listed either on Alternext or on Euronext C (Roulhac 2013b).

Overall, representatives of the corporate sector were not satisfied with the modifications undertaken by NYSE Euronext. They were disappointed that a new SME stock exchange had not been established and they remained sceptical regarding the success of EnterNext and the commitment of the market operator, especially given the takeover by the US-American operator Intercontinental Exchange (ICE) announced in late 2012. 'We wanted a real stock exchange', complained one business representative. 'What we got is a marketing agency. We don't think that it will work that way' (interview 2013060606F). In short, the success of the measures ended with the institutional capacities of the state. Where they met with the resistance rather than the voluntary, self-interested commitment of market actors, as this was the case with the insurance companies, the desired reforms did not conform with the expectations many had put in them.

Besides regulatory changes and efforts to improve the market infrastructure, the state increased its own investments in these market segments. The public investment funds raised their capital invested in listed SMEs: an additional 100 million Euros by the CDC and 300 million by a French sovereign fund (FSI)—considerably more than the 48 million to which private investments had fallen in 2008. In addition, the state bank Oséo (now Bpi) was mandated to set up a joint issuing scheme, endowed with a public guarantee in order to help businesses whose tickets were too small to issue debt on the market on a standalone basis.

In February 2012, Micado France 2018 was launched, the first bond fund dedicated to investments in some 20 listed but unrated medium-sized enterprises. The fund itself is listed on Alternext. The amount of capital raised by individual enterprises ranged from 5 to 20 million Euros with interest rates fixed individually according to the enterprises' risk profile (Roulhac 2012a). Other formats, such as the operations by the agro-alimentary society GIAC mutualize the risk among issuers and hierarchize investors' repayments rights by securitization (GIAC OLT I and II). The time span of these bonds was ten years with an average issuing volume of 2 million Euros per enterprise. In March 2013, Twenty First Capital, a French asset management firm, launched Avenir PME Obligations, a first bond fund that invested in unlisted companies (Diaz 2013). CDC Entreprises and Oséo intervened in several of these operations either by guaranteeing a certain amount of the issued debt or by buying mezzanine debt, that is subordinate forms of debt with higher risks.

The problem of all these funds was, however, that the capital volume actually raised remained below the original expectations—60 million Euros instead of 300 in the case of Micado France and 80 million instead of 160 million initially planned in the case of the GIAC. The initiatives suffered from difficulties finding investors and coordinating the joint issuing operations, because it turned out to be hard to get all the enterprises intending to raise money on the same schedule (also see Diaz 2013; Garrouste 2012; Roulhac 2012b). Here again, the actual success of the measures crucially depended on the commitment and voluntary cooperation of various actors in the light of the incentives and the practicality of the solutions provided.

Despite these difficulties, the efforts did lead to some improvements: The number of SMEs listed on Alternext Paris increased from 119 in 2008 to 167 in 2011 and stabilized at that level. Overall, the capital raised on Alternext by IPOs, capital increases, convertible bonds, and debt obligations increased from 113 million Euros in 2008 to 290 million in 2011 but dropped down to 148 million in 2012 (Giami 2011, 16; 2013, 11, 17). Several joint issuing operations have since been organized in different formats.

Contrary to the previous reforms, which were successful because they coincided with what influential parts of the insurance industry wanted, the developments of market access shows that the outcomes of the reform efforts were crucially conditioned by the scope of influence of state actors and the limits to voluntary cooperation by market actors. Progress on aspects that required the commitment of the market operator, a private company outside direct government influence were limited. In contrast, in areas where the government could act on its own, several measures were implemented.

7.2 Germany: Support for traditional bank lending

In Germany, the renewed support for classic bank intermediation led to a focus on the treatment of corporate credit in the relevant banking regulation. Since the regulatory stipulations for banks are largely harmonized at the European level as part of the common market for financial services, domestic priorities had to transcend the domestic arena and find support in Europe. The following sections deal with how restoring bank lending was defined as a political priority in Germany and how it was, in a next step, brought to the European agenda, becoming a part of the CRR-CRDIV reform package.[3]

---

[3] The politics behind this new SME compromise have also been discussed in Keller (2018).

7.2.1 Defining a new SME compromise

Within Germany, demands to support traditional bank lending translated into concrete reforms through specific, lending-friendly stipulations in the relevant banking regulation (Capital Requirements Directive, CRD). In technical terms, the demand implied lower capital requirements for bank lending to SMEs. Capital requirements are an essential part of modern bank regulation as they define how much equity capital a bank has to hold in order to absorb unforeseen shocks and losses. They put thus a limit to how much credit a bank can offer with a given capital base. Sufficient equity capital de-incentivizes risk taking and allows banks to bear unforeseen losses, while adhering to their other commitments (Tarullo 2008, 15 ff.).

Since the 1970s, a risk-weighted approach to capital requirements has become predominant in banking regulation. Put simply, the underlying rationale is that some bank activities are riskier than others and, hence, potential (unforeseen) losses more probable, and potentially higher, on some bank activities than on others. From this follows in economic terms that the riskier a business is, the more capital a bank needs to hold in order to absorb unforeseen losses. The Basel I framework took this economic functioning principle as the basis for regulatory oversight, defining the riskiness of different bank activities in the form of risk-weights (also see Hüther et al. 2009, 8–15).

Table 7.1 displays the risk weights as they are applied by banks to different classes of debtors under the modified standard approach.[4] As a matter of principle, the assessment of the risk weight to be applied is based on the external rating of a debtor by a credit rating agency. The better the rating, the lower is the risk weight and hence, the lower the amount of capital a bank has to hold against a specific credit risk. The regulatory capital a bank has to hold is calculated as a certain fraction—the so-called capital ratio, 8 per cent under Basel II, 10.5 per cent under Basel III—of the sum of all loans multiplied by the respective risk weight.

However, there are exceptions to the rule: EU member states all have a 0 per cent risk weight, irrespective of their country rating, an exception that

---

[4] The standard approach was introduced with Basel I. Under Basel II, there are two alternative ways to determine the risk weights. The *modified standard approach* allowed the use of external ratings issued by a credit rating agency in order to define the risk weight. Under the *internal risk based approach* (IRB approach, IRBA), banks were allowed to define the risk weights of their borrowers, using their own, internal models in order to estimate the creditworthiness of a borrower (also see Conert 2003, 4–10). The methodologically much more demanding IRBA is primarily used by the big banks. Many smaller banks and almost all German banks still used the modified standard approach, even though it is usually more expensive in terms of required equity capital (interview 2013100902D).

Table 7.1 Risk weights for credit risk according to the standard approach

Credit quality step	1 AAA to AA–	2 A+ to A–	3 BBB+ to BBB	4 BB+ to BB–	5 B+ to B–	6 CCC+ and below
EU member states/ECB	0%	0%	0%	0%	0%	0%
Rated non-EU states	0%	20%	50%	100%	100%	150%
Rated financial institutions	20%	50%	50%	100%	100%	150%
Rated corporations	20%	50%	100%	100%	150%	150%
Non-rated corporations	100%	100%	100%	100%	100%	100%
Retail (including SMEs)	75%	75%	75%	75%	75%	75%

Source: Deutsche Bundesbank. Descriptions only refer to exposures with a residual maturity superior to three months. Additional rules apply under specific conditions and may lead to differing calculations from the ones in the table. The credit quality steps are the ones defined by the EBA for Standard & Poor long-term credit ratings.

contributed to the build-up and the depth of the Euro crisis. In addition, not all debtors—especially smaller ones—have an external rating. In these cases, a uniform risk weight is applied, irrespective of the actual riskiness of the debtor. The risk weight amounts to 100 per cent for unrated businesses and unrated non-EU states and 75 per cent for smaller enterprises (retail exposure). In 2004, with the adoption of Basel II, the decision was made to treat credit to SMEs as a retail exposure and hence apply the lower risk weight if certain criteria are met (so-called SME compromise).[5]

With the overall increase of the capital requirements for credit risk from 8 per cent to 10.5 per cent with Basel III, the amount of capital required for each credit automatically increases. This makes bank lending less attractive from a bank's point of view and bank loans potentially costlier and less abundant for clients (see also Chapter 4). It was this aspect that drew criticism in Germany. In order to offset these potentially unfavourable side effects of the regulatory reforms, a 'financing the economy' coalition formed from 2009

[5] The 75% risk weight is applied to SME lending as long as the exposure of the bank to a specific enterprise does not exceed 1 million Euros, if the annual turnover of the enterprise is below 50 million Euros and as long as certain criteria regarding the granularity of the loan portfolio are met (CRR, art. 114, 120, 121, 122, and 123). The more favourable treatment of SME credit risk compared to the credit risk of larger unrated enterprises, known as the 'SME compromise', was introduced because the credit risk related to smaller businesses was considered more granular and consequently less likely to lead to the build-up of concentration risks, even though smaller businesses have a higher default risk on average (also see EBA 2012, 8).

on. The coalition was composed of representatives from the corporate and the banking sector and joined by politicians and government officials. Their main argument was that SME lending had nothing to do with the outbreak and the propagation of the financial crisis and that it was consequently unfair to 'punish' SME financing because of bank mismanagement that had occurred in other areas of the banks' activities. The coalition lobbied for a new SME compromise, hence, another special regulatory treatment of SME credit in order to support bank lending and ultimately, so the argument went, economic growth.

From the outset, both the German banks and the business sector representatives were highly mobilized on the potential impact of the banking reforms. Substantively, the focus of the debate was on the potential negative effects of the reforms on bank lending and the appropriateness of the capital requirements for credit risk compared to those underlying other bank activities. A study conducted for the Mittelstand association (BVMW 2011, 2) criticized that the regulatory authorities had focused too much on financial stability and too little on economic growth, the availability of bank credit, and the particularities of different national contexts with respect to the funding of the economy. The other employer federations of industry, commerce, and the crafts sector put forward similar arguments (e.g. BDI 2011, 2; DIHK 2011, 1; ZDH 2011, 7).

According to the BVMW's own estimations, the cost of an average SME credit would most probably increase by 54 basis points through the Basel III reforms and the global credit volume would decrease by 2.5 per cent in Germany (BVMW 2011, 26). A study conducted on behalf of the Bavarian Economic Association (vbw) argued that the reforms would lead to an increase of refinancing rates between 30 and 50 basis points for banks, but left it open whether this would result in higher interest rates paid by the banks' customers (vbw 2012). In addition, several employer organizations criticized that the higher Basel III capital requirements were related to two thirds to credit risk and only to one third to trading book activities, even though the losses made during the crisis suggested an inverse ratio (BVMW 2011, 8).

Several federations thereby referred to two publications by German economists (Berg et al. 2011; Erlebach et al. 2010) on bank losses during the financial crisis (e.g. vbw 2012, 60–2, interview 2013101814D; DSGV 2013, 4–5). According to their findings, which were based on a balance sheet analysis of 332 big banks during the crisis, unforeseen losses related to credit risk amounted to 24 per cent of the capital banks had to hold against these risks for most credit institutions (90 per cent quantile). During the crisis, most banks' losses related to credit risk were thus largely covered by the regulatory prescriptions in place. The losses related to the trading book, by contrast, amounted to 255 per cent of risk weighted assets for a large majority of banks (90 per cent quantile). In other words, the losses on trading book activities were in most cases much higher than the capital banks had to hold against these risks according to the regulatory prescriptions in place.

Some form of distortion remains even when taking the 2009 reforms of the trading book activities into account (so-called Basel II.5, transposed into European law by the CRD III). Based on these higher capital requirements, the losses incurred during the crisis would have amounted to 79 per cent. While the new requirements would have covered the de facto losses of most banks during the crisis, they were still, relatively speaking when comparing the actual losses, much lower than the buffers required for credit risk (Berg et al. 2011; Erlebach et al. 2010). The regulatory treatment of credit risk was, in other words, unfavourable compared to the treatment of risks that were related to the trading book.

Based on these insights, the argument put forward was that since banks hold by far the largest share of their capital against credit risk, higher overall capital requirements would 'penalize' credit risk disproportionately and the distorted relation of capital requirements for credit and trading book risks would persist, despite the adjustments made after the crisis (Die Familienunternehmer 2011, 2). In addition to that, several studies aimed to show that current regulatory capital levels for SME credit risk under Basel II were too high compared to the factual losses that occurred. As a result, a sort of cross-subsidization of trading book risks by credit risk occurred that was deemed unjust (BVMW 2011, 5 ff., taken up by vbw 2012, 59–68).[6]

In order to mediate for these distortions, German federations developed suggestions for how the capital cost associated with credit risk could be reduced. Table 7.2 gives an overview of the proposals made by the German employer federations and the federations of the banking sector. Overall, the suggestions focused on two elements: Firstly, a reduction of the risk weight applied to credit risk of smaller businesses both under the standard and the advanced approach and, secondly, on making the SME compromise more

---

[6] The argument elaborated first by Berg et al. (2011) was that the parameter for asset correlation for SME credit risk in the IRBA formula as defined by the regulator was too high. Under IRBA, credit risk comprises two components: a systematic factor, reflecting the extent to which the development of an individual enterprise depends on the development of the economy as a whole and an idiosyncratic factor relating to the individual characteristics of a given enterprise. It is assumed that the former is all the more important, the larger an enterprise is (also see EBA 2012, 24).

Table 7.2 Reform proposals on SME lending

BVMW	Position paper in June 2010 - Reduction of the risk weight to 50% - Increase of the upper limit for annual turnover from 1 to 2 million Euros - Annual increase of the retail threshold should be linked to the development of inflation levels Study from August 2011 - Standard approach: Reduction of the risk weight to 50% for credit up to 1 million Euros and to 70% for enterprises with an annual turnover below 250 million Euros - IRB approach: Increase of the SME definition from an annual turnover of 50 million to 250 million; reduction of the risk weight by 30% to 40% for enterprises with an annual turnover of up to 100 million Euros and by 6% to 30% for enterprises with an annual turnover of up to 250 million through a modification of the asset correlation parameter
ZDH	Position paper from May 2011 - Reduction of the risk weight for retail credit to at least 60% - Redefine the granularity criterion in a more favourable way for smaller credit institutions
BDI	Statement from September 2011 on the European Commission's CRR proposal - Lowering the risk weight to 50% for SMEs with a credit volume < 1 million Euros and to 75% for enterprises with an annual turnover < 250 million Euros - Increase the 1 million Euros credit limit
vbw	Report from January 2012 - Reduction of the risk weights by 30% to 40% - Increase of the 50 million maximum annual turnover and the threshold for the total credit volume from 1 million to 2 million + possibly an adjustment according to the development of inflation
DSGV	- Reduction of the risk weight for SME credit to 55%
BVR	- Reduction of the risk weight for SME credit to 57,14%

Sources: BVMW (2010, 6–7), (2011, 25), ZDH (2011, 8), BDI (2011, 3), vbw (2012, preface, 79–80); DSGV and BVR: interview.

inclusive by extending its scope of application to larger enterprises and higher lending volumes. Two measures were proposed to this end: an increase of the upper limit of the credit volume up to which the SME compromise is applied and an increase of the annual turnover for qualifying enterprises from 50 million to up to 250 million Euros. The demand was also taken up by the AG Mittelstand, a working group composed of members from the corporate and the banking sector founded in 2003, demanding that the risk weight for retail corporate credit should at least be lowered by one third (AG Mittelstand 2011, 3).

7.2.2   The cross-border dynamics of the reforms

How successful was the reform coalition in obtaining more favourable conditions for bank lending? As in France, the demand was supported by a considerable number of actors, including the employer organizations, the banking federations, the Ministry for Economic Affairs, and many parliamentarians. Given the fact that banking regulation is harmonized at the European level, reforms had to be realized there. The Ministry for Economic Affairs threatened not to support the Finance Ministry's proposal on the CRDIV in the cabinet if the latter was not willing to include a stipulation in favour of a new SME compromise. In addition, representatives from the Economic Ministry went to Brussels to meet with representatives from the European Parliament and the Commission, lobbying for a new set of special rules for SME lending (interview 2013120324D). Parallel to this, representatives from the corporate sector approached the chancellery and, after several meetings with Angela Merkel's consultants, aroused her interest in the subject (interview 2013101814D). The SME compromise would have not made it on to the European agenda and even less so into the final regulation without the commitment and the joint lobbying efforts from Germany, joined by representatives from other countries, Italy and Austria in particular.

The financing the economy coalition met, however, with fierce opposition from the regulatory authorities both domestically and at the European level. Based on the quantitative impact studies of the new rules conducted by the Basel Committee, the IMF, and the European Commission, the latter argued that stricter regulatory standards would not constrain bank lending and would, on the contrary, have '*clear net long term economic benefits*' (European Commission 2011c, 52, emphasis in the original), because the benefits in terms of financial stability would outweigh the economic costs associated with the adjustments to the new standards. According to model estimations by the European Commission's econometric services, the regulatory standards for capital and liquidity should lower the risk of systemic financial crises by roughly 70 per cent (European Commission 2011c, fn. 108).

In addition, the European Commission (2011c, 52) argued that SMEs, which depend most heavily on bank credit, were the primary beneficiaries of a smoothed business cycle because smaller businesses are usually more strongly exposed to credit-rationing effects during economic downturns. It also assumed that SMEs would be less strongly affected by stricter regulatory standards than larger enterprises, because banks had tightened their standards more rigorously for the latter since the crisis (European Commission 2011c,

52–4). Regulators in Germany and elsewhere were thus confident that the new rules would not constrain economic growth in an intolerable way and that this was not an issue the real economy should be concerned with.

At the domestic level, when banking and business sector representatives presented their claims of unfair regulatory treatment of SME credit, regulators from the Bundesbank, the supervisory authority BaFin, and the Finance Ministry asked to prove the appropriateness of their claims empirically with their own loan default data. After some back and forth, the savings and the cooperative banks finally agreed to provide the required data and the Bundesbank made its own calculations, concluding that the claims were exaggerated. More generally, the standpoint of the Ministry of Finance, supported by the Bundesbank and BaFin, was that it was not appropriate to modify individual risk weights unilaterally without taking the overall calibration into account, and that, given the results of the impact studies, there was no reason for concern about the economic impact of the reforms (interviews 2013092710D, 2013103018D, 2013103019D).

At the European level, German representatives of the corporate sector approached the Commission first, but the latter was not willing to modify the risk weights (interview 2013101815D). All the Commission was committed to do was to introduce a review clause in its draft and to ask the European Banking Authority (EBA) to make a report by September 2012 on whether a reduction of the risk weights applied to SME credit risk was recommendable (European Commission 2011d, 12–13). The Commission proposal postponed the final decision and mandated the EBA to conduct another study and to write a report within the two years after the implementation of the reform on the factual unforeseen losses of retail exposures compared to those underlying the calculation of the risk weights and to explore whether an increase of the 1 million Euro credit volume limit would be recommendable (European Commission 2011b, 151).

The EBA on its side was very reluctant and emphasized that 'great caution should be exercised in altering the RWs [risk weights] or the threshold for SME Retail exposures to avoid any risk of jeopardising financial stability' (EBA 2012, 9; emphasis omitted), considering the increase of the loan volumes as arbitrary. In its report from September 2012, the EBA emphasized that the financial structure of smaller enterprises was less stable, default probabilities higher, and their activity more strongly affected by economic cycles than those of large enterprises (EBA 2012, 15, 26–9). In addition, the EBA questioned the direct link between regulatory standards and the banks' lending behaviour and its representatives were sceptical whether the presence of a perceived funding gap indeed resulted from the supply of credit. According to the EBA, SME funding was better supported by other mechanisms, such as private equity, debt capital markets, or public guarantees, rather than modifying the risk weights.

As the Commission was not receptive to the demands, and the EBA even less so, lobbying efforts turned to the European Parliament. In October 2010, the Austrian parliamentarian Othmar Karas from the European People's Party (EPP) was nominated rapporteur for the CRR-CRDIV reform package and he was a decisive factor in shaping the Parliament's priorities during the negotiations. Karas involved the Parliament in the debates on the banking reforms early on. By October 2010, the Parliament had internally agreed upon a resolution, which emphasized the need to recognize European distinctiveness regarding corporate financing, and take the impact of the reforms on economic growth and the diversity of Europe's banking landscape more directly into account (European Parliament 2010).

Karas, who represented the position of the Parliament most fiercely in public, was very active in emphasizing that the transposition of Basel III in Europe had to be sensitive to the particularities of the European diversified banking landscape and the role of banks in financing the real economy. In his view, the Basel agreement would favour US-American investment banks. As traditional bank lending is also an important activity for many Austrian banks, creating a regulatory environment that would not disadvantage this model was a priority for him. Karas emphasized that the CRR-CRDIV should be a law both for stabilizing the banking sector and financing the real economy (Karas 2010, 2012).

It may have been a lucky coincidence for the German bank lending coalition that the Parliament had nominated a rapporteur who was sensitive to bank lending issues. In order to be heard by the Austrian, the German association of the skilled crafts sector (ZDH) and the German industry and commerce association (DIHK) approached the Austrian economic chamber (WKÖ) and managed to arrange a high-level meeting with Karas and two German deputies from the Committee on Economic and Monetary Affairs in September 2011 (DIHK et al. 2011a, interview 2013101814D). DIHK, WKÖ, and ZDH welcomed the Commission's efforts to support SME lending in a joint press release, but emphasized that a decrease of the risk weights and an increase of the retail threshold should be introduced without prior analysis by the EBA (DIHK et al. 2011b).

These efforts paid off: The version of the CRR-CRDIV the Parliament adopted in June 2012 included a scaling factor of 0.7619 for SME credit, which offset the effect of the higher capital ratio introduced with Basel III.[7] The capital cost of bank credit for SMEs would thus not change, despite the overall higher capital level introduced under Basel III. The Parliament's draft also increased the upper limit of the loan exposure volume from 1 to 2 million Euros for the standard approach and to 5 million Euros under the IRB approach (European Parliament 2012). In addition, the Parliament introduced a phrase on credit distribution, demanding that the banks' lending decisions should be based on 'customer specific information gleaned from a relationship with the customer and not available on standard credit scores and databases that can be bought in the market' (European Parliament 2012, art. 118-ca) which can be read as an outspoken support of relationship banking.

The Parliament made the SME compromise, besides executive compensation and corporate governance, one of its core demands during the trilogue negotiations—and it was this support that ultimately led to the inclusion in the final draft. The coalition obtained the introduction of the corrective factor, which is applied if the exposure of the bank does not exceed 1.5 million Euros, including subsidiaries and parent institutions in both the retail and the corporate credit risk class. The one million upper limit for retail treatment of corporate credit risk, by contrast, was not modified. During the transition phase up to 2019, in which the higher capital charges were phased in gradually, the capital cost of SME credit for banks was even lower than under Basel II (EBA 2012). Easing the funding of the economy, potentially at the expense of financial stability was successful. Politics trumps banking regulation—as one observer put it.

---

[7] 10.5% [new capital ratio] * 0.7619 = 8% [previous capital ratio].

8

Comparative lessons

More than a decade has passed since the subprime crisis developed into a
fully-fledged financial crisis and from there into a severe economic crisis. The
crisis has had and will have a lasting impact on our understanding of banking.
This applies to the risks and hazards associated with large and highly
interconnected financial institutions that are too big, too complex, and too
interconnected to fail and by that to follow the laws of the market. The same
also holds for the limits of risk management and the effectiveness of banking
supervision. In addition to these rather broad insights, the lessons learnt are,
as the previous chapters have shown, as diverse as the national contexts
affected by the crisis.

The global financial crisis came in the guise of a French and a German
financial crisis and in many other variants alike (also see Hardie and
Howarth 2013b; Mayer et al. 2018; Mayntz 2012a; Thiemann 2018). The
financial crisis was a housing, a financing, a banking, a financial markets, and
a government debt crisis and the impact of these different aspects was not the
same everywhere. These differences had a considerable influence on the ways
in which individual countries and their banking sectors experienced the crisis
and how they responded to it, as the study of the French and the German
cases shows.

Understanding the implications of the crisis, therefore, is a two-level and a
multi-arena issue: Crucial reform initiatives were coordinated within the
framework of the G20 leaders. With respect to banking, they were elaborated
and negotiated by the Basel Committee and at the European level. At the
same time, action was taken at the national level, involving various interest
groups, parliamentarians, and the broader public, beyond the inner circles of
financial expertise. The reform priorities identified in different contexts
followed different logics, depending on the specific institutional and socio-
economic context in which they were embedded.

Differences and diversity will hardly surprise students of comparative
politics as this is their 'bread and butter' business. However, the challenge is
that the diversity observed during the crisis cuts across well-established
categories in political economy, such as liberal and coordinated market

Financial Crises and the Limits of Bank Reform: France and Germany's Ways Into and Out of the Great Recession.
Eileen Keller, Oxford University Press (2021). © Eileen Keller. DOI: 10.1093/oso/9780198870746.003.0008

economies, market-based contrasted with supposedly bank-based financial systems, or majoritarian versus consensus democracies. The crisis has shown that we know too little about the politics of financial regulation in a comparative perspective and the analytic categories that help us understand the complexity and diversity behind contemporary finance. Social learning is one conceptual answer. The following sections summarize the argument and discuss the nature of social learning in response to the crisis. The argument is tested using Bayesian updating and its relevance illustrated by applying it to the US-American and the British crisis responses. The chapter closes with a brief discussion of the theoretical implications of this form of social learning.

8.1 Crisis responses across levels and contexts

The previous chapters analysed how France and Germany experienced and responded to the Great Recession. They showed how decision-makers sought to strike a balance between at least partly diverging legitimate policy aims: increasing financial stability without hampering future economic growth and the competitiveness of their domestic financial sector. These issues were linked to the question of the real economy's access to financial resources and the future financing mix. While the crisis triggered social learning in both countries, in international negotiations in particular, representatives sought not to hamper the competitiveness of their domestic banks.

Starting at the global level, we have seen how France and Germany participated in the negotiations on Basel III in the Basel Committee and its transposition and adaptation within the European Union by the CRR-CRDIV reform package. Representatives from both countries supported overall stricter regulatory standards, but they were concerned with the impact of the reforms on the economic role of the domestic banks and classic bank lending. The concern was similar in both countries, and clearly less pronounced in the United States and the United Kingdom with their more market-based financial systems. Even in the immediate aftermath of the severest financial crisis in decades, negotiating the future of banking was an issue of conflict and competition amongst jurisdictions and competing policy goals.

The analysis moved on, studying how the financial crisis was perceived in both countries. While the discussions in the relevant international fora were highly technical, making abstractions from the various contexts in which banks operate, the domestic debates focused more specifically on the behaviour of the domestic banking sector in the years prior to and during the crisis, considering the implications of the crisis for future developments in both political economies. While the initial government responses to the crisis were fairly similar in both countries with respect to the efforts made to contain the crisis and to stabilize the banks, the ways in which the crisis was widely perceived and the reform options discussed in the subsequent period differed.

In the perception of the broader public, even though the French banks had weathered the turmoil of the subprime crisis fairly well, the financial crisis developed into a severe bank lending crisis, leading to a focus on strengthening alternatives to classic bank intermediation. Trust in the banks' capacity to intermediate financial resources to the real economy had been strongly undermined by the tightening of lending standards with which many banks responded to the uncertainties and losses generated by the crisis. Many entrepreneurs realized that access to bank credit could be hampered from one day to the next. The collective response to these insights was a focus on liberalizing the insurers' investment prescriptions, and reviving SME financial markets.

In Germany, the public, with increasing perplexity and disbelief, discovered from summer 2007 onwards that several German banks, both from the private and the public banking sector, had got into severe difficulties for a variety of reasons. Behind each of these failures was a specific story of how that particular bank had got into trouble. The crisis was not perceived as a crisis of banking or bank intermediation in general, but as one of financial innovation and the risks associated with certain business models. In turn, the collective response was on strengthening traditional banking based on the three-pillar structure, fighting for regulatory stipulations that supported bank lending. As surprising as this may seem, once the initial measures on bank rescue were in place and some reforms on fostering financial stability had been implemented, the responses had more to do with a lowering of regulatory standards and making them more flexible rather than with their tightening.

Even though bank intermediation plays an important role in both countries, it may not entirely surprise students of comparative political economy to see differing responses in France and Germany. After all, their political systems are different, and the structure of the banking sector is not the same. In addition, while Germany has been the textbook case of relationship banking, France is sometimes considered a more hybrid type since the liberal political course of the Socialist government in 1983 (Chapter 2). Were the crisis responses thus not more than politics as usual, following a path-dependent pattern, with Germany confirming its exception with respect to bank intermediation and France going further down the road of financial disintermediation?

At this point of the analysis, the explanatory power of social learning comes into play, which ties the interpretations of the crisis back to specific socio-economic developments in both countries, by which learning was triggered. When we broaden the analysis from the aftermath of the crisis to the two decades before, remarkably similar developments with reversed signs can be found in both countries: increasing reliance on bank intermediation in France and a focus on strengthening market-based banking and financial disintermediation in Germany, reducing the high levels of bank intermediation. In other words, there were similar developments in both countries at different points, irrespective of the existing institutional and structural differences.

In Germany, despite the apparently close and trusting Hausbank relations, many entrepreneurs realized during the 1990s that their access to financial resources was hampered and that the banks were more reluctant to lend— impressions that are remarkably similar to the ones observed in France during the Great Recession. In the light of the observed and assumed further scarcity of classic bank credit under Basel II, the expectations on the conditions for bank lending changed. These developments coincided with widespread beliefs that Germany had to modernize its financial sector and catch up with developments elsewhere, which concerned financial markets, but also banking. The three-pillar structure of the banking sector was increasingly questioned as an obstacle to bank competitivity and asset securitization was promoted as a means to modernize the banking sector. The financial crisis brought these developments to the attention of the broader public. Social learning was linked to the risks associated with asset securitization and financial innovation more generally, leading to a reappraisal of the merits of classic bank intermediation based on the three-pillar system.

In France, the same period was marked by abundant liquidity and many businesses increased their levels of bank debt, thereby becoming more bank-dependent. In the early 2000s, the difficulties many banks had faced in the transition phase from state-dominated banking to increased competition lay behind them. The regulatory changes associated with Basel II passed largely unnoticed by the broader public, including many small business owners. Credit was abundantly available and since the equity levels of French enterprises were higher than in Germany, there was less adaptive pressure in the context of Basel II. Overall, the period was marked by relative stability with respect to the framework in which the banks operated. The French 'Big Bang' of the 1980s had led to the introduction of a framework for asset securitization. It was, however, rather restrictive from a regulatory point of view, and not an activity in which the banks invested massively. Despite the losses incurred by several French banking groups, the subprime crisis had a less devastating impact on their stability. Asset securitization and the risks associated with financial innovation were not the object of social learning.

While the respective reform options chosen in France and Germany in the aftermath of the crisis found considerable support within both countries, they were not uncontested. In both countries, experts hinted to the risks and limits of the respective reform agendas. French technocrats knew that there was no credit crunch during the crisis and that strengthening market access would only profit a small fraction of French businesses. Experts also warned that insurers had little experience in dealing with credit risk. In Germany, resistance came from the Bundesbank, the supervisory authority BaFin, and the Ministry of Finance with respect to the suggestions on lowering the regulatory standards for SME lending. Social learning was, in other words, neither an uncontested nor an even or a completely disinterested process. In both countries, the reforms chosen were supported by a heteroclite coalition of financial sector representatives, the business federations, state representatives, and parliamentarians, advocating policies that were in line with the substance of social learning.

To conclude, more than anything else, the French and the German crisis responses were different because the patterns of stability and change with respect to the perceptions of bank lending and beliefs about financial sector reform in the decade prior to the crisis were different. The drivers of the reforms only become fully comprehensible by placing politics in time, recognizing how the collectively shared understandings of what specific aspects of the political economy, such as the modalities of bank lending or the benefits of financial liberalization, are like and how they will develop in the future change. Let us therefore have a closer examination of where and how social learning occurred in both countries.

8.2 Social learning in response to the crisis

The essence of the social learning approach that structured the previous chapters is that certain political reforms are best understood as the result of an updated, widely shared, but usually not uncontested understanding of a specific aspect of social reality. Social learning can relate to what the society is like, such as gender roles, women's rights, or the role of the church, but also to how the economy works, for instance with respect to the conditions of bank lending, the role of digitalization, or the necessity of making labour markets more flexible. The approach is a conceptual answer to societal, technological, economic, and political change. While it is not a framework that claims applicability to political decision-making in general, it is plausible to assume that ideational change is a major trigger for political change in many cases. Change can be considered an ontological constant because of creative agency.

Social learning is a form of learning because it implies an updating or adjusting of beliefs in the light of new, and thus deemed better, information, leading to changes in the perception or the understanding of a specific social phenomenon. It is a social process because it implies that change can be traced among a broader societal group and even individuals (or groups) that do not believe in the appropriateness of the conclusions drawn have to acknowledge that this has become a social reality, something that is essential for how things are widely perceived, for many others. Let us reconsider the nature of social learning by focusing on the following questions: Where and how did learning occur? What about politicians, party, and electoral politics? What is the role of the institutional context? And, finally, were the lessons learnt inevitable?

8.2.1 Locating true learning

Where and how did social learning occur? Social learning has, as the term indicates, both a cognitive and an interactive component. Even though we can never be entirely sure about personal motivations because we cannot look into people's heads and read their minds, it is reasonable to assume that social learning usually involves 'true' learning on at least one key aspect and by at least one relevant societal group. In a first step, we will focus on descriptive evidence for true learning, as it was presented in the empirical chapters. Its explanatory power will be discussed further in the second part of the chapter, using Bayesian updating.

True learning holds, as questionnaires on bank lending suggest, for the observed changes in widely shared convictions on the conditions of bank lending among small business owners in France during the Great Recession and in Germany during the late 1990s and early 2000s (Chapters 5 and 6). Many entrepreneurs realized that the conditions of bank lending had changed, and they were seriously concerned about this development. It is hard to imagine that there was a hidden agenda behind this, all the more so as entrepreneurs outside the policy-making community held these convictions—a broad group that cannot be manipulated easily. True learning resulted from their own experience with the banks and was further propagated by the business federations and media coverage. The evidence also suggests that there was at least some true learning on the risks of large financial intermediaries that heavily rely on short-term funding in financial markets in the French financial community, including the banks.

With respect to the German experience of the Great Recession, true learning cannot be attributed to one specific societal group. In simplified terms, we can think of true learning in response to the crisis as a bifold phenomenon: In financially informed circles, the crisis led to a better understanding of the financial techniques used by banks and it led to a reappraisal of the risk and benefits associated with asset securitization, the traditional bank lending model, and the merits of a decentral organization of the banking sector along three pillars. While there are limits to the degree to which this will be (publicly) admitted by key actors insofar as the issue touches upon on regulatory deficiencies or political failure, indicators hinting in this direction can be found in the interviews and to some extent also in public statements, such as the expertise of the German Council of Economic Experts (Chapter 6). Among the wider public, true learning related to how parts of the German banking sector had developed in the years prior to the crisis, becoming more market-based—developments many citizens and politicians were not aware of until the crisis. Media coverage played an important role in triggering social learning in this case.

The reform agendas that emerged in both countries responded to these specific, highly salient insights into the crisis. In France, given the perceived reluctance of the banks to engage in bank lending, it was both substantially plausible and politically legitimate to think about alternatives. In Germany, in the light of the devastating consequences of financial innovation, the same applied to the support for traditional bank lending. Decision-makers rallied around these specific salient crisis perceptions, and a coalition supporting a specific set of reforms was formed. Interest groups, whose interests were aligned with these crisis perceptions, profited from the situation, advancing their propositions. This was true for the savings and the cooperative banks in Germany and also for the insurance federation in France.

Inversely, interest groups, whose interests were not aligned with the predominant crisis perception, had difficulties getting heard. This was true for the French banks, which proposed a new tax-incentivized savings product, given the penalizing effect of the Basel III liquidity rules (Chapter 7). In Germany, this applies to reform proposals that argued, as was the case in France, in favour of financial disintermediation, given the risks associated with banking.[1] The Social Democratic Party (SPD), opposition party at that time, took the argument up in a resolution from March 2011, highlighting the difficulties enterprises had in finding financial resources, especially bank credit because of a credit hurdle, persisting financing barriers, and weak equity capital levels. It suggested strengthening alternative sources of funding, private equity in particular, via public investment companies and guarantee banks. In addition, the resolution asked for the introduction of a mechanism for joint bond issuing backed with a public guarantee as implemented in France (Deutscher Bundestag 2011). The resolution did not have much of a political effect and one my wonder why it was adopted at all.

8.2.2 Social learning and the role of politics

Given the broad coalitions which supported the respective reform agenda, including representatives from the financial, the corporate, and the public sector, what was the role of politicians in this process? What about party politics and electoral concerns? In Germany, federal elections took place in 2009 and 2013, leading to the re-establishment of Christian Democrat-led governments headed by Angela Merkel, while the coalition partner changed from the Social Democrats (SPD) to the Liberals (FDP) and back. In the midst of the crisis, Merkel's party (CDU/CSU) profited from crisis management, while some of the SPD's more interventionist policies were rejected by voters in 2009 (Zohlnhöfer 2011). The 2009 election campaign was fairly 'issue-less' and highly candidate-centred, which gave crisis manager Merkel, whose popularity scores were rising, a net advantage over her major competitor from the Social Democrats (Schoen 2011).

---

[1] GBC, a German investment firm, for instance, argued: 'During the last crisis, the banks often turned out not to be a reliable partner anymore and even long-established *Mittelständler* experienced considerable financing problems. Even enterprises which have been publicly listed for many years have reported to us that their house banks had let them down, despite a favourable credit record for decades, that the banks had put credit for important growth projects on ice, which lead to a perilous credit crunch for some time. As a reaction, many enterprises have become more cautious and have considered looking for alternative or supplemental forms of funding. Corporate bonds could be an interesting solution in this context' (GBC Investments 2012, 11; own translation).

In September 2012, a year ahead of the 2013 elections, Peer Steinbrück, who managed the bank bailouts in 2008 as finance minister, undertook a new attempt to 'tame financial markets', publishing a 30-page paper, in which he criticized the lack of change in finance since the crisis, presenting a long list of reform proposals (Steinbrück 2012). However, from a German perspective, the worst of the financial crisis that originated with the subprime crisis and the freezing of the interbank market lay behind the country by the 2013 election. The German economy benefited from a remarkable recovery thanks to the massive use of short-time work, and Angela Merkel profited once more from her crisis management in the context of the European debt crisis. The unpopular measures for supporting Greece were not a major issue during the election because of an informal pre-election consensus between the CDU/CSU and the SPD (Zimmermann 2014), and even though German—like French—banks profited enormously from the Greek bailout, it was not widely perceived as a domestic banking problem.

In France, presidential elections were held in 2012. Crisis manager Nicolas Sarkozy lost the election to his Socialist challenger François Hollande. Like Steinbrück, Hollande sought to capitalize on the limited ambitions of the reforms implemented until then and he famously declared finance to be his main adversary in the electoral campaign.[2] His programme made several reform propositions, including bank restructuring, a financial transaction tax, and the ban of certain speculative financial products alongside maximalist demands in other areas of economic and fiscal policy-making. While the hostility towards finance was of a 'tenor and intensity not seen from the mainstream centre of the party' in years, it resonated with the 'anti-finance discourse and banker bashing' in the wider French political debate since 2008—'with Sarkozy and the mainstream right sporadically advancing similar critiques' (Clift 2012, 108; see also Chapter 5). Even though Sarkozy and Hollande opposed each other on the transaction tax, the Socialist anti-finance agenda operated primarily at a 'rhetorical level and less in the complex realities of policy or regulation', 'deny[ing] in its language what the party conceded to in reality', as was the case in other areas of economic policy-making (Clift 2012, 109, 111). The primary purpose of these proposals therefore was to rally the left and close the ranks.

---

[2] 'Dans cette bataille qui s'engage, je vais vous dire qui est mon adversaire, mon véritable adversaire. Il n'a pas de nom, pas de visage, pas de parti, il ne présentera jamais sa candidature, il ne sera donc pas élu, et pourtant il gouverne. Cet adversaire, c'est le monde de la finance. Sous nos yeux, en vingt ans, la finance a pris le contrôle de l'économie, de la société et même de nos vies' (Hollande 2012).

Overall, the cases studied in the previous chapters suggest that the reform priorities identified were—contrary to the bank bailouts—not the object of major political contention. Given that they responded to widely shared crisis perceptions, and since their purpose ultimately was to guarantee the real economy's access to financial resources, thereby laying the groundwork for future economic growth unhampered by mismanagement in the financial sector, there was no meaningful political opposition to them. It would have been hard to argue against a measure designed to benefit the savings and the cooperative banks, which supported bank lending during the crisis. In a similar vein, given generalized bank bashing in France at that time, who would have wanted to promote a measure that could be framed as (yet another) present for the banks and be against measures that supported alternative funding opportunities for the real economy? The substance of social learning—and by that the ways in which the crisis was widely perceived—narrowed the space for political contestation considerably.

In addition, the reforms pursued in both countries focused on the implications of the crisis for *future* developments. They were much less an inquiry into past government failure. In the French case, as the French banks had weathered the subprime crisis rather well, there was no reason to blame the regulators and supervisors—and by that public authority more generally. Failure, as it was widely perceived, was with the bankers, given their reluctance to support the real economy in a moment of acute economic distress, especially in the light of the government support they had received. In Germany, with the grand coalition governing from 2005 to 2009, parliamentary opposition was weak. The Green and the Left Party lacked the numbers to reach the required 25 per cent quorum for a parliamentary investigation committee on the crisis, which was only achieved for an investigation of the failure of Hypo Real Estate (Elsner 2012).

Contrary to other countries with a major involvement in the crisis, such as the United States or the United Kingdom, there was no general crisis inquiry commission in Germany. With at least one of the two major parties having been in government since the foundation of the federal republic, neither of the two was willing to have an overly critical look into past developments. Moreover, given that the Landesbanken, several of which were severely affected by the crisis, were affiliated with regional governments of various political constellations, it was difficult to clearly identify the culprit. When the attribution of political responsibility for past developments is not clear, it is less likely that financial sector reforms become the object of major political conflict (similarly Ganderson 2020).

8.2.3 Social learning and institutional dispositions

Evidently, the post-crisis reforms were embedded in the respective institutional dispositions of the French and the German political economy. This brings us to the third question, which relates to the role of the institutional settings in shaping social learning and the subsequent political reforms. How decisive were they or, put differently, can we think of social learning as a process that is systematically and consistently shaped by the institutional environment in which it takes place? Given that this research builds on the in-depth study of two cases, there are limits to the generalizability of the observations made. What follows, therefore, is only a preliminary answer.

Social learning implies changing perceptions or an updating of beliefs among people or groups outside the policy-making community. Social learning—the mutual agreement on the relevance of a specific observation which is different from past experience—takes place in the public sphere and is not formally bound to any specific institutional venue of political decision-making. Because of this, there is more flexibility as to how and in which locations it can occur. Media coverage and other channels, especially on the internet, which allow the sharing of information play a considerable role. In addition, the organizations that aggregate and share experiences within a societal group and make them public—such as the business federations in the present case—are an important vector. Considered from this perspective, the media landscape, the organization of interests, but also political access could, in principle, all make a difference.

From a theoretical perspective, the expectation was that the more the situation is open, the more strongly the influence of the institutional settings should be mediated by the situational dynamic and only very fundamental institutional dispositions should matter (Chapter 3). In the cases studied, this seems to be the case. With respect to the early phase of the crisis, the questioning of the status quo, one can identify a more adversarial, confrontational style in France compared to a more consensus-oriented pattern in Germany (Chapter 5). While the conflict with the banks was amplified in France, conflict was avoided in Germany by focusing on the merits of traditional bank lending rather than the developments that had contributed to the depth of the German exposure to the crisis in the first place. At the final stage of formal policy-making, a more prominent role of constraining and enabling aspects of the institutional settings could be observed. These were related to the limits of state influence in France and the opportunity structures resulting from public ownership in banking and the decentral territorial organization in Germany (Chapter 7).

In general terms, with respect to France, this suggests that the picture of a strong hierarchical state, which 'imposes' its solutions on industry from above needs to be nuanced. In the field of financial regulation, given that state authority has been cut back over the past decades, French officials have adopted a rather cooperative style that involves major actors of the marketplace. State authorities have an important coordinative, enabling role, but they often depend on the voluntary, self-interested commitment of the financial industry. With respect to Germany, the cases studied reveal how deeply entrenched the public banking sector is with political life. Both local support for the savings banks and regional support for the Landesbanken— and their mutual integration—limit the room for manoeuvre of the competent federal authorities with respect to furthering market concentration and the effectiveness of bank supervision. The persistence of the diversified German banking landscape may indeed have a strong territorial component.

With respect to the second stage, consensus building, the answer is less clear-cut. One could argue that the French High-level Committee of the marketplace (HCP), whose purpose was to foster the importance and competitiveness of the Parisian marketplace, and which played a considerable role in shaping an agreement, does not have an equally powerful equivalent in Germany. Inversely, the close working relations between the banking and the business federations eased the coordination between the former—a form of cooperation that is less well established in France. In a similar vein, it could be argued that the dependence on a handful of large universal banks in France vs. the fragmented and heterogeneous nature of the German banking system were decisive in shaping the perception of the crisis. One could thus conclude that these specific structural and institutional predispositions were pivotal in shaping the responses to the crisis.

There certainly is some truth in these observations. However, when we take political decisions over a longer time horizon into account in addition to the responses to the crisis, we find both divergent developments within both countries over time and similar developments across contexts at different moments in time. This provides a reason not to overestimate the institutional embeddedness of social learning. Western capitalist democracies are sufficiently open and diversified to allow for a relatively broad spectrum of financial developments and political decisions, depending on the specific ideational context at hand and major changes therein. '[H]istory itself is far richer and less determined than the bare bones of the institutional analysis' which cannot produce a 'science of interest-group influence', as Ellen Immergut (1992, xiv), one of its most forceful proponents, put it.

For instance, while financial markets were not strongly embedded institutionally in the German political economy for a long time, they found their way into it, supported by political reforms when their moment had come, i.e. when it was widely taken for granted that Germany had to catch up with financial developments elsewhere and that the German future financial system would unavoidably be more market-based. In France, while the relations between the banks and their customers were highly conflictual in the aftermath of the crisis, they worked fairly smoothly in the years before. In that sense, there are limits to an understanding of institutions as filters for ideas and the extent to which economic relations are fixed because of the institutional settings in place. Social learning mediates the degree to which various actors profit from their institutional resources, loosening institutional constraints without necessarily offsetting them, especially towards the later stages of the process.

8.2.4 Social learning and contingency

Finally, if the responses to the financial crisis were not institutionally predetermined, were they so ideationally or cognitively because of past developments? Were the lessons learnt inevitable or, put differently, were the responses to the crisis effectively 'baked' into the economy years ago?[3] The social learning approach shares with path dependency arguments the assumption that past developments have an impact on future developments. In that sense, the conclusions possibly drawn from the crisis are bound by past events; social learning is not random. At the same time, social learning diverges from path dependency regarding the mechanism by which they affect future developments. Rather than attributing the 'power of the past' to some form of sunk cost or institutional advantage, it is linked to its collective reassessment. Social learning has a reflexive component that leaves some room for contingency and indeterminacy. This in turn is because there is more than one reasonable way of how past developments related to a phenomenon as complex as the financial crisis can be understood.

---

[3] I am particularly grateful for the comments of one of the reviewers to whom I owe this formulation and who raised several of the points I discuss in this chapter.

Counterfactually speaking, one might argue that the crisis could have been the final proof of the dysfunctionality of the German three-pillar banking system. Public banks, which supposedly follow a public interest mission, were active on the US-American subprime market, entering into ruinous competition with the commercial banks. The existing limits to takeovers across the pillars left Germany without a powerful player at the global level. Many Landesbanken lacked a viable business model well before the crisis and Germany was probably overbanked, especially in the wholesale segment. State guarantees, the desire by many politicians to have a 'para-fiscal facility to fund industrial policy outside parliamentary procedures' (Hellwig 2018, 40), and limits to takeovers across the pillars contributed to the fact that market exit did not occur. Both the large commercial banks and the Landesbanken had to seek profitable business opportunities in market-based banking abroad, given the strong position of both the savings and the cooperative banks in classic bank intermediation, and the dissolution of the Deutschland AG.

One could also argue that given the high costs of the German bailout, and by that the burden for the taxpayer that resulted from bank intermediation, engaging in financial disintermediation could have been the obvious response to the crisis. The German regional stock exchanges could have seized the opportunity as much as the insurance companies, which are relatively restricted in their investments in the real economy (Keller 2014, 142 ff.). Since many German Mittelstand businesses could raise money on the capital markets rather easily—Germany is considered to be the country with the biggest reservoir of companies that could, given their size, maturity etc., raise capital on the markets if they wanted—this adjustment could thus potentially be made without major economic distortions.

In a similar vein, one can make the case for an alternative outcome in France. Given the high levels of bank dependence of many small business owners in France—the large number of very small enterprises is highly unlikely to raise funds on the markets—strengthening traditional bank intermediation would have been a reasonable response to the crisis. All in all, the French banks weathered the subprime crisis fairly well. The French bank bailout was profitable to the state—bank intermediation thus did not create costs for the French taxpayer. The funding problems the French banks faced in the early phase of the crisis were amplified by domestic fiscal and regulatory stipulations, from which they suffered. One could thus argue that the French banks had no choice but to seek funding on the markets in order to grant credit to the real economy. Thanks to the coordinated action of the banks and the state, the liquidity constraint was quickly attenuated and the French economy did not suffer from a credit crunch, despite the unfavourable situation in which the French banks found themselves. Strengthening traditional bank intermediation and easing the funding constraints of the banks by increasing their deposit base could have been a reasonable response to the crisis. As these illustrations show, social learning is informed by past developments, but it is not determined by them.

8.3 Taking learning seriously

Having focused on the empirical side of the argument, let us turn to a couple of considerations that are motivated by methodological and conceptual concerns: A first question ties to the validity of the argument. How can we be sure that social learning rather than something else was driving the reform process? We will draw upon Bayesian updating to complement the answer that has been given to this question by the cross-case and within-case comparison so far. A second issue concerns its relevance. What are the merits of studying the crisis responses and financial sector development through the lens of social learning? This has to do with its analytic appeal in understanding the crisis responses and its applicability to other contexts than the ones analysed in the previous chapters. The section concludes with a short reflection on the implications of this form of social learning for theory building.

8.3.1 Testing for validity

How can we be sure that learning rather than something else was driving the reform process? Learning approaches tie political reforms back to changes in the understanding of a specific aspect of social reality, resulting from the reassessment of past experience and the assimilation of new information. Learning induced policy change unavoidably has to do with the cognitive foundations of a policy and changes therein. The problem with the causal role of learning, as with other ideational approaches, is that it cannot be directly observed (Jacobs 2014). In real life—outside the educational context, where learning is measured by the degree of assimilation of a certain body of predefined knowledge—the operationalization is difficult because one can never be entirely sure whether learning rather than something else motivates behaviour and '[i]t may be impossible to observe the learning activity in isolation from the change requiring explanation' (Bennett and Howlett 1992, 276, 290).

From a methodological point of view, the social learning argument relies on a composite strategy of cross-case and within-case analysis. This set-up discredited the likelihood of certain hypotheses, such as the primacy of the institutional settings or the structure of the banking sector, and established the importance of timing and changing perceptions. In addition to that, the explanatory merit of the social learning hypothesis can be tested using Bayesian updating techniques. Two questions should hereby either increase or decrease our trust in the validity of the argument (van Evera 1997, 31 ff.): Firstly, what is the most important empirical evidence in favour of social learning and how certain can we be that we will see it if learning occurs? Secondly, how specific is the evidence for the social learning explanation? This relates to the compatibility of the evidence with alternative explanations.

Coming to the evidence in favour of social learning: Since learning is not directly observable, a first indicator for learning comes from the statements of key actors. If people change their minds in response to the crisis, assimilate new information, and form new expectations for future developments, it is highly unlikely that no one will say so. If many actors declare that something in their appraisal of the situation has changed—or not—it is reasonable to take these statements seriously. Corresponding evidence has been discussed in Chapters 5 and 6. Let us reconsider only a few characteristic statements here.

One interviewee declared: 'The issue is not whether or not we support it [further disintermediation], *that's how we see* the development of the financial sector. We are moving right now towards *a new world* which is more disintermediated' (interview 2013112936F). This statement from a French business representative is clearly stipulating a change in the perception of the financial environment and the need to recognize this development, irrespective of what it practically implies for business owners. This is also confirmed by a government report that highlighted the need to respond to a 'strong tendency in favour of a partial disintermediation' (Rameix and Giami 2011, 26; own translation). At the other extreme is the refusal of change regarding bank lending in Germany. As one observer put it: 'We *consider* bank credit as the most important external source of financing here. And *I think this will be true for quite some time*' (interview 201312324D). The crisis did not lead to an adjustment of the assumptions on the role of bank credit and its projection in the future. A parliamentarian added: 'I get bashed when I say in panel discussions…that *my imagination is broader* than to *assume* that businesses absolutely need to be financed by classic bank credit' (interview 2013121629D). A cognitively feasible alternative to the analysis that is widely shared is for many others unacceptable.

With respect to financial innovation and market-based banking, that there was no broader awareness of the changes and their relevance for financial stability in Germany can be illustrated by statements from key expert circles. If they did not know, one can reasonably assume that few people did. The then finance minister Peer Steinbrück, for instance, admitted that he had only realized with the crisis the extent to which shadow banking had increased in Germany and the risks associated with it (Steinbrück 2010, 222–3). In a similar vein, the German Council of Economic Experts, which advises the German government on economic policy, declared that with respect to systemic stability, the market-based system could be considered superior to the bank-based system because of a lower concentration of risks in the banks, which had led to financial crises in the past, concluding that 'one could not have expected to observe that the development process of the past years towards a more strongly market-based financial system would lead to particular high systemic instability' (Sachverständigenrat 2007, 122–3; own translation).

Since what individuals say can be biased or even untrue, a second indicator that should increase trust in the validity of the learning argument comes from the breadth of social learning. Indicators for social learning—true learning and the recognition that a specific understanding of the crisis is widely shared—can be found in the statements of financial sector representatives, state representatives, and the business sector (Chapter 5). At the same time, social learning is not bound to the policy-making community. In France, social learning on the changing role of bank intermediation applies above all to French business owners and, to a minor extent, the banks, which adjusted their approach to risk management. Surveys on bank lending and borrowing were a decisive indicator in establishing this aspect (Chapter 6).

With respect to Germany, one indicator for the breadth of social learning can be seen in the extensive media coverage of the crisis as a result of the serial process by which the exposure to the crisis became visible and the case-by-case crisis management reaching well into 2009. Journalistic investigations unveiled dysfunctionalities in managing the crisis and efforts to disguise the difficulties both by bank managers and politicians. Several bank failures were the object of legal proceedings and the process from the bailout to the unwinding of the failing banks was a lengthy one that is ongoing a decade after the crisis. In addition, between 40,000 and 50,000 German savers were directly affected by the breakdown of Lehman Brothers, having lost most of the savings they held in the form of Lehman certificates (Eckert et al. 2013). Media content analyses confirm that the bank bailouts and bank regulation were highly present over a relatively long period with cyclical peaks triggered by individual events (Geiß 2013, 166 ff.; also Englert et al. 2020). While media coverage is a rather rough indicator for individual learning, it is a necessary condition for social learning that is not directly driven by own experience—as in the case of bank lending or the loss of savings—and shows that the issue was salient over an extended period.

The second Bayesian updating technique concerns the compatibility of the evidence with alternative explanations. In principle, it is possible that decision-makers declare that their action was driven by learning although it was not, or that they were actually learning, but they do not say so. On the one hand, learning—and by that at least implicitly admitting that previous knowledge was insufficient or inappropriate—may, for instance, be preferable to admitting having ceded to the pressure of an interest group for personal benefits. On the other hand, it may be uncomfortable for someone who considers themselves an expert in a given field that they had overseen or misjudged something. This may be particularly true for representatives of the competent regulatory and supervisory authorities.

There will never be a final proof on true motivations, and it is better to accept this from the outset. What can be done, however, is to consider the evidence in the light of the most important rival hypotheses, which would impute differing crisis responses—and their ideational framing—to differences in the material interests of key actors and their influence on the decision-making process. An ideational theory is a 'causal theory...in which the content of a cognitive structure influences actors' responses to a choice situation and in which that cognitive structure is *not wholly endogenous* to objective, material features of the choice situation being explained' (Jacobs 2014, 43; own emphasis). Is it possible to show that the priorities identified cannot sufficiently be attributed to the material characteristics of the decision situation and changes therein?

On the aggregate level, one could have expected that in the light of the higher costs of the German bank bailout, there would be an agreement on becoming more independent from the banks, whereas in France, where state support to the banking sector was profitable, there was no reason to lower the levels of bank intermediation. In terms of the objectively given material impact of the crisis, one would thus expect France to stick with bank intermediation, whereas Germany would lower its exposure to the banks. In a similar vein, it has been shown that the difference cannot be attributed to the objective material impact of the crisis with respect to the cost and the availability of bank credit (Chapter 6).

One could also argue that the structural dependence of the business sector from (bank) credit should influence political decision makers' choice on whether or not to reduce bank intermediation. In simplified terms, the smaller businesses are, the less alternatives to credit are available, as so-called life-cycle models of corporate finance suggest (e.g. Berger and Udell 1998, 622–72). Table 8.1 displays the structure of the French and German business sector. In France, micro businesses with less than ten employees make up almost 94 per cent of all enterprises compared to 82 per cent in Germany. In contrast, Germany has a two to three times higher number of businesses in the larger categories. This also applies to their value added, even though the difference between the two countries is less pronounced. On the aggregate level, France can thus be considered structurally more dependent on credit than Germany and strengthening classic bank intermediation would have been a reasonable response to the crisis. From this perspective, it is difficult to understand why the French opted for financial disintermediation whereas the Germans did not.

Finally, considered from a financial power perspective, the French banks appear particularly powerful: A few large banking groups dominate the domestic market, they have a significant implementation abroad and excellent access to decision-makers. Inversely, small German savings and cooperative

Table 8.1   Structure of the corporate sector

	France	Germany	EU-27
I. Share of enterprises per size			
- Micro (<10)	93.8%	81.7%	92.1%
- Small (10–49)	5.2%	15.2%	6.6%
- Medium (50–249)	0.8%	2.6%	1.1%
- Large (>249)	0.2%	0.5%	0.2%
II. Share of value added per size			
- Micro (<10)	26.1%	15.1%	21.1%
- Small (10–49)	17.5%	18.5%	18.3%
- Medium (50–249)	15.0%	20.2%	18.3%
- Large (>249)	41.5%	46.2%	42.4%

Size of enterprises according to the number of employees. Sectors included: Industry, construction, trade, and services.

Source: European Commission (2013a, 2013b).

banks should have much greater difficulty in obtaining favourable political outcomes. Arguably, they have access to local politicians, but what makes business powerful—market dominance or the threat to exit the market—are not at their disposal—or at least not more than for the large French banking groups. The structural power perspective thus has difficulties in explaining a less favourable political outcome for the French banks compared to the German ones.

This is not to deny that the crisis led to changes in the material conditions. This applies to the availability of bank funding on the markets as much as the development of the market for asset-backed securities (ABS) and the availability of bank credit. In this sense, the French and the German responses to the crisis resonate with certain variations in the objectively given material situation. However, it is difficult to understand why they responded to certain objective material incentives—the risk of bank intermediation in the French case, the risk of market-based banking in Germany—and not to others without the form of social learning that occurred. In addition, the magnitude of the reaction is hardly compatible with a narrow definition of interests and the updating of individual preferences.

Having said this, the distinction between an ideational and a materialist explanation cannot be made for all group of actors equally. When the substance of social learning coincides with the predefined material interest of an actor, it may be difficult or even impossible to distinguish between the two empirically with certainty. This is, for instance, the case with lower levels of bank intermediation from the point of view of the insurance sector. This also holds for the merits of traditional bank lending from the perspective of the smaller German banks, reason why the explanatory power of their positioning is lower. In contrast, the positioning of the corporate sector played an important role in the analysis as the changing perceptions that could be traced among French and German businesses are less directly related to a specific form of funding.

Finally, social learning is not a micro-concept. It has an interactive besides a cognitive component. It therefore includes learning about other people's learning and resulting behaviour can in turn be strategically motivated. Social learning—as other theories of learning—is not about cognitions *only* (similarly Bennett and Howlett 1992, 290) and some of the evidence may therefore be compatible with a materialist explanation. However, when the nature and the timing of collective learning is more relevant in shaping individual behaviour than changes in the material conditions, analytic pre-eminence should be given to the former.

8.3.2 Social learning in the US and the UK

Can we expect to see social learning structuring crisis responses in other contexts as well? Since deconstructing social learning is a laborious process, the following reflections are only working hypotheses that certainly deserve closer analysis in another study. In principle, it is likely that a specific understanding of the crisis that resonated with changing beliefs outside the policy-making community shaped the priorities of the post-crisis reform agenda elsewhere as well, but it may relate to different aspects of the crisis and a different set of pre-crisis developments than the ones observed in France and Germany. In the latter two cases, the comparison was articulated around the opposition of banks vs. financial markets and changing perceptions of bank lending, which could be observed in both countries at different moments in time.

Such a pattern may be useful in analysing the crisis responses and financial sector development more generally in other traditionally bank-based financial systems, especially when financial innovation is encouraged. However, it is unlikely that this pattern shaped the crisis responses in countries where financial markets have always played a more prominent role in funding the economy and where financial innovation is considered an integral component of the economic growth model, such as the United States or even more importantly the United Kingdom. Nevertheless, it is plausible that the crisis was also understood in a specific way there, involving changing perceptions beyond the policy-making community. If this is the case, we should expect to see that the content of social learning limited the influence of certain actors, while supporting others whose policy proposals were in line with it. Can we find preliminary evidence for social learning in the US-American and the British context?

In the United States, social learning may have been linked to the origins of the crisis in the housing market and the limits of the American dream of homeownership, and by that potentially of credit-based welfare. In the years prior to the crisis, seemingly everyone could become a homeowner—even with little or no capital, as the emergence of so-called NINJA credits (No Income, No Job, No Assets) shows. Debt levels, both in the form of mortgages and consumer credit, rose from 120 per cent of disposable income to over 180 per cent before the crisis (Gräf 2009, 6). With the crisis, house prices fell and many homeowners defaulted on their debt, leading to a reassessment of the risk and limits of credit-based real estate (and potentially credit-based consumption more generally). The financial crisis affected people outside the policy-making community directly, as was the case with the changing conditions on bank lending in France. The images of families camping in tents because they had lost their homes kept circulating through the media, creating considerable awareness for the issue. Between 2007 and 2010, family homelessness increased by 20 per cent (Hunter et al. 2014, 3), nurturing the emergence of the Occupy Wall Street Movement. The Wall Street Reform and Consumer Protection Act (also called Dodd-Frank Act) from July 2010, the major reform law in response to the crisis, articulates this insight. The Consumer Protection Bureau it entailed is one of its core elements and represents considerable progress in consumer protection (Kastner 2017). Research along these lines would have to explore the centrality of this crisis narrative relative to others in the media, among American citizens, and key stakeholders in addition to representatives of the policy-making community and explore its impact on limiting vs. furthering interest group prevalence during the policy-making process.

The British case appears fairly complex. On the aggregate level, the United Kingdom was the second most affected country. Contrary to Germany, where banks bought toxic assets abroad, the British crisis was at least in part 'home made' with a domestic housing bubble and the existence of a domestic ABS market of considerable size, mortgage-backed securities in particular, which imploded with the crisis. By 2007, about 18 per cent of all mortgages were securitized and sold off balance (see also Turner 2009, 29 ff.). In the early phase of the crisis, several banks suffered from liquidity problems. This was most prominently the case with Northern Rock, leading to a bank run in September 2007, when the news spread that it needed an emergency loan from the Bank of England. The crisis thus both affected ordinary citizens as depositors and (mortgage) borrowers and had a negative impact on lending to SMEs.

More importantly even, the financial crisis led to a questioning of the British growth model and its overreliance on the 'City'. The United Kingdom was the jurisdiction 'where narratives about the social contribution of finance [we]re most highly developed' (Engelen et al. 2011, 179). Political decision-makers 'genuinely believed that what was good for the banking industry would be good for the UK economy' (Bell and Hindmoor 2014a, 4), favouring a light-touch approach to financial regulation. With the crisis, this was seriously questioned and British preferences on banking regulation underwent a 'dramatic shift': The 'fiscal burden of bailing out two of the UK's largest banks sent shockwaves through the political establishment' leading to a '*broad cross-party consensus* that the existing banking regulatory system was fundamentally broken' (Hungin and James 2018, 339; emphasis added). In 2010, Nick Clegg (2010), Deputy Prime Minister from the Liberal Democrats, wrote:

> For years our prosperity has been pinned on financial wizardry in London's Square Mile, with other sectors and other regions left behind. That imbalance left us hugely exposed when the banking crisis hit. And now Britain has a budget deficit higher than at any time since the Second World War. It's time to correct that imbalance. We need to spread growth across the whole country, and across all sectors. We need to rediscover our talent for building and making things.

As was the case in France, bank bashing was widespread in response to the crisis and further fuelled by public trials, insensitive appearances of bankers in public, and the Libor scandal. Government support to the banking sector came with comparatively unfavourable conditions (Woll 2014) and 'protecting taxpayers became an acute electoral priority for all the main political parties' (Howarth and James 2020, 43). Rebalancing the economy was 'the new mantra' (Gardiner et al. 2012, 4) and the topic profited from a 'cross-party commitment' (Hunt 2013, xv), which can be seen as an indicator for social learning.

In parallel, leading figures from the regulatory authorities, including the then Governor of the Bank of England, Mervyn King, his chief economist Andrew Haldane, and the chairman of the Financial Services Authority, Adair Turner, stand out with their tough stances in public on the need for reform. Top British regulators advanced fairly radical positions, questioning the merits of financial innovation (Turner 2012) and comparing the financial system to biological food ecosystems, where systemic instability increases when the number and the strength of the interactions among species pass a certain threshold (Haldane and May 2011).[4] This is in stark contrast with Germany where this was clearly not the case.

Social learning on the limits, costs, and downsides of financial innovation and finance-led growth is also reflected by the reforms implemented in response to the crisis. The British defended fairly intransigent positions during both international and European banking reforms of bank capital

---

[4] The increase of intra-financial linkages, which made up for most of the sector's growth over the past years, together with an increasing homogeneity in business models, drawing heavily on wholesale borrowing and the trading of credit derivatives, led to a highly instable system, which was fragile to cascade-like movements (Haldane and May 2011).

(Chapter 4; Bell and Hindmoor 2017b; James 2016; James and Quaglia 2020). Domestically, the reform on bank ring fencing, separating retail banking from investment banking went further than in many other countries. The success of the British reforms was attributed to political factors that are compatible with the social learning hypothesis. Ganderson (2020) finds that the reform resulted from electoral politics with stricter rules for finance having been an issue for all major parties during the general election in May 2010. Massoc (2020, 139 f.) explains the success of the British reforms with the fact that the issue had become salient, which is one implication of social learning. She highlights the role of an independent commission, which allowed the ' "anti-TBTF" factions to carry weight in policymaking'. Social learning can explain why such a commission was established in the first place in addition to tactical considerations by the governing parties.

Ring fencing was most prominently defended by the Liberal Democratic candidate Vince Cable who declared that 'I think what we said *resonated with people*' (cited in Ganderson 2020, 209; emphasis added), which can be seen as an indicator of how the crisis was perceived in the broader public. Ganderson finds that Members of Parliament 'with relevant interests and expertise from all major political parties *worked amiably* on a broad range of questions concerning the future of finance, and throughout the process, the banks lacked a figure in Parliament prepared to publicly defend them and voice concerns' (Ganderson 2020, 213; emphasis added). Cross-party agreement and the lack of support for interests that were not aligned with the general perception of the crisis are in line with what one would expect from a social learning perspective.

Finally, social learning has explanatory power from a comparative perspective with respect to differing outcomes of reforms on bank structure. Howarth and James (2020) attribute the stricter British reforms on ring fencing compared to those implemented in France and Germany to differing agenda setting dynamics. Whereas the French and the German reform hardly affected the domestic banks' business models, only separating a limited set of proprietary trading activities, the British reform had considerable implications, 'imposing some of the highest capital requirements in the world on UK banks' (Howarth and James 2020, 35). The authors attribute the British outcome to venue shifting and the expansion of the conflict, leading to the mobilization of a broad coalition in support of it. When we wonder why this was the case in the United Kingdom, but not in France and Germany, the nature of social learning in both countries discussed in the previous chapters may provide at least a partial answer.

In Germany, universal banking along the pillar structure was considered a remedy rather than a root cause of the crisis. In the French case, while banking intermediation by large banks came under pressure, the answer, which was supported by a broad coalition of actors, focused on alternatives to bank intermediation rather than the separation of bank activities into separate entities (Chapter 5). In addition, the balanced universal banking model of a strong engagement in retail alongside investment banking was seen as the reason why the French banks weathered the subprime crisis comparatively well (Howarth 2013). Even though bank structural reforms were mentioned in election programmes and discussed in both countries, they were not forcefully endorsed by decision-makers.

Neither in France nor in Germany was universal banking as such seen as a major root cause of the crisis. The fact that legislation was adopted at all was a pre-emptive move in order to avoid more constraining European legislation (Hardie and Macartney 2016), given competitive concerns with respect to the position of US-American banks (Massoc 2020). The general perception of the role of universal banking may indeed have been different in other contexts, such as the United States, which does not have a long-standing tradition in this regard. Indeed, the repeal of the Glass-Steagall Act in 1999, which had introduced separate banking in the United States in the aftermath of the Great Depression, led to a higher financial sector concentration and by that to the problem of too big to fail, which was considered as one of the root causes of the crisis.

8.3.3 Studying how ideas change

The social learning approach that structured the previous chapters is part of a well-established, growing branch in economics (e.g. Foote et al. 2012; Shiller 2020), economic sociology (e.g. Beckert 2016; Bronk 2009), policy analysis (e.g. Baumgartner and Jones 1993; Kingdon 1995; Sabatier and Jenkins-Smith 1988, 1993), and comparative and international political economy (e.g. Béland and Cox 2010; Blyth 2002; Campbell 1998; Culpepper 2008; Goldstein and Keohane 1993a; Hay 2010; Jacobsen 1995; Schmidt 2002), on ideas—mental constructs of various kinds—and discourse—contextualized verbal exchanges on them—as a conceptual answer to societal change resulting from economic, scientific, or technical progress, and the uncertainty created by it. Social learning addresses the challenges of policy-making in complex, innovation- and competition-driven societal subsystems.

The form of social learning presented in the previous chapters makes contributions to ideational scholarship in institutional analysis, the literature on policy-related learning, and the branch of economic sociology that deals with decision-making under conditions of uncertainty. Compared to other ideational approaches, social learning has several specificities. Social learning puts the analytic focus on changing perceptions or beliefs which were previously taken for granted. Thus, it has a focus that can be clearly identified. Social learning concentrates on how widely a specific interpretation is shared and how influential it is relative to alternative understandings in shaping collective cognitions. By focusing on changes in widely shared perceptions or assumptions, it provides an explanation as to how the institutionalized status quo can be overcome, legitimizing certain policies at the expense of others, and easing vs. hindering access for different interest groups.

Social learning is less instrumental than a discourse, whose primary purpose often is to generate and to legitimize a policy programme (Schmidt 2002, 210). It gives the broader public outside the policy-making community a more active role than being the recipient of a communicative discourse, whose primary function is to be a 'mass process of public persuasion' (Schmidt 2008, 310),[5] tying political decisions back to economic and societal change. Contrary to other approaches, focusing on epistemic communities (Haas 1992), advocacy coalitions (Sabatier and Jenkins-Smith 1988), or knowledge regimes (Campbell and Pedersen 2014), social learning locates the shaping of policy-relevant features in the public sphere, involving changing perceptions and experiences that transcend the policy-making community and expert circles.

Social learning takes some contingency from ideational factors, since the ideas that matter are those that fit the situation particularly well in the perception of a relevant number of actors given the reassessment of past developments and adjustments in the projections on the future. Analytic pre-eminence is not given to the ideational factors as such, but to the ways in which they become influential because they are shared among a relevant group of actors and further propagated by them. The decisive moment is when a specific understanding—or idea—among others becomes a social fact that cannot easily be refuted. It then has a social as well as a cognitive reality.

At the same time, this approach to institutional change leaves room for creative agency since there is no automatic path-dependent reproduction of the institutions in place and no lesson that can automatically be drawn from a

---

[5] However, note that the recipients can also take a more active role, participating in the communicative discourse when they are politically active (Schmidt 2008, 310).

specific situation. Rather, the institutional set-up needs to be adapted in the light of the new shared understanding of what the situation is about, which requires consensus through coalition building. The process of restoring collectively valid assumptions about the functioning of the economy is decisive. Further developments are not path-dependent, but they form a developmental path since they are informed, but not determined, by previous developments.

The social learning approach developed in the previous chapters contributes to the literature on policy-oriented learning by refocusing the concept on ideas that are widely shared. Social learning as opposed to other forms, such as policy, organizational, or bureaucratic learning, has been strongly marked by a paradigmatic understanding of policy change, which borrowed from the philosophy of science (Hall 1993). From this perspective, major or radical policy change is driven by failure, contestation, experimentation, and the emergence of alternative authority when the interpretative framework, in which policy-making takes place, is no longer deemed valid (Hall 1993). Such an approach seemed to be particularly appropriate in the area of economic policy-making where policies could be derived from encompassing economic doctrines and it was fruitfully applied to major changes in macro-economic policy-making in the post-war era from state interventions, Keynesianism, and embedded liberalism to free(er) markets, monetarism, and neoliberalism (Blyth 2002; Hall 1986, 1993).

However, explaining ideational change at the level of coherent policy paradigms has not proved helpful since the onset of financial globalization and this also applies to the global financial crisis. While some new elements were implemented with respect to macroprudential regulation (Baker 2013, 2014), recognizing that it is insufficient to focus on the financial soundness of individual financial institutions, most of the regulatory response to the crisis does not challenge conventional wisdom with respect to risk management and the intellectual micro-rationalist and macro-equilibristic framework in which it is embedded. In a similar vein, little has changed with respect to the ways in which economics is taught at universities (e.g. Bowles and Carlin 2020, 192 f.). At the same time, the crisis has seen a—brief—revival of Keynesian demand management and massive state interventions when large financial institutions were collapsing—even in jurisdictions that were deemed highly liberal.

Since the onset of globalization, the world economy has been embedded in a kind of 'resilient liberalism' (Schmidt and Thatcher 2013), a malleable ideational framework that combines an emphasis on markets with varying degrees of state intervention, depending on the situation and the specific context at hand. Thinking about economic policy-making in terms of coherent paradigms that change when anomalies occur has little explanatory value. As Mark Blyth (2013, 208) put it with respect to the fact that the efficient market hypothesis survived the financial crisis: 'if you ever wanted an empirical disconfirmation of a social science theory, here it is; and it only cost (to date) $4 trillion to run the experiment'.

Rather than associating social learning with paradigm change (only), a promising way of rethinking the concept could therefore be to focus on ideas that become policy relevant because they are *widely shared* at a given moment in time, highlighting a specific aspect of a complex social phenomenon selectively, and studying the mechanisms of how this occurs. In a similar vein, Baumgartner (2013, 251) defined ideas as a paradigm when they are 'widely shared by an entire policy community'. Such an approach abandons the assumption of internal coherence and incommensurability of Peter Hall's original formulation, which has been heavily criticized (see Carstensen 2015 for an overview). Coherence and consistency may not necessarily be defining and cognitively relevant features of an influential ideational framework in a complex, uncertain world.

Finally, social learning has implications for action theory by providing a more nuanced conceptualization of decision-making under conditions of uncertainty. Much theorizing, both in economics and in sociology, has had a strong bias in the status quo, focusing on contexts in which agents can conform to the social norms of the networks and social relations in which they are embedded, or be treated as if they inferred their interests from stable utility functions (Chapter 3). While such a framework has explanatory power with respect to routine behaviour, it insufficiently captures economic agents' behaviour in a changing environment and with respect to fundamental choices. These latter decision situations are insufficiently depicted by a risk framework, requiring a conceptualization in terms of uncertainty, where meaning is (re-)constituted in social interactions of sense-making and the collective interpretation of the situation.

A growing line of research in economic sociology responded to these insights by focusing on the future orientation of economic action, where actors anticipate or imagine future states of the world that are different from the past (e.g. Beckert 2016; Beckert and Bronk 2018; Tavory and Eliasoph 2013). In this context, social learning may help to square the cycle between the restlessness of capitalist societies and their institutional embeddedness (Beckert and Ergen 2020, 4), suggesting that a future orientation that goes beyond the stipulation that any decision implies anticipation—or imagination—of its effects is heightened in some moments and on some aspects of economic activity. This is, for instance, the case with creative product development or investment decisions, whereas the status quo often is a sufficiently good predictor for many other aspects of economic activity, such as the conditions for bank lending, taxation, labour markets, or social security. While economic agents will have to deal with potential changes in these areas as well, they will usually focus their heightened future orientation on aspects that are the most relevant to their individual business success.

Related to this is a second insight from the empirical processes studied in the previous chapters. Changes in collectively held beliefs not only result from creative actors imagining alternative states of the world in their pursuit of profit, but also from the painful realization that past circumstances are no longer valid and that there is a need to adapt to this (which may result from other agents' innovations). In this case, the reassessment of past developments and an interpretation of the implications for future developments may play a more prominent role. In moments of economic crisis, it is likely that the future will be articulated in antagonism to past events. This may be different from the proactive shaping of future states with respect to the relative weight different groups of actors have in the absence of crises. Studying different contexts for social learning and their implications comparatively could be a promising line for future research.

Social learning matters once we broaden our horizon to consider actor behaviour over longer periods of time. In this case, the decision-making environment cannot be considered as an invariant background condition. Actors must adjust their understandings of the situation, which goes beyond a Bayesian updating. When a certain number of actors change their expectations with respect to the general framework in which economic activity is embedded, chances are high that these changes will be consolidated by political reforms. Further fields that would be interesting from the perspective of social learning include the study of the spread of the sense of urgency to act on climate change, the gaining pace of the digital revolution, the emergence and the bursting of bubbles, as well as other dynamics in financial markets, such as investor confidence, perceptions of debt sustainability, or speculative attacks.

Undoubtedly, the big question is why some ideas are more influential than others. Social learning suggests that those ideas that fit the situation particularly well in the general perception are the ones that are likely to crowd out other ideas. This does not necessarily imply that the average voter 'learns' or is aware of a specific development, but it implies that a specific understanding is widely shared beyond the policy-making community, as was the case with changing perceptions on the conditions of bank lending or the realization that the traditional bank lending model insufficiently described what (some) German banks actually do. When policies resonate with widespread beliefs, it is likely that politicians will endorse and support them in public.

Substantially, this is more than a tautological statement after the fact because the fact that social learning concerns a wider audience involving non-specialist circles has implications with respect to the cognitive content of the ideas that are likely to be influential. Social learning usually has to make abstractions from a complex reality. Many situations that require political reform result from a complex constellation of causes. Social learning selectively highlights one or a few aspects of them. One implication of the selectivity of social learning, therefore, is that it tends to overestimate the relevance of certain aspects while neglecting others. It does not necessarily lead to optimal—or even good—policy outcomes.

Defining successful ideas as those that fit the situation particularly well in the general perception involves an element of superiority of a specific idea relative to others. However, one might still wonder if there was not an alternative, equally appropriate idea that has not become dominant. This brings us back the question of ideational (Carstensen and Schmidt 2015) or productive (Woll 2014) power. It is plausible to assume that the ideas adopted resonate with certain background ideational structures that enjoy superior authority 'in structuring thought at the expense of other ideas' (Carstensen and Schmidt 2015, 329). This may lead to the fact that crises, as other societal challenges, are more easily understood in terms of their implications for economic growth or competitiveness, rather than for social justice or biodiversity. Future research along these lines would be highly desirable and could potentially contribute to the explanation of the crisis of contemporary democracies.

9

The nature of crisis responses

While the effects of the Great Recession are still perceptible more than a decade after the crisis, when looking at the impact it has had on public debt levels in many countries or on the restructuring process some fragilized banks are still undergoing, the window for the political response to the crisis is long closed. In some respects, the pendulum has even begun to swing back from re-regulation towards deregulation and the loosening of standards. In the United States, the Volcker rule, one of the hallmarks of the Dodd-Frank Reform Act from 2010, was watered down by President Trump, who had made the repeal of the entire Reform Act a campaign promise. With respect to one of the most fundamental problems the crisis had revealed, namely moral hazard resulting from financial institutions that are too big to fail, one has to recognize that both in the United States and in Europe the largest banks have been growing even further and bank sector concentration is in many cases higher than before the crisis. JPMorgan Chase—the largest bank outside Asia—almost doubled its assets between 2006 and 2017 (White and Mehmood 2017). It may well be that in financial ecosystems 'evolutionary forces have often been survival of the fattest rather than the fittest' (Haldane and May 2011, 351). How has banking developed since the crisis and what can we learn from the politics of bank reform studied in the previous chapters for the management of future banking crises?

9.1 Banking since the crisis

Despite forces of inertia, the context in which European banks operate has undergone considerable transformations since the beginning of the crisis. Beyond the changes discussed in the previous chapters, they relate to the low interest environment, ongoing financial innovation, and technological change. New services providers, such as Apple, Samsung, or Amazon, and a variety of fintechs have entered core areas of banking, such as payments or the provision of credit, providing their services online. Changes have also resulted from the creation of a banking union. In 2014, the authority over bank

Financial Crises and the Limits of Bank Reform: France and Germany's Ways Into and Out of the Great Recession.
Eileen Keller, Oxford University Press (2021). © Eileen Keller. DOI: 10.1093/oso/9780198870746.003.0009

supervision was transferred to the European Banking Authority (EBA). Large banks are supervised directly by European instead of national teams, and a European regime for bank resolution and recovery was adopted.

While the regulatory and supervisory regime under which European banks operate will further converge under the effect of banking union, the previous chapters suggest that multiple sources for divergence with a direct impact on banking persist as a result of the differing set-ups of national banking sectors and bank profiles, overall economic performance and economic policy, the functioning of funding relations, and differences in the salience of different aspects of banking. As this book shows, a truly integrated market for banking cannot easily be realized through regulatory change alone since financial practices do not automatically follow the incentives regulatory change is supposed to bring about.

In the Euro area, the importance of banks relative to other financial institutions in terms of global assets is lower than before the crisis (45 per cent in 2015 compared to 53 per cent in 2006; CGFS 2018, 80). Many banks divested some more risky trading activities and focused on core business areas, such as commercial banking. Banks are less leveraged, they hold higher equity levels, and more assets deemed liquid. In parallel, wholesale funding has shrunk in favour of deposits. Cross-border banking has decreased considerably, especially in the Euro area (-40 per cent between 2007 and 2016; CGFS 2018, 24). At the same time, financial sector concentration is higher and shadow banking has not been reduced univocally (Bell and Hindmoor 2017a). Bank profitability is much lower than before the crisis and given the low interest environment and sluggish growth (at best) in Europe, some banks may be tempted or even feel they have no choice but to engage in riskier activities in order to meet the return expectations of their shareholders, bearing risks that could lead to a new crisis (see also CGFS 2018).

While the French banks suffer from the low interest environment and relatively high operating costs, they recovered from the crisis. In the past years, the insurance business and asset management have contributed the most to bank profits. Competition on investment banking has been fierce, the reason why the French groups refocused on core activities in this area. As far as bank intermediation is concerned, lending to SMEs gathered pace from 2017 onwards, following a pronounced period of deceleration in the aftermath of the crisis. The proportion of SMEs obtaining at least 75 per cent of the investment credit they applied for reached almost 97 per cent by the end of 2018. While the annual growth rate of debt of SMEs stagnated between 2011 and 2014 (0.3 per cent contrary to 4.8 and 6.4 per cent for medium and large enterprises), it increased by 5 per cent between late 2014 and 2018, which suggests that many SMEs have incorporated the new standards and that the situation has normalized (HCSF 2019, 26 ff.).

The situation for the German banks—especially those that were directly affected by the crisis—is more challenging. Deutsche Bank, by far the largest German bank, which was proud not to have asked for state support during the crisis is suffering from write-downs and costly dispute settlement in the United States and with the Libor scandal, amounting to over 10 billion Euros in total (Hellwig 2018). The bank, which celebrated its 150th anniversary in 2020, has lost 95 per cent of its market value since the crisis. A merger with Commerzbank, which has not recovered from the crisis either, did not come to fruition in 2019. The large banks lost market shares in the credit attribution business to the other banking groups, the savings and the cooperative banks in particular, which are more profitable than the large banks (Sachverständigenrat 2019, 207 ff.). Overall, German banks are the least profitable in Europe. Even though the consolidation process has gathered pace—since 2008, the number of independent banks has shrunk by 20 per cent—bank income is stagnating and the cost-income ratio increasing (Sinn and Thoben 2019).

As far as the public Landesbanken are concerned, the crisis led to the consolidation and downsizing of the sector, a change of the legal form[1] in some cases, and to a partial privatization, resulting from the prescriptions by the European Commission in return for state support during the crisis. Six Landesbanken have ceased to exist as independent public banks since the beginning of the crisis. Three of them were merged with other Landesbanken, one was merged with a savings bank. HSH Nordbank—now Hamburg Commercial Bank—was privatized and sold to a US-American group of investors under the lead of the hedge fund Cerberus. WestLB is still being wound up. Of the five remaining regional public banks, Nord LB made significant write-downs over the past years and needed an additional 3.5 billion Euros in the form of equity capital and guarantees from its owners in 2019 in order to avoid a breakdown. The Landesbanken are still the least profitable part of the German banking sector, overcapacities may persist, and it is unclear if corporate governance has improved with the continued

---

[1] The private form of a joint-stock company (AG, Aktiengesellschaft) instead of a public law form (AöR, Anstalt öffentlichen Rechts).

presence of politicians on the supervisory boards (Hallerberg and Markgraf 2018).[2]

How consequential are the reforms implemented in both countries with regard to the future role of the banks? The French reforms, supporting a move away from bank intermediation, were certainly not meant to be a complete overhaul of the corporate funding landscape and they have not altered the financing structure of the economy fundamentally. Nevertheless, they gave an impetus for developments in one specific direction. In addition, French businesses obviously also profit from the special European rules on SME lending promoted by Germany, but how much they actually benefit from these dispositions depends on the extent to which banks succeeded in rebuilding the trust that was undermined with the crisis.

In Germany, the reforms focusing on the regulatory treatment of bank credit were seen as a means to stabilize traditional bank lending and the historic specificity of the pillar structure that had been undermined for decades with respect to many of the functioning principles that shaped the emergence and persistence of the tripartite configuration in the first place. The financial crisis had a stabilizing effect in this regard, even more so as the large German commercial banks face severe difficulties. Overall, the reforms initiated in response to the crisis conform to the pattern of incrementalism that has been found in other areas of financial sector reforms (e.g. Mayntz 2012a; Moschella and Tsingou 2013).

An alternative way of interpreting the responses implemented in the aftermath of the crisis is to juxtapose them against alternative solutions that have not been implemented. Even though crises come to be understood in a specific way, excluding by that numerous alternative outcomes, one can think of further-reaching policy proposals that are in line with the differing understandings of the crisis observed in both countries. Since the crisis revealed the risks associated with market-based banking, why was there not a fiercer reaction on fighting this development in Germany, especially in the public banking sector? Similarly, since the crisis lay bare the risks associated with large-scale bank intermediation in France, why was there not more support for policies that would limit the size of the French banking groups drastically? In order to understand why, one has to turn to the nature of the politics of banking reform.

---

[2] Hau and Thum (2009) found a lack of financial competence on the supervisory boards of German banks, the Landesbanken in particular, that is correlated with the concerned bank's losses during the crisis.

9.2   The politics of bank reform

While the drastic experience of the crisis will certainly not lead to the avoidance of future financial crises, studying past crisis responses is useful with respect to the identification of the processes that structure crisis reactions and the nature of the policy responses financial or banking crises tend to produce. Bank reforms are influenced by competitive concerns, they are the object of competing and at least in part conflicting policy aims, and they are shaped by a deeply entrenched predisposition of contemporary capitalist economies towards the promise of future economic growth. Crisis responses are shaped by the interactive social reconstruction of the causes of the crisis and the dynamics of mobilization and coalition-building following from it.

A key insight from the previous chapters is that crises tend to be understood in a specific way that selectively highlights certain aspects of it at the expense of others and they can lead to herd-like, self-reinforcing behaviour. Financial crises are multidimensional events, resulting from a complex constellation of causes. Macroeconomic imbalances, loose monetary policy, the limits of risk management, market, regulatory, supervisory, and political failure are all part of what is generally considered as having contributed to the emergence, the propagation, and the depth of the crisis. There is not one single understanding of the causes and consequences of a crisis that has cognitive superiority relative to all others with respect to the role and the relative weight attributed to different elements and processes having contributed to it.

To illustrate, one can interpret the global financial crisis as a crisis that primarily resulted from market failure—imperfect markets that led to suboptimal aggregate outcomes because of various deficiencies. Alternatively, the crisis can be seen as the result of state failure because it would have been the responsibility of the latter to avoid the former on a large scale. One could also argue that states are structurally incapable of regulating global finance effectively because of competition and capital mobility, shifting the explanation to a completely different level. Since there is not one single understanding of the origins and the consequences of the crisis that has cognitive superiority relative to all others, diagnosing the crisis ultimately is a social process.

With respect to the ways in which a crisis becomes politically salient, the selectivity with which a crisis is widely perceived increases even further because it relies on simplified representations. These result from a social learning process, which selectively highlights specific aspects of the crisis in the light of previously widely shared assumptions that are no longer deemed valid. The object of social learning is not the financial crisis per se, but specific developments having contributed to it, the behaviour of a specific subset of actors, and related to this, specific implications of the crisis. Financial trends and crises may be global, but their dynamics and implications are local.

Despite selectivity and simplification, it would be inappropriate to reduce social learning to mere misperceptions (Jervis 1976). The insights of social learning as such can be considered reasonably well-founded. For instance, that the hopes set in asset securitization and market-based banking as a means to modernize and boost the banking sector in Germany prior to the crisis were fairly optimistic can hardly be refuted in retrospect. In a similar vein, there is some truth in the French realization of the risks for borrowers when banks revise their lending criteria abruptly in the face of a crisis.

At the same time, one should bear in mind that selectivity creates bias. One implication of social learning, therefore, is that it tends to overemphasize the relevance of certain aspects while neglecting others. For instance, while the American market for asset-backed securities was affected by substantial write-downs, the European ABS market was stable throughout the crisis, and aggregate losses lower than in the corporate bond market (Bechtold 2012, 26). Nevertheless, the whole topic was a 'hot potato' in Germany. While learning usually has a positive connotation, social learning, as other forms of policy-oriented learning, does not necessarily lead to optimal policy outcomes if one assumes that optimal policies can be identified (e.g. Dunlop et al. 2020).

Bias is further amplified by the effects social learning has on the subsequent policy-making process because of its impact on shaping the reform agenda. The ways in which a crisis is understood collectively legitimize certain claims at the expense of others, and therefore ease access for some interest groups while hampering it for others. The emergence of a broader coalition in favour of a policy solution that is in line with social learning defines what is politically feasible. During crises, political agendas are driven by events and their collective interpretation, not by political programmes. If governments want to shape characteristics of the political economy, they should preferably do so in periods of relative calm because the room for manoeuvre and the proactive shaping of coalitions is larger than in moments of acute situational stress. The management of crises is a political task, but it is not necessarily one where politicians are in the driving seat.

Substantively, the previous chapters highlight the key role of a real economy–finance nexus in shaping reforms. In countries where the financial sector is not considered a key sector in its own right because of the substantial revenues it generates as a major international financial centre, the way in which reforms are articulated in terms of their impact on the real economy is decisive, tipping the scale in one specific direction (similarly Pagliari and Young 2013). While research on financialization has focused on how a logic of financial returns has spread even further across the economy and society (for an overview see van der Zwan 2014), the influence of the real economy in shaping financial sectors is less well understood (but see Deeg and Braun 2020; O'Sullivan 2007; Röper 2017). In political terms, reforms have good chances of succeeding when the interests of the real economy and the financial sector converge.

Even in the aftermath of a severe crisis, the window of opportunity for stricter regulation is limited. As long as the financial sector is not discredited entirely, failure in one area can lead to the strengthening of other areas, including the loosening of regulatory prescriptions. In addition, even though it is not necessarily the case, especially when considering a longer time horizon, policies that increase financial stability are often seen as an antagonist to economic growth or welfare. Put differently, the choice for stricter regulation only contributes to one among several equally legitimate policy aims. Given these circumstances, measures which further economic growth are likely to outweigh regulatory concerns, since financial stability lacks an equally potent advocate. Fostering financial stability by implementing stricter regulation has immediate, measurable costs and diffuse, uncertain future benefits.

Only in the immediate aftermath of an acute crisis, in which the shock of the disaster is fresh and broader attention high enough, can we expect stricter regulation to find sufficient support. Politicians may promote this if they think it might pay off on election day. Regulatory and supervisory agencies may work in that direction, but there are also limits, given regulatory competition and the extent to which a crisis that is diagnosed as having resulted from regulatory failure undermines the authority of the agency concerned. The financial crisis has led to some civil society mobilization, but it has remained less influential than in other areas, such as climate change, which brings back the question of how policy-relevant knowledge is constructed and how financial literacy of the population can be enhanced.

Finally, if there is one single most important lesson to be drawn from the crisis, it is the insight into how strong the bias towards the promise of growth in capitalist societies ultimately is. Growth-promoting policies are an equally legitimate policy goal as fostering financial stability and the former has decidedly a larger army of advocates. Potential negative effects on macroeconomic developments are a legitimate argument against stricter regulations and this also holds in the aftermath of a major crisis, given the overall challenging economic environment. These limits also became clear in the discussions on the need for further reforms. As one regulator reported about a meeting of the EBA's Board of supervisors:

> In this meeting, it became clear that if we wanted to feel even better and safer, we would have to do more. But that would mean that the production of loans as it is practised these days would be strongly limited and that bank credit to the real economy would become much more expensive. But that's the price that we would have to pay. Everything would become a bit more 'real'. At the moment, liquidity is abundant. We always talk about the financial crisis and say: 'Bad United States, where these subprime loans had been issued.' But that fits quite nicely into the broader picture of loose monetary policies worldwide in order to pamper the real economy and to get out of the economic trough. All of that has been massively driven by a political logic.   (Interview 2013103019)

Knowing about this crisis may help us respond differently when the next crisis hits.

List of interviews

Financial industry

France

Organization	Division
AF2i	Management Board
AFG	International affairs
AFIC	Legal and fiscal affairs
ASF	Corporate finance
Europlace	Research
FBF	European and international affairs
	Research on banking and financial activities
	Retail banking
FFSA	Research on economic and financial affairs (twice)
BNP Paribas France	Big corporate clients
BNP Paribas Ile-de-France	Maison des Entrepreneurs, Management Board (twice)
BPCE France	Development, corporate clients
Crédit Agricole Ile-de-France	Corporate clients
Finance Innovation	SME finance

Germany

Organization	Division
BdB	Banking supervision
	Corporate finance
BVR	Risk analysis
	Liaison Office Parliament and European Politics
DSGV	Savings banks politics and banking supervision
GDV	Capital investments
VAB	Management Board
vdp	Management Board
VÖB	Banking supervision and foreign trade
Börse Stuttgart	Financial products
Commerzbank	Group risk management
Deutsche Bank	DB research, division banking, financial markets, regulations

Organization	Division
Deutsche Börse	Manager issuer and primary market relations
Deutsches Aktieninstitut	Division for capital market policies
KSK Ludwigsburg	Bank management and controlling
Société Générale	Covered bond origination
TSI GmbH	Management Board

Public sector

France

Organization	Division
ACP	International banking issues
AMF	Regulation and international affairs
	Regulation of listed corporations
Assemblé nationale	Deputy of the Parti Socialiste
Banque de France	Division on financial and monetary statistics, twice
	Observatory on enterprises
	Division on research and coordination of financial regulation
	Division on market operations
Banque de France, Ile-de-France	Management Board
CDC Entreprises	Investment capital
Minefi	Médiation du crédit
Oséo/bpi, Ile-de-France	Management Board
Trésor	Bank issues
	Trade policies and investment
	Unit on the economic analysis of the financial sector

Germany

Organization	Division
BaFin	Banking supervision
BMF	Financial market policies
BMWi	SME finance
	Fundamental issues of SME policies
Deutsche Bundesbank	Supervision law and international banking supervision
Deutsche Bundesbank, Berlin-Brandenburg	Creditworthiness analysis and securities
Deutscher Bundestag	Two members of the Financial Committee
KfW	Capital markets-related forms of financing

Corporate sector

France

Organisation	Division
APCMA	Economic action
AFTE	Management Board
ASMEP-ETI	Management Board
CCI Paris	Economy and finance
CGPME, Ile-de-France	Management Board
Medef	Economy and finance
Middlenext	Management Board

Germany

Organization	Division
ASU—Die Familienunternehmer	Fundamental macroeconomic issues
BDI	Economic and industrial policies, corporate finance, and financial markets
DIHK	Money, currency, corporate finance, and corporate stability
ZDH	Division for economic, energy, and environmental policies
ZGV—Der Mittelstandsverbund	Management division

References

Abbott, Kenneth W., and Duncan Snidal. 1998. 'Why States Act through Formal International Organizations'. *Journal of Conflict Resolution* 42 (1): 3–32.

Acharya, Viral, and Philipp Schnabl. 2009. Do Global Banks Spread Global Imbalances? The Case of Asset-Backed Commercial Paper During the Financial Crisis of 2007–09. Paper presented at the 10th Jacques Polak Annual Research Conference. http://www.imf.org/external/np/res/seminars/2009/arc/pdf/acharya.pdf (Accessed 4 August 2012).

Adler, Emanuel. 1997. 'Seizing the Middle Ground: Constructivism in World Politics'. *European Journal of International Relations* 3 (3): 319–63.

Admati, Anat R., and Martin Hellwig. 2013. *The Bankers' New Clothes: What's Wrong with Banking and What to Do about It.* Princeton, NJ: Princeton University Press.

AFG, AMAFI, Europlace, Medef, and PME Finance. 2013. *PEA-PME. Conditions de mise en oeuvre. Document de travail.* http://www.pmefinance.org/documents/PEA%20PME%20Conditions%20de%20mise%20en%20oeuvre%20v5bis%2017%20juillet%20 2013.pdf (Accessed 19 February 2014).

AFTE. 2012. *Le financement des entreprises industrielles et commerciales. La position de l'AFTE.* http://www.afte.com/files/afte/Position_paper_AFTE_Financement_entreprises_pour_CP.pdf (Accessed 6 February 2014).

AG Mittelstand. 2009. *Vorschläge zu Eigenkapitalanforderungen sorgfältig prüfen! AG Mittelstand warnt vor Gefährdung der Kreditversorgung.* http://www.dihk.de/presse/meldungen/meldung011892 (Accessed 12 March 2014).

AG Mittelstand. 2011. *Basel III: Unternehmensfinanzierung im Mittelstand sichern.* http://www.vdb-info.de/media/file/1479.20111130_Positionspapier_AG_Mittelstand_Basel__III.pdf (Accessed 2 August 2014).

Aglietta, Michel. 1997. *La crise bancaire en France et dans le monde.* Centre d'Etudes Prospectives et d'Informations Internationales. La Lettre du CEPII, 155. http://www.cepii.fr/PDF_PUB/lettre/1997/let155.pdf (Accessed 24 March 2013).

Allen, Franklin, Michael K. Chui, and Angela Maddaloni. 2004. 'Financial Systems in Europe, the USA, and Asia'. *Oxford Review of Economic Policy* 20 (4): 490–508.

Allen, Franklin, and Douglas Gale. 2000. *Comparing Financial Systems.* Cambridge, MA: MIT Press.

Amable, Bruno. 2005. *Les cinq capitalismes: Diversité des systèmes économiques et sociaux dans la mondialisation.* Paris: Seuil.

AMAFI. 2013. *Financement des ETI. Vers un marché organisé des 'Euro Private Placements' ou 'Euro PP'—Propositions de l'AMAFI.* http://www.amafi.fr/images/stories/pdf/docs/juridique/13-44.pdf (Accessed 23 February 2014).

AMF. 2013. *Stratégie 2013–2016.* http://www.amf-france.org/Publications/Consultations-publiques/Archives.html?docId=workspace%3A%2F%2FSpacesStore%2Fc3329dba-8805-4375-84c9-797780218e26 (Accessed 7 February 2013).

AMF, and ACP. 2013. *Guide du financement participatif (crowdfunding) à destination des plates-formes et des porteurs de projet.* https://acpr.banque-france.fr/agrements-et-autorisations/le-financement-participatif-crowdfunding.html (Accessed 10 July 2014).

André-Leruste, Cécile. 2011. *Quel avenir pour le financement à long terme des entreprises non cotées?* Chambre de Commerce et de l'Industrie de Paris. http://www.etudes.cci-paris-idf.fr/rapport/306-financement-entreprises-non-cotees (Accessed 7 February 2014).

Angelkort, Asmus, and Alexander Stuwe. 2011. *Basel III and SME Financing*. Friedrich Ebert Stiftung. http://library.fes.de/pdf-files/managerkreis/08507.pdf (Accessed 9 March 2014).

Ansolabehere, Stephen, John de Figueiredo, and James M. Snyder. 2003. 'Why Is There so Little Money in U.S. Politics?' *The Journal of Economic Perspectives* 17 (1): 105–30.

Aussannaire, Patrick. 2010. 'L'Allemagne craint les effets de Bâle 3 pour son système bancaire'. *Agefi Quotidien*, 29 July. http://www.agefi.fr/articles/l-allemagne-craint-les-effets-de-bale-3-pour-son-systeme-bancaire-1145950.html (Accessed 2 August 2014).

Autorité de Contrôle Prudentiel. 2013. *Rapport Annuel 2010*. http://www.acp.banque-france.fr/fileadmin/user_upload/acp/publications/rapports-annuels/2012-rapport-annuel-activite-acp.pdf (Accessed 14 July 2013).

Autret, Florence. 2011. 'L'accouchement de la directive CRD4 s'annonce difficile'. *Agefi Quotidien*, 23 June. http://www.agefi.fr/articles/l-accouchement-de-la-directive-crd4-s-annonce-difficile-1180214.html (Accessed 23 March 2014).

Avouyi-Dovi, Sanvi, Rémy Lecat, Charles O'Donnell, Benjamin Bureau, and Jean-Pierre Villetelle. 2016. 'Les crédits aux entreprises à taux particulièrement bas en France'. *Bulletin de la Banque de France* 203: 5–17.

BaFin. 2002. *Geschäftsbericht 2001 des Bundesaufsichtsamtes für das Kreditwesen*. http://www.bafin.de/SharedDocs/Downloads/DE/Jahresbericht/dl_jb_2001_bakred.pdf?__blob=publicationFile&v=5 (Accessed 3 January 2013).

BaFin. 2003. *Jahresbericht 2002—Teil A*. http://www.bafin.de/SharedDocs/Downloads/DE/Jahresbericht/dl_jb_2002_a.pdf?__blob=publicationFile&v=10 (Accessed 14 January 2013).

BaFin. 2004. *Jahresbericht 2003—Teil A*. http://www.bafin.de/SharedDocs/Downloads/DE/Jahresbericht/dl_jb_2003_a.pdf;jsessionid=9B24C7C5F0248A7908381C1C92125685.1_cid290?__blob=publicationFile&v=8 (Accessed 14 January 2013).

Baker, Andrew. 2010. 'Restraining Regulatory Capture? Anglo-America, Crisis Politics and Trajectories of Change in Global Financial Governance'. *International Affairs* 86 (3): 647–63.

Baker, Andrew. 2013. 'The New Political Economy of the Macroprudential Ideational Shift'. *New Political Economy* 18 (1): 112–39.

Baker, Andrew. 2014. 'Varieties of Economic Crisis, Varieties of Ideational Change: How and Why Financial Regulation and Macroeconomic Policy Differ'. *New Political Economy* 20 (3): 342–66.

BAKred. 1997. *Jahresbericht 1996*. http://www.bafin.de/SharedDocs/Downloads/DE/Jahresbericht/dl_jb_1996_bakred.pdf?__blob=publicationFile&v=5 (Accessed 3 January 2013).

BAKred. 1998. *Jahresbericht 1997*. http://www.bafin.de/SharedDocs/Downloads/DE/Jahresbericht/dl_jb_1997_bakred.pdf?__blob=publicationFile&v=6 (Accessed 3 January 2013).

BAKred. 1999. *Jahresbericht 1998*. http://www.bafin.de/SharedDocs/Downloads/DE/Jahresbericht/dl_jb_1998_bakred.pdf?__blob=publicationFile&v=5 (Accessed 3 January 2013).

BAKred. 2000. *Jahresbericht 1999*. http://www.bafin.de/SharedDocs/Downloads/DE/Jahresbericht/dl_jb_1999_bakred.html?nn=2818588 (Accessed 28 December 2012).

Banque de France. 2010. *De la crise financière à la crise économique*. Documents et débats, 3.

Banque de France. 2012. *Le marché Alternext*. Référentiel des Financements des Entreprises, 231. http://www.banque-france.fr/fileadmin/user_upload/banque_de_france/La_Banque_de_France/pdf/fiche_231-BDF-Marche-Alternext.pdf (Accessed 11 February 2014).

Banque de France. 2014. 'Le référentiel des financements des entreprises'. https://entreprises.banque-france.fr/accompagnement-des-entreprises/le-referentiel-des-financements-des-entreprises (Accessed 3 February 2014).

Barth, James R., Gerard Caprio, and Ross Levine. 2012. *Guardians of Finance: Making Regulators Work for Us*. Cambridge, MA: MIT Press.

Basel Committee. 2006. *Basel II: International Convergence of Capital Measurement and Capital Standards: Comprehensive Version*. http://www.bis.org/publ/bcbs128.pdf (Accessed 17 August 2014).

Basel Committee. 2009. *Enhancements to the Basel II framework*. http://www.bis.org/publ/bcbs157.pdf (Accessed 17 August 2014).

Basel Committee. 2010a. *Basel III: A global regulatory framework for more resilient banks and banking systems*. http://www.bis.org/publ/bcbs189_dec2010.pdf (Accessed 28 February 2014).

Basel Committee. 2010b. *Basel III: International framework for liquidity risk measurement, standards and monitoring*. http://www.bis.org/publ/bcbs188.pdf (Accessed 28 February 2014).

Basel Committee. 2010c. *Group of Governors and Heads of Supervision announces higher global minimum capital standards*. http://www.bis.org/press/p100912.pdf (Accessed 3 March 2014).

Basel Committee. 2010d. *Results of the comprehensive quantitative impact study*. https://www.bis.org/publ/bcbs186.pdf (Accessed 2 August 2014).

Basel Committee. 2010e. *The Group of Governors and Heads of Supervision reach broad agreement on Basel Committee capital and liquidity reform package*. Annex. Press Release. http://www.bis.org/press/p100726.htm (Accessed 28 February 2014).

Basel Committee. 2013. *Group of Governors and Heads of Supervision endorses revised liquidity standard for banks*. http://www.bis.org/press/p130106.htm (Accessed 4 March 2014).

Basel Committee. 2017. *Basel III: Finalising post-crisis reforms*. https://www.bis.org/bcbs/publ/d424.pdf (Accessed 23 September 2018).

Baumgartner, Frank R. 2013. 'Ideas and Policy Change'. *Governance* 26 (2): 239–58.

Baumgartner, Frank R., and Bryan D. Jones. 1993. *Agendas and Instability in American Politics*. Chicago: University of Chicago Press.

BdB, and DIHK. 2011. *Folgen von Basel III für den Mittelstand*. http://www.dihk.de/presse/meldungen/2013-05-15-basel-iii-publikation (Accessed 9 March 2014).

BDI. 2011. *Stellungnahme zum Verordnungsvorschlag der Europäischen Kommission zur Umsetzung von Basel III*. http://www.bdi.eu/images_content/KonjunkturStandortUndWettbewerb/Basel_III_deutsch.pdf (Accessed 12 March 2014).

Beach, Derek, and Rasmus Pedersen. 2013. *Process-Tracing Methods: Foundations and Guidelines*. Ann Arbor: University of Michigan Press.

Béal, Laure. 1997. 'La titrisation en 1996'. *Bulletin de la Banque de France* 48: 113–26.

Bechtold, Hartmut. 2012. 'ABS zwischen Investorenvertrauen, Regulierung und Zentralbankpolitik'. *Kreditwesen* 2012 (8): 22–6.

Beckert, Jens. 1996. 'What is Sociological about Economic Sociology? Uncertainty and the Embeddedness of Economic Action'. *Theory and Society* 25 (6): 803–40.

Beckert, Jens. 2013. 'Imagined Futures: Fictional Expectations in the Economy'. *Theory and Society* 42 (3): 219–40.

Beckert, Jens. 2016. *Imagined Futures: Fictional Expectations and Capitalist Dynamics.* Cambridge, MA: Harvard University Press.

Beckert, Jens, and Richard Bronk, eds. 2018. *Uncertain Futures: Imaginaries, Narratives, and Calculation in the Economy.* Oxford and New York: Oxford University Press.

Beckert, Jens, and Timur Ergen. 2020. *Transcending History's Heavy Hand: The Future in Economic Action.* Max Planck Institute for the Study of Societies. MPIfG Discussion Paper, 20/3.

Béland, Daniel, and Robert H. Cox, eds. 2010. *Ideas and Politics in Social Science Research.* Oxford and New York: Oxford University Press.

Bell, Stephen. 2012. 'The Power of Ideas: The Ideational Shaping of the Structural Power of Business'. *International Studies Quarterly* 56 (4): 661–73.

Bell, Stephen, and Andrew Hindmoor. 2014a. 'Taming the City? Ideas, Structural Power and the Evolution of British Banking Policy Amidst the Great Financial Meltdown'. *New Political Economy* 20 (3): 454–74.

Bell, Stephen, and Andrew Hindmoor. 2014b. 'The Ideational Shaping of State Power and Capacity: Winning Battles but Losing the War over Bank Reform in the US and UK'. *Government and Opposition* 49 (3): 342–68.

Bell, Stephen, and Andrew Hindmoor. 2015. *Masters of the Universe, Slaves of the Market.* Cambridge, MA: Harvard University Press.

Bell, Stephen, and Andrew Hindmoor. 2017a. 'Are the Major Global Banks Now Safer? Structural Continuities and Change in Banking and Finance since the 2008 Crisis'. *Review of International Political Economy* 25 (1): 1–27.

Bell, Stephen, and Andrew Hindmoor. 2017b. 'Structural Power and the Politics of Bank Capital Regulation in the United Kingdom'. *Political Studies* 65 (1): 103–21.

Bender, Hanno. 2011. 'Kreditmediator: "Der Einzelhandel ist benachteiligt": Interview mit Hans-Joachim Metternich'. *Der Handel,* 13 November. http://www.derhandel.de/news/finanzen/pages/Finanzierung-Kreditmediator-Der-Einzelhandel-ist-benachteiligt-7977.html?i_searchword=kreditmediation (Accessed 4 February 2013).

Bennett, Colin, and Michael Howlett. 1992. 'The Lessons of Learning: Reconciling Theories of Policy Learning and Policy Change'. *Policy Sciences* 25 (3): 275–94.

Berg, Tobias, Bernhard Gehra, and Michael Kunisch. 2011. 'A Certification Model for Regulatory Arbitrage: Will Regulatory Arbitrage Persist under Basel III?' *The Journal of Fixed Income* 21 (2): 39–56.

Berger, Allen, and Gregory Udell. 1998. 'The Economics of Small Business Finance: The Roles of Private Equity and Debt Markets in the Financial Growth Cycle'. *Journal of Banking and Finance* 22: 613–73.

Berger, Karine, and Dominique Lefebvre. 2013. *Dynamiser l'épargne financière des ménages pour financer l'investissement et la compétitivité: Rapport au Premier Ministre.* http://www.tresor.economie.gouv.fr/File/383682 (Accessed 10 February 2014).

Berger, Suzanne, and Ronald Dore. 1996. *National Diversity and Global Capitalism.* Ithaca, NY: Cornell University Press.

Berman, Sheri. 2013. 'Ideational Theorizing in the Social Sciences since "Policy Paradigms, Social Learning, and the State"'. *Governance* 26 (2): 217–37.

Bernhagen, Patrick, and Thomas Bräuninger. 2005. 'Structural Power and Public Policy: A Signaling Model of Business Lobbying in Democratic Capitalism'. *Political Studies* 53 (1): 43–64.

Beyer, Jürgen. 2002. *Deutschland AG a.D.: Deutsche Bank, Allianz und das Verflechtungszentrum großer deutscher Unternehmen.* MPIfG Working Paper, 02/4. http://www.mpifg.de/pu/workpap/wp02-4/wp02-4.html (Accessed 2 August 2014).

Beyer, Jürgen, and Martin Höppner. 2003. 'The Disintegration of Organised Capitalism: German Corporate Governance in the 1990s'. *West European Politics* 26 (4): 179–98.

Birouk, Omar, and Laetitia Cassan. 2012. 'La titrisation en France'. *Bulletin de la Banque de France* 190: 99–112.

Bluhm, Katharina, and Bernd Martens. 2008. 'Change within Traditional Channels: German SMEs, the Restructuring of the Banking Sector, and the Growing Shareholder-Value Orientation'. In *Change in SMEs: Towards a New European Capitalism?*, eds. Katharina Bluhm and Rudi Schmidt. Basingstoke: Palgrave Macmillan, 39–57.

Blyth, Mark. 2002. *Great Transformations: Economic Ideas and Institutional Change in the Twentieth Century*. Cambridge and New York: Cambridge University Press.

Blyth, Mark. 2013. 'Paradigms and Paradox: The Politics of Economic Ideas in Two Moments of Crisis'. *Governance: An International Journal of Policy, Administration, and Institutions* 26 (2): 197–215.

BMF. 2010. *Responses to the Commission's Working Document 'Consultation regarding further possible changes to the Capital Requirements Directive'*. https://circabc.europa.eu/faces/jsp/extension/wai/navigation/container.jsp (Accessed 2 April 2014).

BMWi. 2009. *Wirtschaftsfonds Deutschland: Das Kredit- und Bürgschaftsprogramm der Bundesregierung.* http://www.existenzgruender.de/imperia/md/content/pdf/podcast-pdfs/podcast_wirtschfonds-deutschland.pdf (Accessed 16 August 2014).

BMWi. 2010. *Schlaglichter der Wirtschaftspolitik: Monatsbericht Mai 2010.* http://www.bmwi.de/Dateien/BMWi/PDF/Monatsbericht/schlaglichter-der-wirtschaftspolitik-05-2010,property=pdf,bereich=bmwi,sprache=de,rwb=true.pdf (Accessed 16 August 2014).

BMWi Mittelstandsbeirat. 2011. *Resolution zum Thema 'Basel III'*. http://bmwi.de/BMWi/Redaktion/PDF/M-O/mittelstandsbeirat-resolution-zum-thema-basel-iii,property=pdf,bereich=bmwi2012,sprache=de,rwb=true.pdf (Accessed 2 August 2014).

BMWi Wissenschaftlicher Beirat. 2010. *Reform von Bankenregulierung und Bankenaufsicht nach der Finanzkrise: Gutachten.* http://www.bmwi.de/DE/Mediathek/Publikationen/publikationen-archiv,did=344680.html (Accessed 10 March 2014).

Bordet, Marie. 2008. 'René Ricol l'homme qui fait trembler les banquiers'. *Le Point*, 20 November, 58–61.

Bossone, Biagio. 1999. *What Makes Banks Special? A Study on Banking, Finance, and Economic Development*. Washington, DC: World Bank. http://elibrary.worldbank.org/content/workingpaper/10.1596/1813-9450-2408 (Accessed 15 April 2013).

Bourdieu, Pierre. 1989. *La noblesse d'Etat: Grandes écoles et esprit de corps*. Paris: Editions de Minuit.

Bouvier, Jean. 1973. *Un siècle de banque française*. Paris: Hachette.

Bowles, Samuel, and Wendy Carlin. 2020. 'What Students Learn in Economics 101: Time for a Change'. *Journal of Economic Literature* 58 (1): 176–214.

Braithwaite, John, and Peter Drahos. 2000. *Global Business Regulation*. Cambridge and New York: Cambridge University Press.

Braun, Michael, Axel Flemming, and Wolfgang Labuhn. 2004. *Signal für den Umbruch im Bankenwesen? Der Streit um den Verkauf der Sparkasse Stralsund*. Deutschlandfunk. http://www.dradio.de/dlf/sendungen/hintergrundpolitik/228287/ (Accessed 19 January 2013).

Bronk, Richard. 2009. *The Romantic Economist: Imagination in Economics*. Cambridge and New York: Cambridge University Press.

Brunella, Bruno, Alexandra D'Onofrio, and Immacolata Marino. 2018a. 'Financial Structure and Corporate Investment in Europe'. In *Finance and Investment: The*

European Case, eds. Colin Mayer, Stefano Micossi, Marco Onado, Marco Pagano, and Andrea Polo. Oxford: Oxford University Press, 15–56.

Brunella, Bruno, Giacomo Nocera, and Andrea Resti. 2018b. 'Are Risk-Based Capital Requirements Detrimental to Corporate Lending? Evidence from Europe'. In *Finance and Investment: The European Case*, eds. Colin Mayer, Stefano Micossi, Marco Onado, Marco Pagano, and Andrea Polo. Oxford: Oxford University Press, 327–34.

Brunner, Allan, Jörg Decressin, Daniel Hardy, and Beata Kudela. 2004. *Germany's Three-Pillar Banking System: Cross-Country Perspectives in Europe*. IMF Occasional Paper, 233.

Brunnermeier, Markus. 2009. 'Deciphering the Liquidity and Credit Crunch 2007–2008'. *Journal of Economic Perspectives* 23 (1): 77–100.

Brunnermeier, Markus, Andrew Crocket, Charles Goodhart, Avinash D. Persaud, and Hyun Shin. 2009. *The Fundamental Principles of Financial Regulation*. Geneva and London: International Center for Monetary and Banking Studies and Centre for Economic Policy Research.

Buder, Matthäus, Max Lienemeyer, Marcel Magnus, Bert Smits, and Karl Soukup. 2011. *The Rescue and Restructuring of Hypo Real Estate*. European Commission. Competition Policy Newsletter, 3.

Buiter, Willem. 2008. *Central Banks and Financial Crises*. LSE Discussion Papers, 619. London School of Economics and Political Science.

Busch, Andreas. 2004. 'National Filters: Europeanisation, Institutions, and Discourse in the Case of Banking Regulation'. *West European Politics* 27 (2): 310–33.

Busch, Andreas. 2008. *Banking Regulation and Globalization*. Oxford: Oxford University Press.

BVMW. 2010. *Bankenregulierung—Forderungen und Positionen des Mittelstands*. http://www.bvmw.de/uploads/media/BVMW-Positionspapier-Bankenregulierung.pdf (Accessed 9 March 2014).

BVMW. 2011. *Auswirkungsstudie Basel III. Die Folgen für den deutschen Mittelstand: Eine wissenschaftliche Studie durchgeführt von Dr. Tobias Berg, Humboldt-Universität zu Berlin und PD Dr. Martin Uzik, Bergische Universität Wuppertal im Auftrag des Bundesverband mittelständische Wirtschaft*. http://www.bvmw.de/fileadmin/download/Bund/basel_III_studie.pdf (Accessed 9 March 2014).

BWHT, IHK, SVBW, and bwgv. 2012. *Gemeinsame Resolution zu 'Basel III'*. http://www.handwerk-bw.de/uploads/tx_rdepublications/bwht-resolution-basel-iii.pdf (Accessed 19 March 2014).

Cabannes, Pierre-Yves, Vincent Cottet, Yves Dubois, Claire Lelarge, and Michaël Sicsic. 2013. 'Les ajustements des entreprises françaises pendant la crise de 2008/2009'. In *L'économie française—comptes et dossiers*, ed. INSEE. Paris: INSEE, 53–67.

Calomiris, Charles W., and Stephen H. Haber. 2014. *Fragile by Design: The Political Origins of Banking Crises and Scarce Credit*. Princeton, NJ: Princeton University Press.

Campbell, John L. 1998. 'Institutional Analysis and the Role of Ideas in Political Economy'. *Theory and Society* 27 (3): 377–409.

Campbell, John L. 2004. *Institutional Change and Globalization*. Princeton, NJ: Princeton University Press.

Campbell, John L. 2010. 'Institutional Reproduction and Change'. In *The Oxford Handbook of Comparative Institutional Analysis*, eds. Glenn Morgan, John L. Campbell, Colin Crouch, Ove Pedersen, and Richard Whitley. Oxford and New York: Oxford University Press, 87–116.

Campbell, John L., and Ove K. Pedersen. 2014. *The National Origins of Policy Ideas: Knowledge Regimes in the United States, France, Germany, and Denmark*. Princeton, NJ: Princeton University Press.

Carlat, Thomas. 2013. 'Le risque entreprises au menu du bilan des assureurs'. *Agefi Hebdo*, 18 July. http://www.agefi.fr/articles/le-risque-entreprises-au-menu-du-bilan-des-assureurs-1277202.html (Accessed 21 February 2014).

Carmassi, Jacopo, Stefano Micossi, and Daniel Gros. 2009. 'The Global Financial Crisis: Causes and Cures'. *JCMS: Journal of Common Market Studies* 47 (5): 977–96.

Carpenter, Daniel P. 2014. 'Detecting and Measuring Capture'. In *Preventing Regulatory Capture: Special Interest Influence and How to Limit It*, eds. Daniel P. Carpenter and David A. Moss. New York: Cambridge University Press, 57–68.

Carpenter, Daniel P., and David A. Moss. 2014. 'Introduction'. In *Preventing Regulatory Capture: Special Interest Influence and How to Limit It*, eds. Daniel P. Carpenter and David A. Moss. New York: Cambridge University Press, 1–22.

Carstensen, Martin B. 2015. 'Bringing Ideational Power into the Paradigm Approach: Critical Perspectives on Policy Paradigms in Theory and Practice'. In *Policy Paradigms in Theory and Practice*, eds. John Hogan and Michael Howlett. London: Palgrave Macmillan, 295–318.

Carstensen, Martin B., and Vivien A. Schmidt. 2015. 'Power through, over and in Ideas: Conceptualizing Ideational Power in Discursive Institutionalism'. *Journal of European Public Policy* 23 (3): 318–37.

Cassou, Pierre-Henri. 2001. 'Seize ans de réorganisaiton bancaire en France'. *Revue d'économie financière* 61 (1): 13–30.

Cayssials, Jean-Luc, Dominique Durant, Olivier Vigna, and Jean-Pierre Villetelle. 2008. 'La situation financière des sociétés non financières en France 1995–2006: Baisse du taux d'épargne et recours accru à l'endettement'. *Bulletin de la Banque de France* 170: 29–48.

Cayssials, Jean-Luc, and Elisabeth Kremp. 2010. 'Les PME de l'industrie manufacturière en France. Un positionnement intermédiaire par rapport à huit autres pays européens'. *Bulletin de la Banque de France* 180: 49–63.

Cayssials, Jean-Luc, Elisabeth Kremp, and Christophe Peter. 2007. 'Dix années de dynamique financière des PME en France'. In *Petites et moyennes entreprises. Bulletin de la Banque de France*. Numéro spécial, 31–48.

Cayssials, Jean-Luc, and François Servant. 2011. 'La situation financière des PME'. In *PME 2011: Rapport sur l'évolution des PME*, ed. Oséo, 45–68.

CDC. 2012. *Lancement des fonds d'investissement nova 1 et nova 2 pour les PME et ETI cotées*. http://www.pme-bourse.fr/fileadmin/medias/Initiative_de_place/Dossier_presse_fonds_nova_couv.pdf (Accessed 18 February 2014).

CDU, CSU, and SPD. 2013. *Deutschlands Zukunft gestalten: Koalitionsvertrag zwischen CDU, CSU und SPD*. https://www.cdu.de/sites/default/files/media/dokumente/koalitionsvertrag.pdf (Accessed 4 February 2013).

Cerny, Philip G. 1989. 'The "Little Big Bang" in Paris: Financial Market Deregulation in a Dirigiste System'. *European Journal of Political Research* 17 (2): 169–92.

CGFS. 2018. *Structural Changes in Banking after the Crisis*. CGFS Papers, 60. Bank for International Settlements.

CGPME. 2011. *Financement des entreprises. Propositions de la CGPME*. http://www.cgpme.fr/economies/voir/30/propositions-de-la-cgpme-pour-le-financement-des-entreprises (Accessed 7 February 2013).

Chertok, Grégoire, Jean-Alain de Malleray, and Phillippe Pouletty, eds. 2009. *Le financement des PME*. Paris: La Documentation française.

Clegg, Nick. 2010. 'We must build a new kind of economy to create a stronger, balanced Britain'. *The Yorkshire Post*, 28 June.

Clemens, Elisabeth S., and James M. Cook. 1999. 'Politics and Institutionalism: Explaining Durability and Change'. *Annual Review of Sociology* 25: 441–66.

Clift, Ben. 2012. 'Le Changement? French Socialism, the 2012 Presidential Election and the Politics of Economic Credibility amidst the Eurozone Crisis'. *Parliamentary Affairs* 66 (1): 106–23.

Coleman, William D. 1993. 'Reforming Corporatism: The French Banking Policy Community, 1941–1990'. *West European Politics* 16 (2): 122–43.

Coleman, William D. 1994. 'Policy Convergence in Banking: A Comparative Study'. *Political Studies* 42 (2): 274–92.

Coleman, William D. 1996. *Financial Services, Globalization and Domestic Policy Change*. Basingstoke: Macmillan.

Companies Observatory. 2012. 'SMEs in Europe: Disparities between Countries and Sectors Were Greater in 2010 than Before the Crisis'. In *Quarterly Selection of Articles*. Vol. 26, ed. Banque de France, 25–51.

Conert, Jens. 2003. *Basel II—Die Überarbeitung der Eigenkapitalregelungen der Kreditinstitute im Fokus von Wirtschafts- und Wettbewerbspolitik*. Institute for Law and Finance Working paper series, 14. http://www.ilf-frankfurt.de/uploads/media/ILF_WP_014.pdf (Accessed 17 March 2014).

Conseil National du Crédit. 1995. 'Synthèse du rapport "Risque de crédit"'. *Bulletin de la Banque de France* 21: 91–6.

Couppey-Soubeyran, Jézabel, Olivier Garnier, and Jean-Paul Pollin, eds. 2012. *Le financement de l'économie dans le nouveau contexte réglementaire*. Paris: La Documentation française.

Cour des comptes. 2012a. *L'Etat et le financement de l'économie: Rapport public thématique*. http://www.ccomptes.fr/Publications/Publications/L-Etat-et-le-financement-de-l-economie (Accessed 7 February 2014).

Cour des comptes. 2012b. *La politique en faveur de l'assurance-vie. Rapport public thématique.* http://www.ccomptes.fr/Publications/Publications/La-politique-en-faveur-de-l-assurance-vie (Accessed 10 February 2014).

Cour des comptes. 2013. *Rapport public annuel 2013*. https://www.ccomptes.fr/Publications/Publications/Rapport-public-annuel-2013 (Accessed 17 April 2017).

Crouch, Colin. 2011. *The Strange Non-Death of Neoliberalism*. Cambridge: Polity Press.

Crouch, Colin, and Wolfgang Streeck. 1997a. 'Introduction: The Future of Capitalist Diversity'. In *Political Economy of Modern Capitalism: Mapping Convergence and Diversity*, eds. Colin Crouch and Wolfgang Streeck. London: Sage, 1–18.

Crouch, Colin, and Wolfgang Streeck, eds. 1997b. *Political Economy of Modern Capitalism: Mapping Convergence and Diversity*. London: Sage.

Culpepper, Pepper D. 2003. *Creating Cooperation: How States Develop Human Capital in Europe*. Ithaca, NY: Cornell University Press.

Culpepper, Pepper D. 2005. 'Institutional Change in Contemporary Capitalism: Coordinated Financial Systems since 1990'. *World Politics* 57 (2): 173–99.

Culpepper, Pepper D. 2008. 'The Politics of Common Knowledge: Ideas and Institutional Change in Wage Bargaining'. *International Organization* 62 (1): 1–33.

Culpepper, Pepper D. 2011. *Quiet Politics and Business Power: Corporate Control in Europe and Japan*. Cambridge and New York: Cambridge University Press.

Culpepper, Pepper D., and Raphael Reinke. 2014. 'Structural Power and Bank Bailouts in the United Kingdom and the United States'. *Politics & Society* 42 (4): 427–54.

Dal Bo, Ernesto. 2006. 'Regulatory Capture: A Review'. *Oxford Review of Economic Policy* 22 (2): 203–25.

Daruvala, Toos, Miklos Dietz, Philipp Härle, Joydeep Sengupta, Matthias Voelkl, and Eckhart Windhagen. 2012. *The Triple Transformation: Achieving a Sustainable Business Model.* McKinsey. http://www.mckinsey.de/suche/2nd_McK_annual_review_on_the_banking_industry_October_2012.pdf (Accessed 9 April 2014).

Dattels, Peter, and Laura Kodres. 2009. 'Further Action Needed to Reinforce Signs of Market Recovery'. IMF. http://www.imf.org/external/pubs/ft/survey/so/2009/RES042109C. htm (Accessed 9 March 2014).

Dayal, Ranu, Gerold Grasshoff, Douglas Jackson, Philippe Morel, and Peter Neu. 2011. *Facing New Realities in Global Banking: Risk Report 2011.* Boston Consulting Group. http://www.bcg.de/documents/file93568.pdf (Accessed 9 March 2014).

Deeg, Richard. 1999. *Finance Capitalism Unveiled: Banks and the German Political Economy.* Ann Arbor: University of Michigan Press.

Deeg, Richard. 2005. 'Change from Within: German and Italian Finance in the 1990s'. In *Beyond Continuity: Institutional Change in Advanced Political Economies,* eds. Wolfgang Streeck and Kathleen A. Thelen. Oxford and New York: Oxford University Press, 169–202.

Deeg, Richard. 2009. 'The Rise of Internal Capitalist Diversity? Changing Patterns of Finance and Corporate Governance in Europe'. *Economy and Society* 38 (4): 552–79.

Deeg, Richard, and Benjamin Braun. 2020. 'Strong Firms, Weak Banks: The Financial Consequences of Germany's Export-Led Growth Model'. *German Politics* 29 (3): 358–81.

Deeg, Richard, and Gregory Jackson. 2007. 'Towards a More Dynamic Theory of Capitalist Variety'. *Socio-Economic Review* 5 (1): 149–79.

Deutsche Bundesbank. 1999. *Monatsbericht Oktober 1999: 51. Jahrgang Nr. 10.* http://www.bundesbank.de/Redaktion/DE/Downloads/Veroeffentlichungen/Monatsberichte/1999/1999_10_monatsbericht.pdf?__blob=publicationFile (Accessed 28 March 2013).

Deutsche Bundesbank. 2007. 'La situation économique des PME depuis 1997 en Allemagne'. In *Petites et moyennes entreprises. Bulletin de la Banque de France.* Numéro spécial, 49–64.

Deutsche Bundesbank. 2009. 'Die Entwicklung der Kredite an den privaten Sektor in Deutschland während der globalen Finanzkrise'. *Monatsbericht* (September): 17–36.

Deutsche Bundesbank. 2011. *Basel III—Leitfaden zu den neuen Eigenkapital- und Liquiditätsregeln für Banken.* Frankfurt am Main.

Deutsche Bundesbank. 2012. *Verzeichnis der Kreditinstitute und ihrer Verbände sowie der Treuhänder für Kreditinstitute in der Bundesrepublik Deutschland.* http://www.bundesbank.de/Redaktion/DE/Downloads/Bundesbank/Aufgaben_und_Organisation/verzeichnis_der_kreditinstitute_und_ihrer_verbaende.pdf?__blob=publicationFile (Accessed 5 December 2012).

Deutsche Bundesbank. 2015a. 'Strukturelle Entwicklungen im deutschen Bankensektor'. *Monatsbericht* (April): 33–59.

Deutsche Bundesbank. 2015b. 'Zur jüngeren Entwicklung der Buchkredite an nichtfinanzielle Unternehmen im Euro-Raum'. *Monatsbericht* (September): 15–41.

Deutscher Bundestag. 2007. *Internetnutzung: Globale Entwicklung und Darstellung empirischer Daten.* https://www.bundestag.de/blob/414768/797fa31a4e17ca56bef9ebb6fb0306fc/wd-10-070-07-pdf-data.pdf (Accessed 13 August 2020).

Deutscher Bundestag. 2010. *Antrag der Fraktionen CDU/CSU, SPD, FDP und BÜNDNIS 90/DIE GRÜNEN: Stabilisierung des Finanzsektors—Eigenkapitalvorschriften für Banken angemessen überarbeiten.* http://dip21.bundestag.de/dip21/btd/17/017/1701756.pdf (Accessed 17 March 2014).

Deutscher Bundestag. 2011. *Antrag der Abgeordneten Peter Friedrich* et al. *und der Fraktion der SPD: Finanzierungsbedingungen des Mittelstands verbessern.* http://dip21.bundestag. de/dip21/btd/17/052/1705229.pdf (Accessed 2 August 2014).

Deutscher Bundestag. 2012. *Antrag der Fraktion der SPD Umsetzung von Basel III: Finanzmärkte stabilisieren—Realwirtschaft stärken—Kommunalfinanzierung sichern.* http://dip21.bundestag.de/dip21/btd/17/091/1709167.pdf (Accessed 17 March 2014).

Dialogforum Finanzstandort Deutschland. 2012. *Finanzstandort Deutschland: Bericht Nr. 8–2012.* http://www.die-deutsche-kreditwirtschaft.de/uploads/media/IFD_ Finanzstandort-Bericht_Nr8_2012D.pdf (Accessed 5 December 2012).

Diaz, Xavier. 2013. 'Un premier FCPR d'obligations non cotées de PME'. *Agefi Hebdo*, 7 March. http://www.agefi.fr/articles/un-premier-fcpr-d-obligations-non-cotees-de-pme-1259582.html (Accessed 17 February 2014).

Die Familienunternehmer. 2011. *Auswirkungen der Reformen der Bankenaufsicht berücksichtigen! Kreditvergabe der Banken, Sparkassen und genossenschaftlichen Kreditinstitute: Gutachten im Auftrag von Die Familienunternehmer—ASU e.V., angefertigt von Univ.-Prof. Dr. Thomas Hartmann-Wendels.* https://www.familienunternehmer.eu/uploads/ tx_wfmedienpr/gutachten_basel_III.pdf (Accessed 9 March 2014).

DIHK. 2011. *DIHK-Anmerkungen zur Umsetzung von Basel III in europäisches Recht.* http://www.sihk.de/linkableblob/haihk24/starthilfe/downloads/1422746/.4./data/ Stellungnahme_zur_Umsetzung_von_Basel_III-data.pdf (Accessed 13 March 2014).

DIHK, WKÖ, and ZDH. 2011a. *Basel III. Deutsche und österreichische Wirtschaft treten gemeinsam für Verbesserungen bei Unternehmenskrediten ein.* http://www.zdh.de/ fileadmin/user_upload/themen/wirtschaft/Basel_III/20110920_gemeinsame_PM.pdf (Accessed 17 March 2014).

DIHK, WKÖ, and ZDH. 2011b. *Basel III: Stabilität des Finanzsystems stärken, Unternehmensfinanzierung sichern.* http://www.dihk.de/presse/meldungen/2011-09-20-basel (Accessed 17 March 2014).

Dill, Alexander. 2011. 'Das plötzliche Verschwinden der Initiative Finanzstandort Deutschland'. telopolis. heise online. https://www.heise.de/tp/features/Das-ploetzliche-Verschwinden-der-Initiative-Finanzstandort-Deutschland-3503349.html (Accessed 13 August 2020).

Djankov, Simeon, Jürgen Ligi, Ingrida Simonyte, Ivan Miklos, Elena Salgado, Anders Borg, Peter Norman, and George Osborne. 2011. *Letter addressed to the EU Commissioners Michael Barnier and Olli Rehn.* http://www.secure-finance.com/analyses/1110.pdf (Accessed 2 August 2014).

Djelic, Marie-Laure. 2010. 'Institutional Perspectives: Working towards Coherence or Irreconcilable Diversity?' In *The Oxford Handbook of Comparative Institutional Analysis*, eds. Glenn Morgan, John L. Campbell, Colin Crouch, Ove Pedersen, and Richard Whitley. Oxford and New York: Oxford University Press, 15–40.

Djelic, Marie-Laure, and Sigrid Quack, eds. 2003a. *Globalization and Institutions: Redefining the Rules of the Economic Game.* Cheltenham, UK and Northampton, MA: Edward Elgar.

Djelic, Marie-Laure, and Sigrid Quack. 2003b. 'Theoretical Building Blocks for a Research Agenda Linking Globalization and Institutions'. In *Globalization and Institutions: Redefining the Rules of the Economic Game*, eds. Marie-Laure Djelic and Sigrid Quack. Cheltenham, UK and Northampton, MA: Edward Elgar, 15–34.

DSGV. 2013. *Wettbewerbliche Benachteiligung dezentraler bzw. kleinteiliger Bankmarktstrukturen durch eine undifferenzierte Regulierung.*

Dunlop, Claire A., Scott James, and Claudio M. Radaelli. 2020. 'Can't Get No Learning: The Brexit Fiasco through the Lens of Policy Learning'. *Journal of European Public Policy* 27 (5): 703–22.

EBA. 2012. *Assessment of SME Proposals for CRD IV/CRR.* http://www.eba.europa.eu/documents/10180/16148/EBA-SME-Report.pdf (Accessed 2 August 2014).

ECB. 2007. *Corporate Finance in the Euro Area.* Occasional Paper Series, 63.

ECB 2015. 'The Fiscal Impact of Financial Sector Support during the Crisis'. *ECB Economic Bulletin* 6: 74–87.

Eckert, Daniel, Karsten Seibel, and Holger Zschäpitz. 2013. 'Die Illusion von der sicheren Geldanlage'. *Die Welt,* 7 September. https://www.welt.de/finanzen/article119796323/Die-Illusion-von-der-sicheren-Geldanlage.html (Accessed 19 August 2020).

Edwards, Jeremy, and Sheilagh Ogilvie. 1996. 'Universal Banks and German Industrialization: A Reappraisal'. *The Economic History Review* 49 (3): 427–46.

Eichengreen, Barry. 2015. *Hall of Mirrors: The Great Depression, the Great Recession, and the Uses—and Misuses—of History.* London and New York: Oxford University Press.

Elsner, Dirk. 2012. *Untersuchungsausschuss zur Aufarbeitung der Finanzkrise durch Bundestag scheitert an notwendiger Mehrheit: Interview mit Gerhard Schick.* Blick Log. http://www.blicklog.com/2012/03/12/gerhard-schick-untersuchungsausschuss-zur-aufarbeitung-der-finanzkrise-durch-bundestag-scheitert-an-notwendiger-mehrheit/ (Accessed 26 June 2020).

Engelen, Ewald, Ismail Ertürk, Julie Froud, Sukhdev Johal, Adam Leaver, Mick Moran, Adriana Nilsson, and Karel William. 2011. *After the Great Complacence: Financial Crisis and the Politics of Reform.* Oxford and New York: Oxford University Press.

Englert, Mario R., Christopher Koch, and Jens Wüstemann. 2020. 'The Effects of Financial Crisis on the Organizational Reputation of Banks: An Empirical Analysis of Newspaper Articles'. *Business & Society* 59 (8): 1519–1553.

Epstein, Rachel A. 2017. *Banking on Markets: The Transformation of Bank–State Ties in Europe and Beyond.* Oxford and New York: Oxford University Press.

Erlebach, Jörg, Gerold Grasshoff, and Tobias Berg. 2010. 'Die Effekte von Basel III: Gleiche Bedingungen im Bank- und Handelsbuch?' *Die Bank* 10: 54–60.

European Commission. 2010. *Possible further changes to the capital requirements directive.* http://ec.europa.eu/internal_market/consultations/docs/2010/crd4/consultation_paper_en.pdf (Accessed 7 April 2014).

European Commission. 2011a. *Commission Staff Working Paper Impact Assessment. Accompanying the document Regulation of the European Parliament and the Council on prudential requirements for the credit institutions and investment firms (SEC(2011) 949 final.*

European Commission. 2011b. *Proposal for a regulation of the European Parliament and of the Council on prudential requirements for credit institutions and investment firms. Part III.* http://eur-lex.europa.eu/LexUriServ/LexUriServ.do?uri=COM:2011:0452:FIN:EN:PDF (Accessed 3 March 2014).

European Commission. 2011c. *Commission Staff Working Paper Impact Assessment. Accompanying the document Regulation of the European Parliament and the Council on prudential requirements for the credit institutions and investment firms.* SEC(2011) 949 final. http://ec.europa.eu/internal_market/bank/docs/regcapital/CRD4_reform/IA_reg-ulation_en.pdf (Accessed 11 July 2013).

European Commission. 2011d. *Proposal for a regulation of the European Parliament and of the Council on prudential requirements for credit institutions and investment firms. Part I.* http://eur-lex.europa.eu/LexUriServ/LexUriServ.do?uri=COM:2011:0452:FIN:EN:PDF (Accessed 3 March 2014).

European Commission. 2013a. *SBA Fact Sheet France.* http://ec.europa.eu/enterprise/policies/sme/facts-figures-analysis/performance-review/files/countries-sheets/2013/france_en.pdf (Accessed 31 May 2014).

European Commission. 2013b. *SBA Fact Sheet Germany.* http://ec.europa.eu/enterprise/policies/sme/facts-figures-analysis/performance-review/files/countries-sheets/2013/germany_en.pdf (Accessed 31 May 2014).

European Council. 2012. *Report from Presidency to Permanent Representatives Committee (Part 2).* http://register.consilium.europa.eu/doc/srv?l=EN&f=ST%208879%202012%20INIT (Accessed 2 August 2014).

European Council. 2013. *Statements on the adoption of the legislative act.* http://register.consilium.europa.eu/doc/srv?l=EN&t=PDF&gc=true&sc=false&f=ST%2010853%202013%20ADD%201 (Accessed 23 March 2014).

European Parliament. 2010. *European Parliament resolution of 7 October 2010 on Basel II and revision of the Capital Requirements Directives.* http://www.europarl.europa.eu/sides/getDoc.do?pubRef=-//EP//NONSGML+TA+P7-TA-2010-0354+0+DOC+PDF+V0//EN (Accessed 17 March 2014).

European Parliament. 2012. *Report on the proposal for a regulation of the European Parliament and of the Council on prudential requirements for credit institutions and investment firms: Amendments by the European Parliament to the Commission Proposal.* http://www.europarl.europa.eu/sides/getDoc.do?pubRef=-//EP//NONSGML+REPORT+A7-2012-0171+0+DOC+PDF+V0//EN (Accessed 2 August 2014).

Fabra, Paul. 1985. 'Banking Policy under the Socialists'. In *Economic Policy and Policy-Making under the Mitterrand Presidency, 1981–1984*, eds. Howard Machin and Vincent Wright. London: Pinter, 173–83.

Fay, Sophie. 2019. 'CAC 40: Que les gros contribuables lèvent le doigt!' *L'Obs*, 2 July, 36–40.

FBF. 2010. *Response to the public consultation on the capital requirement directive ('CRD IV').* http://ec.europa.eu/internal_market/consultations/2010/crd4_en.htm (Accessed 7 April 2014).

FFSA. 2013. Overview of the French market of direct SME lending. Unpublished presentation.

Figueiredo, John de, and Brian Richer. 2013. *Advancing Empirical Research on Lobbying.* NBER Working Paper, 19698.

Financial Stability Board. 2018. *Implementation and Effects of the G20 Financial Regulatory Reforms: 4th Annual Report.*

FMSA. 2016. *Historischer Überblick über die Maßnahmen des SoFFin.* https://www.fmsa.de/de/oeffentlichkeit/c_soffin/ (Accessed 26 October 2017).

Foote, Christopher, Kristopher Gerardi, and Paul Willen. 2012. *Why Did So Many People Make So Many Ex Post Bad Decisions? The Causes of the Foreclosure Crisis.* Federal Reserve Bank of Atlanta Working Paper Series, 2012–07.

Forbes, William, Sheila O. Donohoe, and Jörg Prokop. 2015. 'Financial Regulation, Collective Cognition, and Nation State Crisis Management'. *The Journal of Risk Finance* 16 (3): 284–302.

Forissier, Nicolas. 2009. *Rapport d'information relatif au financement en fonds propres des PME.* Assemblée nationale 1547. http://www.assemblee-nationale.fr/13/rap-info/i1547.asp (Accessed 10 February 2014).

Franke, Günter. 2000. *Deutsche Finanzmarktregulierung nach dem Zweiten Weltkrieg zwischen Risikoschutz und Wettbewerbssicherung.* CoFE Diskussionspapiere, 2000/31. http://nbn-resolving.de/urn:nbn:de:bsz:352-opus-5811 (Accessed 4 August 2012).

Friderichs, Hans, Bernard Paranque, and Annie Sauvé. 1999. 'Structures de financement des entreprises en France et en Allemagne: influence des facteurs institutionnels'. In *Modes de financement des entreprises allemandes et françaises: Projet de recherche commun de la Deutsche Bundesbank et de la Banque de France*, eds. Annie Sauvé and Manfred Scheuer. Paris and Frankfurt am Main: Banque de France and Deutsche Bundesbank, 47–122.

Frieden, Jeffry A. 1991. 'Invested Interests: The Politics of National Economic Policies in a World of Global Finance'. *International Organization* 45 (4): 425–51.

Frieden, Jeffry A. 1999. 'Actors and Preferences in International Relations'. In *Strategic Choice and International Relations*, eds. David A. Lake and Robert Powell. Princeton, NJ: Princeton University Press, 39–76.

Froud, Julie, Michael Moran, Adriana Nilsson, and Karel Williams. 2010. 'Wasting a Crisis? Democracy and Markets in Britain after 2007'. *Political Quarterly* 81 (1): 25–38.

Froud, Julie, Adriana Nilsson, Michael Moran, and Karel Williams. 2012. 'Stories and Interests in Finance: Agendas of Governance before and after the Financial Crisis'. *Governance* 25 (1): 35–59.

G20. 2008. *Declaration of the Summit on Financial Markets and the World Economy, November 15, 2008, Washington DC.* http://www.g20.utoronto.ca/2008/2008declaration 1115.html (Accessed 26 February 2012).

G20. 2009. *Declaration on Strengthening the Financial System. London Summit, 2 April 2009.* http://www.g20.utoronto.ca/summits/2009london.html (Accessed 28 February 2014).

G20. 2010. *The Seoul Summit Document. November 12, 2010.* http://www.g20.utoronto.ca/summits/2010seoul.html (Accessed 28 February 2014).

Gabrielli, Daniel. 2007. 'L'accès des PME aux financements bancaires'. In *Petites et moyennes entreprises. Bulletin de la Banque de France*. Numéro spécial, 21–9.

Gammelin, Cerstin. 2018. 'Jede Familie zahlt 3000 Euro für Finanzkrise'. *Sz.de*, 12 September. https://www.sueddeutsche.de/wirtschaft/finanzkrise-kosten-deutschland-1.4126273 (Accessed 13 August 2020).

Ganderson, Joseph. 2020. 'To Change Banks or Bankers? Systemic Political (In)action and Post-Crisis Banking Reform in the UK and the Netherlands'. *Business and Politics* 22 (1): 196–223.

Garabedian, Alexandre. 2013. 'BNP Paribas et Tikehau sont les premiers gagnants des fonds PME de Place'. *Agefi Quotidien*, 11 July. http://www.agefi.fr/articles/bnp-paribas-et-tikehau-sont-les-premiers-gagnants-des-fonds-pme-de-place-1276779.html (Accessed 21 February 2014).

Gardiner, Ben, Ron Martin, and Peter Tyler. 2012. *Spatially Unbalanced Growth in the British Economy*. Working Paper CGER, 1. Centre for Geographical Economic Research.

Garrouste, Frédérique. 2012. 'Micado, premier fonds d'obligations midcaps, touche au but'. *Agefi Hebdo*, 12 April. http://www.agefi.fr/articles/micado-premier-fonds-d-obligations-midcaps-touche-au-but-1218888.html (Accessed 17 February 2014).

GBC Investments. 2012. *GBC Best of m:access II.2012.* http://www.gbc-ag.de/ (Accessed 2 March 2014).

Geiß, Stefan. 2013. 'Entwicklung und Wettbewerb der Deutungsmuster. Konkurrierende Frames und Deutungshoheit in der Krisenberichterstattung'. In *Lehman Brothers und die Folgen*, eds. Oliver Quiring, Hans M. Kepplinger, Mathias Weber, and Stefan Geiß. Wiesbaden: Springer VS, 153–83.

Genders, Sascha. 2013. *Basel III—Auswirkungen auf den Mittelstand in Mainfranken aus Sicht von Unternehmen und Banken*. Schriftenreihe der IHK Würzburg-Schweinfurt, 35.

http://www.wuerzburg.ihk.de/fileadmin/user_upload/pdf/Existenzgruendung/5969_ Basel_III_lowres.pdf (Accessed 19 March 2014).

George, Alexander L., and Andrew Bennett. 2005. *Case Studies and Theory Development in the Social Sciences*. Cambridge, MA: MIT Press.

Gerken, Arno, Frank Guse, Matthias Heuser, Davide Monguzzi, Olivier Planteve, and Thomas Poppensieker. 2013. *Between Deluge and Drought: The Divided Future of European Bank-Funding Markets*. McKinsey Working Papers on Risk, 41. http://www.mckinsey.com/client_service/risk/latest_thinking (Accessed 9 April 2014).

Germain, Randall D. 1997. *The International Organization of Credit: States and Global Finance in the World-Economy*. Cambridge and New York: Cambridge University Press.

Gerring, John. 2007. *Case Study Research: Principles and Practices*. Cambridge: Cambridge University Press.

Gerschenkron, Alexander. 1962. *Economic Backwardness in Historical Perspective: A Book of Essays*. Cambridge, MA: Belknap Press of Harvard University Press.

Giami, Thierry. 2011. *Rapport annuel 2010 de l'Observatoire du financement des entreprises par le marché*. http://www.pme-bourse.fr/fileadmin/medias/Rapport_annuel/2010_Rapport_Observatoire_200611.pdf (Accessed 17 February 2014).

Giami, Thierry. 2013. *Rapport annuel 2012 de l'Observatoire du financement des entreprises par le marché*. http://www.pme-bourse.fr/fileadmin/medias/Rapport_annuel/Rapport_Observatoire_version_finale.pdf (Accessed 17 February 2014).

Giami, Thierry, and Marc Lefèvre. 2009. *Faciliter l'accès au marché des petites et moyennes entreprises à la recherche de capitaux*. CDC and NYSE Euronext. http://www.pme-bourse.fr/publications/etudes-et-rapports.html (Accessed 10 February 2014).

Goldstein, Judith, and Robert O. Keohane, eds. 1993a. *Ideas and Foreign Policy: Beliefs, Institutions, and Political Change*. Ithaca, NY: Cornell University Press.

Goldstein, Judith, and Robert O. Keohane. 1993b. 'Ideas and Foreign Policy: An Analytical Framework'. In *Ideas and Foreign Policy: Beliefs, Institutions, and Political Change*, eds. Judith Goldstein and Robert O. Keohane. Ithaca, NY: Cornell University Press, 3–30.

Goodhart, Charles A. 2010. 'How Should We Regulate Bank Capital and Financial Products? What Role for "Living Wills"?' In *The Future of Finance: The LSE Report*. London: LSE, 165–86.

Gräf, Bernhard. 2009. *Die internationale Finanzkrise: Ursachen, Ausprägungen und Ausblick*. Frankfurt: DB Research.

Granovetter, Mark. 1985. 'Economic Action and Social Structure: The Problem of Embeddedness'. *The American Journal of Sociology* 91 (3): 481–510.

Griffith-Jones, Stephany, José Ocampo, and Ariane Ortiz. 2009. Building on the Counter-Cyclical Consensus: A Policy Agenda. Paper prepared for the High-level Roundtable in Brussels on October 12, 2009, Towards Basel III? Regulating the Banking Sector after the Crisis. http://www.stephanygj.net/papers/Counter-Cyclical-Regulation.pdf (Accessed 13 August 2020).

Grossman, Emiliano. 2006. 'Europeanization as an Interactive Process: German Public Banks Meet EU State Aid Policy'. *JCMS: Journal of Common Market Studies* 44 (2): 325–48.

Grossman, Emiliano, and Patrick Leblond. 2011. 'European Financial Integration: Finally the Great Leap Forward?' *JCMS: Journal of Common Market Studies* 49 (2): 413–35.

Grossman, Richard. 2010. *Unsettled Account: The Evolution of Banking in the Industrialized World since 1800*. Princeton, NJ: Princeton University Press.

Guinnane, Timothy. 2002. 'Delegated Monitors, Large and Small: Germany's Banking System, 1800–1914'. *Journal of Economic Literature* 40 (March): 73–124.

Guinouard, François, Elisabeth Kremp, and Marina Randriamisaina. 2013. 'Accès au crédit des PME et ETI: fléchissement de l'offre ou moindre demande? Les enseignements d'une nouvelle enquête trimestrielle auprès des entreprises'. *Bulletin de la Banque de France* 192: 35–44.

Guyony, Sylvie, and Frédérique Garrouste. 2013. 'Liquidité bancaire – Les grands travaux'. *Agefi Hebdo*, 25 March. http://www.agefi.fr/articles/liquidite-bancaire-les-grands-travaux-1269755.html (Accessed 8 April 2014).

Haas, Peter M. 1992. 'Introduction: Epistemic Communities and International Policy Coordination'. *International Organization* 46 (1): 1–35.

Hackethal, Andreas. 2004. 'German Banks and Banking Structure'. In *The German Financial System*, eds. Jan P. Krahnen and Reinhard H. Schmidt. Oxford and New York: Oxford University Press, 71–105.

Haldane, Andrew, Simon Brennan, and Vasileios Madouros. 2010. 'What Is the Contribution of the Financial Sector: Miracle or Mirage?' In *The Future of Finance: The LSE Report*. London: LSE, 87–120.

Haldane, Andrew G., and Robert M. May. 2011. 'Systemic Risk in Banking Ecosystems'. *Nature* 469 (7330): 351–5.

Hall, Peter A. 1986. *Governing the Economy: The Politics of State Intervention in Britain and France*. New York: Oxford University Press.

Hall, Peter A. 1989. 'Conclusion: The Politics of Keynesian Ideas'. In *The Political Power of Economic Ideas: Keynesianism Across Nations*, ed. Peter A. Hall. Princeton, NJ: Princeton University Press, 361–91.

Hall, Peter A. 1993. 'Policy Paradigms, Social Learning, and the State: The Case of Economic Policymaking in Britain'. *Comparative Politics* 25 (3): 275–96.

Hall, Peter A. 2008. 'Systematic Process Analysis: When and How to Use It'. *European Political Science* 7 (3): 304–17.

Hall, Peter A., and Daniel Gingerich. 2004. *Varieties of Capitalism and Institutional Complementarities in the Macroeconomy: An Empirical Analysis*. MPIfG Discussion Paper, 04/5. http://www.mpifg.de/pu/mpifg_dp/dp04-5.pdf (Accessed 4 August 2012).

Hall, Peter A., and David W. Soskice. 2001a. 'An Introduction to Varieties of Capitalism'. In *Varieties of Capitalism: The Institutional Foundations of Comparative Advantage*, eds. Peter A. Hall and David W. Soskice. Oxford and New York: Oxford University Press, 1–70.

Hall, Peter A., and David W. Soskice, eds. 2001b. *Varieties of Capitalism: The Institutional Foundations of Comparative Advantage*. Oxford and New York: Oxford University Press.

Hall, Peter A., and Kathleen A. Thelen. 2009. 'Institutional Change in Varieties of Capitalism'. *Socio-Economic Review* 7 (1): 7–34.

Hall, Richard, and Alan Deardorff. 2006. 'Lobbying as Legislative Subsidy'. *American Political Science Review* 100 (1): 69–84.

Hall, Richard L., and Frank W. Wayman. 1990. 'Buying Time: Moneyed Interests and the Mobilization of Bias in Congressional Committees'. *The American Political Science Review* 84 (3): 797–820.

Hallerberg, Mark, and Jonas Markgraf. 2018. 'The Corporate Governance of Public Banks before and after the Global Financial Crisis'. *Global Policy* 9 (2): 43–53.

Handke, Stefan, and Hubert Zimmermann. 2012. 'Institutional Change in German Financial Regulation'. In *Crisis and Control: Institutional Change in Financial Market Regulation*, ed. Renate Mayntz. Frankfurt am Main: Campus Verlag, 119–42.

Hanke, Thomas. 2013. 'Den Mittelstand im Blick'. *Handelsblatt*, 2 March, 32.

Hardie, Iain, and David Howarth. 2009. 'Die Krise but not La Crise? The Financial Crisis and the Transformation of German and French Banking Systems'. *JCMS: Journal of Common Market Studies* 47 (5): 1017–39.

Hardie, Iain, and David Howarth. 2013a. 'A Peculiar Kind of Devastation: German Market-Based Banking'. In *Market-Based Banking and the International Financial Crisis*, eds. Iain Hardie and David Howarth. Oxford: Oxford University Press, 103–24.

Hardie, Iain, and David Howarth, eds. 2013b. *Market-Based Banking and the International Financial Crisis*. Oxford: Oxford University Press.

Hardie, Iain, David Howarth, Sylvia Maxfield, and Amy Verdun. 2013. 'Banks and the False Dichotomy in the Comparative Political Economy of Finance'. *World Politics* 65 (4): 691–728.

Hardie, Iain, and Huw Macartney. 2016. 'EU Ring-Fencing and the Defence of Too-Big-to-Fail Banks'. *West European Politics* 39 (3): 503–25.

Hau, Harald, and Marcel Thum. 2009. 'Subprime Crisis and Board (In-)competence: Private versus Public Banks in Germany'. *Economic Policy* 24 (60): 701–52.

Hautcœur, Pierre-Cyrille, Paul Lagneau-Ymonet, and Angelo Riva. 2011. 'Finance et économie réelle. Les marchés financiers français: une perspective historique'. *Cahiers français* 361: 8–12.

Hautefeuille, Arnould, and Abderrahim Doulazmi. 2009. *Des PME aux ETI: quels financements alternatifs pour les entreprises?* Chambre de Commerce de l'Industrie de Paris. http://www.etudes.cci-paris-idf.fr/rapport/102 (Accessed 7 February 2014).

Hay, Colin. 1996. 'Narrating Crisis: The Discursive Construction of the "Winter of Discontent"'. *Sociology* 30 (2): 253–77.

Hay, Colin. 1999. 'Crisis and the Structural Transformation of the State: Interrogating the Process of Change'. *The British Journal of Politics and International Relations* 1 (3): 317–44.

Hay, Colin. 2010. 'Ideas and the Construction of Interests'. In *Ideas and Politics in Social Science Research*, eds. Daniel Béland and Robert H. Cox. Oxford and New York: Oxford University Press, 65–82.

Hay, Colin. 2020. 'Does Capitalism (Still) Come in Varieties?' *Review of International Political Economy* 27 (2): 302–19.

Hayward, Jack. 1986. *The State and the Market Economy: Industrial Patriotism and Economic Intervention in France*. Brighton: Wheatsheaf Books.

HCSF. 2019. *Rapport annuel 2019 du Haut Conseil de Stabilité Financière*. Paris.

Heclo, Hugh. 1974. *Modern Social Politics in Britain and Sweden: From Relief to Income Maintenance*. New Haven: Yale University Press.

Helleiner, Eric. 1994a. 'Freeing Money: Why Have States Been More Willing to Liberalize Capital Controls than Trade Barriers?' *Policy Sciences* 27 (4): 299–318.

Helleiner, Eric. 1994b. *States and the Reemergence of Global Finance: From Bretton Woods to the 1990s*. Ithaca, NY: Cornell University Press.

Helleiner, Eric. 2014. *The Status Quo Crisis: Global Financial Governance after the 2008 Financial Meltdown*. Oxford and New York: Oxford University Press.

Hellwig, Martin. 2008. *Systemic Risk in the Financial Sector: An Analysis of the Subprime-Mortgage Financial Crisis*. Preprints of the Max Planck Institute for Research on Collective Goods, 2008/43.

Hellwig, Martin. 2010. *Capital Regulation after the Crisis: Business as Usual?* Preprints of the Max Planck Institute for Research on Collective Goods Bonn, 2010/31. http://www.coll.mpg.de/pdf_dat/2010_31online.pdf (Accessed 4 December 2012).

Hellwig, Martin. 2018. *Germany and the Financial Crises 2007–2017: Paper presented at the 4th Annual Macroprudential Conference of the Swedish Riksbank, June 2018*. https://www.riksbank.se/globalassets/media/konferenser/2018/germany-and-financial-crises-2007-2017.pdf (Accessed 24 July 2020).

Helmke, Gretchen, and Steven Levitsky. 2004. 'Informal Institutions and Comparative Politics: A Research Agenda'. *Perspectives on Politics* 2 (4): 725–40.

Hirschman, Albert O. 1970. *Exit, Voice, and Loyalty: Responses to Decline in Firms, Organizations, and States*. Cambridge, MA: Harvard University Press.

Hollande, François. 2012. *Discours du Bourget.* https://www.nouvelobs.com/election-presidentielle-2012/sources-brutes/20120122.OBS9488/l-integralite-du-discours-de-francois-hollande-au-bourget.html (Accessed 13 August 2020).

Höpner, Martin, and Lothar Krempel. 2003. *The Politics of the German Company Network.* MPIfG Working Paper, 03/9. http://www.mpi-fg-koeln.mpg.de/pu/workpap/wp03-9/wp03-9.html (Accessed 2 August 2014).

Howarth, David. 2013. 'France and the International Financial Crisis: The Legacy of State-Led Finance'. *Governance* 26 (3): 369–95.

Howarth, David, and Scott James. 2020. 'The Politics of Bank Structural Reform: Business Power and Agenda Setting in the United Kingdom, France, and Germany'. *Business and Politics* 22 (1): 25–51.

Howarth, David, and Lucia Quaglia. 2013. 'Banking on Stability: The Political Economy of New Capital Requirements in the European Union'. *Journal of European Integration* 35 (3): 333–46.

Hüfner, Felix. 2010. *The German Banking System: Lessons from the Financial Crisis.* OECD Economics Department Working Papers, 788. http://dx.doi.org/10.1787/5kmbm80pjkd6-en (Accessed 4 August 2012).

Hugo, Victor. 2010 [1877]. *Histoire d'un crime: Déposition d'un témoin.* Paris: La fabrique.

Hungin, Harpal, and Scott James. 2018. 'Central Bank Reform and the Politics of Blame Avoidance in the UK'. *New Political Economy* 24 (3): 334–49.

Hunt, Tristram, ed. 2013. *Rebalancing the British Economy.* London: Civitas: Institute for the Study of Civil Society.

Hunter, Julie, Paul Linden-Retek, Sirine Shebaya, and Samuel Halpert. 2014. *Welcome Home: The Rise of Tent Cities in the United States.* Yale Law School and the National Law Center on Homelessness and Poverty. https://www.homelesshub.ca/resource/welcome-home-rise-tent-cities-united-state (Accessed 13 August 2020).

Hüther, Michael, Manfred Jäger, Martin Hellwig, and Thomas Hartmann-Wendels. 2009. *Arbeitsweise der Bankenaufsicht vor dem Hintergrund der Finanzmarktkrise: Gutachten im Auftrag des Bundesfinanzministeriums.* Forschungsberichte aus dem Institut der Deutschen Wirtschaft Köln, 63.

Igan, Deniz, and Thomas Lambert. 2019. 'Bank Lobbying: Regulatory Capture and Beyond'. In *The Political Economy of Financial Regulation*, eds. Emilios Avgouleas and David C. Donald. Cambridge and New York: Cambridge University Press, 129–59.

IMF. 2009. *France. Selected Issues.* IMF Country Report No. 09/233. http://www.imf.org/external/pubs/ft/scr/2009/cr09233.pdf (Accessed 4 August 2012).

Immergut, Ellen M. 1992. *Health Politics: Interests and Institutions in Western Europe.* Cambridge and New York: Cambridge University Press.

Insurance Europe, and Oliver Wyman. 2013. *Funding the Future: Insurers' Role as Institutional Investors.* http://www.insuranceeurope.eu/uploads/Modules/Publications/funding-the-future.pdf (Accessed 21 February 2014).

Jabko, Nicolas. 2012. 'International Radicalism, Domestic Conformism: France's Ambiguous Stance on Financial Reforms'. In *Crisis and Control: Institutional Change in Financial Market Regulation*, ed. Renate Mayntz. Frankfurt am Main: Campus Verlag, 97–118.

Jabko, Nicolas, and Elsa Massoc. 2012. 'French Capitalism under Stress: How Nicolas Sarkozy Rescued the Banks'. *Review of International Political Economy* 19 (4): 562–85.

Jackson, Gregory. 2010. 'Actors and Institutions'. In *The Oxford Handbook of Comparative Institutional Analysis*, eds. Glenn Morgan, John L. Campbell, Colin Crouch, Ove Pedersen, and Richard Whitley. Oxford and New York: Oxford University Press, 63–86.

Jackson, Gregory, and Richard Deeg. 2006. *How Many Varieties of Capitalism? Comparing the Comparative Institutional Analyses of Capitalist Diversity.* MPIfG Discussion Paper, 06/2. http://www.mpifg.de/pu/mpifg_dp/dp06-2.pdf (Accessed 4 August 2012).

Jackson, Gregory, and Richard Deeg. 2008. 'From Comparing Capitalisms to the Politics of Institutional Change'. *Review of International Political Economy* 15 (4): 680–709.

Jacobs, Alan. 2014. 'Process Tracing the Effects of Ideas'. In *Process Tracing: From Metaphor to Analytic Tool*, eds. Andrew Bennett and Jeffrey T. Checkel. Cambridge: Cambridge University Press, 41–73.

Jacobsen, John K. 1995. 'Much Ado About Ideas: The Cognitive Factor in Economic Policy'. *World Politics* 47 (2): 283–310.

James, Scott. 2016. 'The Domestic Politics of Financial Regulation: Informal Ratification Games and the EU Capital Requirement Negotiations'. *New Political Economy* 21 (2): 187–203.

James, Scott, and Lucia Quaglia. 2020. *The UK and Multi-Level Financial Regulation: From Post-Crisis Reform to Brexit*. Oxford: Oxford University Press.

Jervis, Robert. 1976. *Perception and Misperception in International Politics*. Princeton, NJ: Princeton University Press.

Jessop, Bob. 2014. 'Variegated Capitalism, das Modell Deutschland, and the Eurozone Crisis'. *Journal of Contemporary European Studies* 22 (3): 248–60.

Joint Economic Committee. 1976. *A Symposium on the 40th Anniversary of the Joint Economic Committee*. US Congress, Washington, DC.

Kadushin, Charles. 1995. 'Friendship Among the French Financial Elite'. *American Sociological Review* 60 (2): 202–21.

Kahneman, Daniel, Paul Slovic, and Amos Tversky, eds. 1982. *Judgment Under Uncertainty: Heuristics and Biases*. Cambridge and New York: Cambridge University Press.

Kaminsky, Graciela L., and Carmen M. Reinhart. 1999. 'The Twin Crises: The Causes of Banking and Balance-of-Payments Problems'. *American Economic Review* 89 (3): 473–500.

Kapstein, Ethan B. 1989. 'Resolving the Regulator's Dilemma: International Coordination of Banking Regulations'. *International Organization* 43 (2): 323–47.

Kapstein, Ethan B. 1994. *Governing the Global Economy: International Finance and the State*. Cambridge, MA: Harvard University Press.

Karas, Othmar. 2010. 'Basel III kommt: Und das Europäische Parlament gestaltet mit'. *Der Wirtschaftstreuhänder* 5–6: 12–13.

Karas, Othmar. 2012. *Basel III/CRD 4: Banken stabilisieren und Wachstum finanzieren*. http://arc.eppgroup.eu/press/showpr.asp?prcontroldoctypeid=1&prcontrolid=11181&prcontentid=18693&prcontentlg=de (Accessed 17 March 2014).

Kastner, Lisa. 2017. 'Tracing Policy Influence of Diffuse Interests: The Post-Crisis Consumer Finance Protection Politics in the US'. *Journal of Civil Society* 13 (2): 130–48.

Kay, John. 2010. 'Should We Have "Narrow Banking"?' In *The Future of Finance: The LSE Report*. London: LSE, 217–34.

Keller, Eileen. 2014. 'Negotiating the Future of Banking: The Coalitional Dynamics of Collective Preference Formation in France and Germany after the Crisis'. Dissertation, Humboldt-Universität zu Berlin.

Keller, Eileen. 2018. 'Noisy Business Politics: Lobbying Strategies and Business Influence after the Financial Crisis'. *Journal of European Public Policy* 25 (3): 287–306.

Keller, Eileen. 2019. 'Relationship Banking: An "Endangered Species"? Evidence from Germany'. In *The Making of Finance: Perspectives from the Social Sciences*, eds. Isabelle Chambost, Marc Lenglet, and Yamina Tadjeddine. London: Routledge, 152–60.

Keohane, Robert O. 1984. *After Hegemony: Cooperation and Discord in the World Political Economy*. Princeton, NJ: Princeton University Press.

Kertzer, Joshua D., and Dustin Tingley. 2018. 'Political Psychology in International Relations: Beyond the Paradigms'. *Annual Review of Political Science* 21 (1): 319–39.

Kindleberger, Charles. 1984. *A Financial History of Western Europe*. London: Allen & Unwin.

Kindleberger, Charles P., and Robert Z. Aliber. 2005. *Manias, Panics and Crashes: A History of Financial Crises*. 5th ed. New York: Palgrave Macmillan.

Kingdon, John W. 1995. *Agendas, Alternatives, and Public Policies*. 2nd ed. New York: HarperCollins.

Kitschelt, Herbert, Peter Lange, Gary Marks, and John Stephens, eds. 1999. *Continuity and Change in Contemporary Capitalism*. Cambridge: Cambridge University Press.

Knight, Frank H. 1921. *Risk, Uncertainty, and Profit: A Thesis Presented to the Faculty of the Graduate School of Cornell University for the Degree of Doctor of Philosophy*. Boston and New York: Houghton Mifflin Company.

Krahnen, Jan P., and Reinhard H. Schmidt. 2004. 'Taking Stock and Looking Ahead: The German Financial System at the Crossroads'. In *The German Financial System*, eds. Jan P. Krahnen and Reinhard H. Schmidt. Oxford and New York: Oxford University Press, 485–514.

Krämer-Eis, Helmut, Claudia Schneider, and Christoph Tiskens. 2001. 'Die Verbriefung von Mittelstandskrediten durch die KfW'. *Beiträge zur Mittelstands- und Strukturpolitik* 16: 24–30.

Krasner, Stephen D., ed. 1983. *International Regimes*. Ithaca, NY: Cornell University Press.

Kremp, Elisabeth, and Claude Piot. 2014. 'Le ralentissement du crédit bancaire aux PME en France'. *Revue d'économie financière* 114: 91–103.

Kremp, Elisabeth, and Patrick Sevestre. 2013. 'Did the Crisis Induce Credit Rationing for French SMEs?' *Journal of Banking & Finance* 37 (10): 3757–72.

Krüger, Markus. 2011. *Wirtschaftsfonds Deutschland nur wenig genutzt*. BI Bankinformation. https://www.bankinformation.de/index.php?option=com_content&view=article&id=336:wirtschaftsfonds-deutschland-nur-wenig-genutzt&catid=27:aus-der-branche&Itemid=144 (Accessed 16 August 2014).

Krugman, Paul R. 2009. *The Return of Depression Economics and the Crisis of 2008*. New York: W. W. Norton.

Kwak, James. 2014. 'Cultural Capture and the Financial Crisis'. In *Preventing Regulatory Capture: Special Interest Influence and How to Limit It*, eds. Daniel P. Carpenter and David A. Moss. New York: Cambridge University Press, 71–98.

La Porta, Rafael, Florencio Lopez-de-Silanes, Andrei Shleifer, and Robert Vishny. 1996. *Law and Finance*. NBER Working Paper, 5661. http://piketty.pse.ens.fr/files/LaPortaetal1998.pdf (Accessed 30 June 2014).

La Porta, Rafael, Florencio Lopez-de-Silanes, Andrei Shleifer, and Robert Vishny. 1997. 'Legal Determinants of External Finance'. *The Journal of Finance* 52 (3): 1131–50.

Lacoue-Labarthe, Dominique. 2001. *Les banques en France: Privatisation, restructuration, consolidation*. Paris: Economica.

Lacroix, Renaud, and Jérémi Montoronès. 2009. 'Analyse de la portée des résultats du Bank Lending Survey au regard des données de crédit'. *Bulletin de la Banque de France* 178 (4): 21–33.

Laeven, Luc, and Fabian Valencia. 2010. *Resolution of Banking Crises: The Good, the Bad, and the Ugly*. IMF Working Paper, WP/10/146. http://www.imf.org/external/pubs/ft/wp/2010/wp10146.pdf (Accessed 4 August 2012).

Lagarde, Christine. 2009. *Faciliter l'accès au marché des petites et moyennes entreprises à la recherche de capitaux: Dossier de presse*. Minefi. http://www.economie.gouv.fr/files/finances/presse/dossiers_de_presse/091012pme_capitaux.pdf (Accessed 13 February 2014).

Lambert, Alain. 1996. *Banques: votre santé nous intéresse*. Commission des Finances du Sénat. Rapport 52. http://www.senat.fr/rap/r96-52/r96-52_mono.html#toc19 (Accessed 12 March 2013).

Landrot, Antoine. 2012. 'Le superviseur français s'inquiète de dérives sur la transposition de Bâle 3'. *Agefi Quotidien*, 28 June. http://www.agefi.fr/articles/le-superviseur-francais-s-inquiete-de-derives-sur-la-transposition-de-bale-3-1229775.html (Accessed 2 August 2014).

Lane, Christel, and Geoffrey Wood. 2009. 'Capitalist Diversity and Diversity within Capitalism'. *Economy and Society* 38 (4): 531–51.

Lane, Christel, and Geoffrey Wood, eds. 2012. *Capitalist Diversity and Diversity within Capitalism*. London and New York: Routledge.

Lanxade, Thibault. 2011. *Small Business Act: Propositions du MEDEF pour aller plus loin en Europe et en France*. Medef. http://www.thibaultlanxade.com/files/medef_small_business_act_janvier_2012.pdf (Accessed 13 February 2014).

Le Monde.fr. 2010. 'Les banques s'engagent sur 96 milliards d'euros de credit pour les PME'. 6 March. http://www.lemonde.fr/economie/article/2010/03/05/les-banquiers-a-nouveau-attendus-a-l-elysee_1314699_3234.html (Accessed 10 February 2014).

Les Echos. 2008. 'Les banques françaises face aux critiques'. 12 November, 30.

Lieberson, Stanley. 1991. 'Small N's and Big Conclusions: An Examination of the Reasoning in Comparative Studies Based on a Small Number of Cases'. *Social Forces* 70 (2): 307–20.

Liebert, Christian. 2009. 'Credit Mediation'. *Banque de France—Quarterly Selection of Articles* 16: 83–96.

Lindblom, Charles E. 1977. *Politics and Markets: The World's Political Economic Systems*. New York: Basic Books.

Loriaux, Michael. 1991. *France after Hegemony: International Change and Financial Reform*. Ithaca, NY: Cornell University Press.

Lund, Susan, Asheet Mehta, James Manyika, and Diana Goldshtein. 2019. *A Decade after the Global Financial Crisis: What Has (and Hasn't) Changed?* McKinsey. https://www.mckinsey.com/industries/financial-services/our-insights/a-decade-after-the-global-financial-crisis-what-has-and-hasnt-changed#part1 (Accessed 5 August 2020).

Lütz, Susanne. 2002. *Der Staat und die Globalisierung von Finanzmärkten: Regulative Politik in Deutschland, Großbritannien und den USA*. Frankfurt: Campus Verlag.

Lütz, Susanne. 2003. *Convergence within National Diversity: A Comparative Perspective on the Regulatory State in Finance*. MPIfG Discussion Paper, 03/7. http://www.mpifg.de/pu/mpifg_dp/dp03-7.pdf (Accessed 4 August 2012).

Macartney, Huw. 2009. 'Variegated Neo-Liberalism: Transnationally Oriented Fractions of Capital in EU Financial Market Integration'. *Review of International Studies* 35 (2): 451–80.

Macartney, Huw, David Howarth, and Scott James. 2020. 'Bank Power and Public Policy since the Financial Crisis'. *Business and Politics* 22 (1): 1–24.

McCarty, Nolan. 2014. 'Complexity, Capacity, and Capture'. In *Preventing Regulatory Capture: Special Interest Influence and How to Limit It*, eds. Daniel P. Carpenter and David A. Moss. New York: Cambridge University Press, 99–123.

Mahoney, James, and Kathleen A. Thelen, eds. 2010. *Explaining Institutional Change: Ambiguity, Agency, and Power in Historical Institutionalism*. Cambridge: Cambridge University Press.

March, James G. 1994. *A Primer on Decision Making: How Decisions Happen*. New York: Free Press.

Massoc, Elsa. 2018. 'Banking on States: Divergent European Trajectories of Finance after the Crisis'. Dissertation, University of California.

Massoc, Elsa. 2020. 'Banks, Power, and Political Institutions: The Divergent Priorities of European States towards "Too-Big-to-Fail" Banks: The Cases of Competition in Retail Banking and the Banking Structural Reform'. *Business and Politics* 22 (1): 135–60.

Mayer, Chris, Karen Pence, and Shane M. Sherlund. 2008. *The Rise in Mortgage Defaults*. Washington: Federal Reserve Board. Finance and Economics Discussion Series, 2008–59. https://www.federalreserve.gov/pubs/feds/2008/200859/200859pap.pdf (Accessed 13 August 2020).

Mayer, Colin, Stefano Micossi, Marco Onado, Marco Pagano, and Andrea Polo, eds. 2018. *Finance and Investment: The European Case*. Oxford: Oxford University Press.

Mayntz, Renate, ed. 2012a. *Crisis and Control: Institutional Change in Financial Market Regulation*. Frankfurt am Main: Campus Verlag.

Mayntz, Renate. 2012b. 'Institutional Change in the Regulation of Financial Markets: Questions and Answers'. In *Crisis and Control: Institutional Change in Financial Market Regulation*, ed. Renate Mayntz. Frankfurt am Main: Campus Verlag, 7–28.

Mehta, Jal. 2010. 'The Varied Roles of Ideas in Politics: From "Whether" to "How"'. In *Ideas and Politics in Social Science Research*, eds. Daniel Béland and Robert H. Cox. Oxford and New York: Oxford University Press, 23–46.

Melitz, Jacques. 1990. 'Financial Deregulation in France'. *European Economic Review* 34: 394–402.

Michel, Anne. 2009. 'Crédit aux PME: le gouvernement fait pression sur les banques'. *Le Monde*, 15 September, 14.

Mill, John S. 1882. *A system of logic, ratiocinative and inductive: Being a connected view of the principles of evidence, and the methods of scientific investigation*. New York: Harper & Brothers.

Minefi. 2009. *Accord de place sur la médiation du crédit aux entreprises*. http://www.fbf.fr/fr/files/877DQR/Accord_place_mediation_credit_entreprises_2009.pdf (Accessed 6 February 2014).

Minefi, Banque de France, and ACP. 2010. *Response to European Commission's consultations paper on CRDIV*. http://ec.europa.eu/internal_market/consultations/2010/crd4_en.htm (Accessed 2 April 2014).

Moran, Michael. 1988. 'Thatcherism and Financial Regulation'. *The Political Quarterly* 59 (1): 20–7.

Moran, Michael. 1991. *The Politics of the Financial Services Revolution: The USA, UK, and Japan*. Basingstoke: Macmillan.

Moran, Michael. 1992. 'Regulatory Change in German Financial Markets'. In *The Politics of German Regulation*, ed. Kenneth Dyson. Aldershot and Brookfield, VT: Dartmouth, 137–58.

Moravcsik, Andrew. 1991. 'Negotiating the Single European Act: National Interests and Conventional Statecraft in the European Community'. *International Organization* 45 (1): 19–56.

Morgan, Glenn, Richard Whitley, and Eli Moen, eds. 2005. *Changing Capitalisms? Internationalism, Institutional Change, and Systems of Economic Organization*. Oxford: Oxford University Press.

Morin, François. 2000. 'A Transformation in the French Model of Shareholding and Management'. *Economy and Society* 29 (1): 36–53.

Morton, Rebecca, and Charles Cameron. 1992. 'Elections and the Theory of Campaign Contributions: A Survey and Critical Analysis'. *Economics and Politics* 4 (1): 79–108.

Moschella, Manuela, and Eleni Tsingou, eds. 2013. *Great Expectations, Slow Transformations: Incremental Change in Post-Crisis Regulation*. Colchester: ECPR Press.

Mügge, Daniel. 2010. *Widen the Market, Narrow the Competition: Banker Interests and the Making of a European Capital Market.* Colchester: ECPR Press.

Mügge, Daniel, and Bart Stellinga. 2010. 'Absent Alternatives and Insider Interests in Postcrisis Financial Reform'. *dms—der moderne staat—Zeitschrift für Public Policy, Recht und Management* 2: 321–38.

Nelson, Stephen C., and Peter J. Katzenstein. 2014. 'Uncertainty, Risk, and the Financial Crisis of 2008'. *International Organization* 68 (2): 361–92.

Nési, Christian. 2005. 'Modernisation du régime juridique français de la titrisation'. *Bulletin de la Banque de France* 133: 69–75.

Neukirchen, Eva. 2012. 'Kreditmediator macht sich überflüssig'. *WirtschaftsWoche*, 21 February. http://www.wiwo.de/unternehmen/mittelstand/mittelstand-kreditmediator-macht-sich-ueberfluessig-seite-all/6236044-all.html (Accessed 4 February 2014).

Nölke, Andreas. 2011. *Transnational Economic Order and National Economic Institutions: Comparative Capitalism Meets International Political Economy.* MPIfG Working Paper, 11/3. http://www.mpifg.de/pu/workpap/wp11-3.pdf (Accessed 4 August 2012).

Noyer, Christian. 1990. *Banques: La règle du jeu.* Paris: Dunod.

NYSE Euronext. 2012. *Pour la création de la 'Bourse de l'entreprise'. Projet d'orientation stratégique.* http://j7.agefi.fr/documents/liens/201207/04-MJCXHNCKBOBGWZN.pdf (Accessed 16 February 2014).

O'Sullivan, Mary. 2007. 'Acting Out Institutional Change: Understanding the Recent Transformation of the French Financial System'. *Socio-Economic Review* 5 (3): 389–436.

Pagliari, Stefano, and Kevin Young. 2013. 'Leveraged Interests: Financial Industry Power and the Role of Private Sector Coalitions'. *Review of International Political Economy* 21 (3): 575–610.

Panetta, Fabio, Thomas Faeh, Giuseppe Grande, Corrinne Ho, Michael King, Aviram Levy, Federico Signoretti, and Marco Taboga. 2009. *An Assessment of Financial Sector Rescue Programmes.* BIS Papers, 48. http://www.bis.org/publ/bppdf/bispap48.pdf (Accessed 6 August 2012).

Paris Europlace. 2012. *20 propositions pour relancer le financement de l'économie et la croissance durable: Livre blanc 2012–2015.* http://www.paris-europlace.net/files/Livre_Blanc_Paris_EUROPLACE_20-03-2012 (Accessed 10 February 2014).

Paris Europlace. 2013. *Financement des Entreprises et de l'Économie Française: pour un retour vers une croissance durable: Rapport du Groupe de travail FINECO.* http://www.paris-europlace.net/files/Rapport_FINECO_Paris_EUROPLACE.pdf (Accessed 7 February 2014).

Pastré, Olivier. 2006. *Les enjeux économiques et sociaux de l'industrie bancaire: Rapport réalisé sous l'égide du CCSF.* http://www.fbf.fr/fr/files/87ZK46/Rapport_pastre_ccsf_industrie_bancaire_2006.pdf (Accessed 12 February 2013).

Perez, Sofia A. 1998. 'Systemic Explanations, Divergent Outcomes: The Politics of Financial Liberalization in France and Spain'. *International Studies Quarterly* 42 (4): 755–84.

Pierson, Paul. 2000. 'Increasing Returns, Path Dependence, and the Study of Politics'. *The American Political Science Review* 94 (2): 251–67.

Pierson, Paul. 2004. *Politics in Time: History, Institutions, and Social Analysis.* Princeton, NJ: Princeton University Press.

Piliu, Fabien. 2011. 'Bercy veut ménager les PME inquiètes de l'accès au crédit'. *La Tribune*, 20 September, 2–3.

Pince, Arnaud, Oliver Hubert, and Yannick Le Gall. 2013. *Le Financement de l'économie par les assureurs et les nouveaux Fonds de Prêt à l'Economie (FPE).* Newsletter of the legal firm De Pardieu Brocas Maffei. http://www.de-pardieu.com/web/Vous-accompagner/

Les-publications/Le-Financement-de-l-economie-par-les-assureurs-et-les-nouveaux-Fonds-de-Pret-a-l-Economie-FPE (Accessed 21 February 2014).

Plattner, Dankwart. 2001. *Unternehmensfinanzierung im Umbruch. Die Finanzierungsperspektiven deutscher Unternehmen im Zeichen von Finanzmarktwandel und Basel II. Auswertung der Unternehmensbefragung 2001.* KfW. https://www.kfw.de/Download-Center/Konzernthemen/Research/PDF-Dokumente-Unternehmensbefragung/Unternehmensbefragung-2001-lang.pdf (Accessed 9 May 2013).

Plattner, Dankwart. 2002. *Unternehmensfinanzierung in schwierigem Fahrwasser. Wachsende Finanzierungsprobleme im Mittelstand. Auswertung der Unternehmensbefragung 2002.* KfW. https://www.kfw.de/Download-Center/Konzernthemen/Research/PDF-Dokumente-Unternehmensbefragung/Unternehmensbefragung-2002-lang.pdf (Accessed 10 May 2013).

Plessis, Alexandre. 2003. *Histoire des banques en France.* FBF. http://www.fbf.fr/fr/files/88AFWG/Histoire_banques_France.pdf (Accessed 8 March 2013).

Pohl, Manfred. 1976. *Einführung in die deutsche Bankengeschichte: Die Entwicklung des gesamten deutschen Kreditwesens.* Frankfurt am Main: Knapp.

Pohl, Manfred. 1982. 'Die Entwicklung des deutschen Bankwesens zwischen 1848 und 1870 – The Development of the German Banking System between 1848 and 1870'. In *Deutsche Bankengeschichte: Band 2: Das deutsche Bankwesen 1806–1848*, eds. Günther Ashauer, Karl Born, Wolfram Engels, Ernst Klein, Manfred Pohl, and Wilhelm Treue. Frankfurt am Main: Knapp, 143–220.

Polster, Armin. 2004a. *Erste Schritte bei der Reform des Sparkassensektors in Italien: Bildung von großen Universalbanken mit weiterem Potenzial.* Deutsche Bank Research. EU-Monitor Finanzmarktspezial, 17. http://www.dbresearch.de/PROD/DBR_INTERNET_DE-PROD/PROD0000000000178254/EU-Monitor+Nr_+17%3A+Erste+Schritte+bei+der+Reform+des+Sparkassensektors+in++Italien%3A+Bildung+von+gro%C3%9Fen+Universalbanken+mit+weiterem+Potenzial.pdf (Accessed 13 April 2013).

Polster, Armin. 2004b. *Gelungene Sparkassenreform in Schweden: Gesamter Bankenmarkt profitiert von Privatisierung und Konsolidierung.* Deutsche Bank Research. EU-Monitor Finanzmarktspezial, 14. http://www.dbresearch.de/PROD/DBR_INTERNET_DE-PROD/PROD0000000000080714/EU-Monitor+Nr_+14%3A+Gelungene+Sparkassenreform+in+Schweden%3A+Gesamter+Bankenmarkt+profitiert+von+Privatisierung+und+Konsolidierung.pdf (Accessed 10 February 2013).

Polster, Armin. 2005. *Frankreichs Sparkassenreform: Plus ça change, plus ça reste—presque—le même.* Deutsche Bank Research. EU-Monitor Finanzmarktspezial, 22. http://www.dbresearch.de/PROD/DBR_INTERNET_DE-PROD/PROD0000000000185140/EU-Monitor+Nr_+22%3A+Frankreichs+Sparkassenreform%3A+Plus+%C3%A7a+change,+plus+%C3%A7a+reste+-+presque+-+le+m%C3%AAme.PDF (Accessed 10 February 2013).

Prost, Jeanne-Marie. 2013. *Plus de 20 000 emplois préservés depuis janvier 2013: Communiqué de presse.* Minefi. http://www.economie.gouv.fr/files/files/directions_services/media-teurducredit/pdf/CP___JUILLETVF_2013.pdf (Accessed 4 February 2013).

Przeworski, Adam, and Michael Wallerstein. 1988. 'Structural Dependence of the State on Capital'. *The American Political Science Review* 82 (1): 11–29.

Quaglia, Lucia. 2010. *Governing Financial Services in the European Union: Banking, Securities and Post-Trading.* London and New York: Routledge.

Quaglia, Lucia, and Aneta Spendzharova. 2017. 'Post-Crisis Reforms in Banking: Regulators at the Interface between Domestic and International Governance'. *Regulation & Governance* 11 (4): 422–37.

Ragin, Charles C. 1987. *The Comparative Method: Moving beyond Qualitative and Quantitative Strategies*. Berkeley: University of California Press.

Rameix, Gérard. 2011. *Rapport de Gérard RAMEIX sur l'accès au financement des TPE*. Médiation nationale du crédit aux entreprises and Observatoire du financement des entreprises. http://www.economie.gouv.fr/files/files/directions_services/mediateur-ducredit/pdf/Rapport_Financement_TPE__2011.pdf (Accessed 13 July 2014).

Rameix, Gérard, and Thierry Giami. 2011. *Rapport sur le financement des pme-eti par le marché financier: adressé à François Baroin, ministre de l'économie, des finances et de l'industrie*. http://www.tresor.economie.gouv.fr/File/337296 (Accessed 12 May 2013).

Ranné, Omar. 2005. 'Kreditverbriefung und Mittelstandsfinanzierung'. *Mittelstands- und Strukturpolitik* 33: 43–66.

Rathbun, Brian C. 2007. 'Uncertain about Uncertainty: Understanding the Multiple Meanings of a Crucial Concept in International Relations Theory'. *International Studies Quarterly* 51 (3): 533–57.

Reinhart, Carmen M., and Kenneth S. Rogoff. 2009. *This Time Is Different: Eight Centuries of Financial Folly*. Princeton, NJ: Princeton University Press.

Risse, Thomas. 2000. '"Let's Argue!": Communicative Action in World Politics'. *International Organization* 54 (1): 1–39.

Rivaud-Danset, Dorothée, Emmanuelle Dubocage, and Robert Salais. 2001. *Comparison between the financial structure of SMES and that of large enterprises (LES) using the BACH database*. Directorate-General Economic and Financial Affairs, European Commission. European Economy—Economic Papers, 155. http://ec.europa.eu/economy_finance/publications/publication928_en.pdf (Accessed 18 July 2014).

Rixen, Thomas. 2013. 'Why Reregulation after the Crisis Is Feeble: Shadow Banking, Offshore Financial Centers, and Jurisdictional Competition'. *Regulation & Governance* 7 (4): 435–59.

Röper, Nils. 2017. 'German Finance Capitalism: The Paradigm Shift Underlying Financial Diversification'. *New Political Economy* 23 (3): 366–90.

Rottmann, Horst, and Timo Wollmershäuser. 2013. 'A Micro Data Approach to the Identification of Credit Crunches'. *Applied Economics* 45 (17): 2423–41.

Roulhac, Bruno de. 2012a. 'Le premier fonds obligataire dédié aux ETI voit le jour'. *Agefi Quotidien*, 8 February. http://www.agefi.fr/articles/le-premier-fonds-obligataire-dedie-aux-eti-voit-le-jour-1210369.html (Accessed 20 August 2014).

Roulhac, Bruno de. 2012b. 'Les PME disposent de deux outils obligataires pour se financer'. *Agefi Quotidien*, 27 September. http://www.agefi.fr/articles/les-pme-disposent-de-deux-outils-obligataires-pour-se-financer-1239094.html (Accessed 17 February 2014).

Roulhac, Bruno de. 2013a. 'Nyse Euronext lance EnterNext pour inciter les PME à lever des capitaux'. *Agefi Hebdo*, 25 April. http://www.agefi.fr/articles/nyse-euronext-lance-enternext-pour-inciter-les-pme-a-lever-des-capitaux-1270426.html   (Accessed 17 February 2014).

Roulhac, Bruno de. 2013b. 'Le promoteur non coté Réalités lance la première IBO "high yield"'. *Agefi Quotidien*, 4 June. http://www.agefi.fr//articles/imprimer.aspx?id=1271732 (Accessed 21 August 2014).

Roulhac, Bruno de. 2013c. 'Le PEA-PME verra le jour début 2014'. *Agefi Quotidien*, 27 August. http://www.agefi.fr/articles/le-pea-pme-verra-le-jour-debut-2014-1283368.html (Accessed 21 February 2014).

Royer, Amélie. 2012. 'Etat des lieux du financement des PME par les assureurs'. In *L'Innovation dans l'assurance au Pôle Finance Innovation: restitution des travaux*. Vol. 2 of *Livre Blanc de l'assurance*, ed. Finance Innovation. Paris: Finance Innovation, 230–49.

Rudant, Gaetan, and Olivier Genain. 2010. *Rapport du groupe de travail: Accès au financement*. Etats Généraux de l'industrie. http://archives.dgcis.gouv.fr/2012/www. industrie.gouv.fr/archive/sites-web/etats-generaux-industrie/fileadmin/documents/ Nationnal/documents/Acces_au_financement/EGI_-_acces_aux_financements.pdf (Accessed 7 February 2014).

Ruggie, John G. 1982. 'International Regimes, Transactions, and Change: Embedded Liberalism in the Postwar Economic Order'. *International Organization* 36 (2): 379–415.

Sabatier, Paul, and Hank Jenkins-Smith. 1988. 'An Advocacy Coalition Framework of Policy Change and the Role of Policy-Oriented Learning Therein'. *Policy Sciences* 21 (2–3): 129–68.

Sabatier, Paul, and Hank Jenkins-Smith, eds. 1993. *Policy Change and Learning: An Advocacy Coalition Approach*. Boulder, CO: Westview Press.

Sabry, Faten, and Chudozie Okongwu. 2009. 'How Did We Get Here? The Story of the Credit Crisis'. *The Journal of Structured Finance* 15 (1): 53–70.

Sachverständigenrat. 2004. *Erfolge im Ausland—Herausforderungen im Inland: Jahresgutachten 2004/05*.

Sachverständigenrat. 2005. *Die Chance nutzen—Reformen mutig voranbringen: Jahresgutachten 2005/06*.

Sachverständigenrat. 2007. *Das Erreichte nicht verspielen: Jahresgutachten 2007/08*.

Sachverständigenrat. 2008. *Das deutsche Finanzsystem. Effizienz steigern—Stabilität erhöhen.: Expertise im Auftrag der Bundesregierung*.

Sachverständigenrat. 2019. *Den Strukturwandel Meistern. Jahresgutachten 2019/2020*.

Sarkozy, Nicolas. 2008. *Le discours de Nicolas Sarkozy à Toulon, jeudi 25 septembre*. https:// www.lemonde.fr/politique/article/2008/09/25/le-discours-de-nicolas-sarkozy-a-toulon_1099795_823448.html (Accessed 13 August 2020).

Sauvé, Annie, and Manfred Scheuer, eds. 1999. *Modes de financement des entreprises allemandes et françaises: Projet de recherche commun de la Deutsche Bundesbank et de la Banque de France*. Paris and Frankfurt am Main: Banque de France and Deutsche Bundesbank.

Scharpf, Fritz W. 1997. *Games Real Actors Play: Actor-Centered Institutionalism in Policy Research*. Boulder, CO: Westview Press.

Schildbach, Jan. 2008. *Banken in Europa: Die stille (R)evolution. Entscheidend sind die letzten 10 Jahre, nicht 10 Monate*. Deutsche Bank Research. EU-Monitor Finanzmarktspezial, 54. http://www.dbresearch.de/PROD/DBR_INTERNET_DE-PROD/PROD000000 0000225819/Banken+in+Europa%3A+Die+stille+%28R%29Evolution.pdf (Accessed 30 October 2012).

Schmidt, Vivien A. 2000. 'Still Three Models of Capitalism? The Dynamics of Economic Adjustment in Britain, Germany, and France'. In *Die politische Konstitution von Märkten*, eds. Roland M. Czada and Susanne Lütz. Wiesbaden: Westdeutscher Verlag, 38–72.

Schmidt, Vivien A. 2002. *The Futures of European Capitalism*. Oxford: Oxford University Press.

Schmidt, Vivien A. 2008. 'Discursive Institutionalism: The Explanatory Power of Ideas and Discourse'. *Annual Review of Political Science* 11 (1): 303–26.

Schmidt, Vivien, and Mark Thatcher, eds. 2013. *European Political Economy: Resilient Liberalism through Boom and Bust*. Cambridge: Cambridge University Press.

Schmitter, Philippe. 2008. 'The Design of Social and Political Research'. In *Approaches and Methodologies in the Social Sciences: A Pluralist Perspective*, eds. Donatella Della Porta and Michael Keating. Cambridge: Cambridge University Press, 263–96.

Schoen, Harald. 2011. 'Merely a Referendum on Chancellor Merkel? Parties, Issues and Candidates in the 2009 German Federal Election'. *German Politics* 20 (1): 92–106.

Searle, John R. 1995. *The Construction of Social Reality*. New York: Free Press.

Seikel, Daniel. 2011. *Wie die Europäische Kommission Liberalisierung durchsetzt. Der Konflikt um das öffentlich-rechtliche Bankenwesen in Deutschland*. MPIfG Discussion Paper, 11/16. http://www.mpifg.de/pu/mpifg_dp/dp11-16.pdf (Accessed 19 January 2013).

Seikel, Daniel. 2013. *Der Kampf um öffentlich-rechtliche Banken: Wie die Europäische Kommission Liberalisierung durchsetzt*. Frankfurt: Campus.

Shiller, Robert. 2013. 'Is Economics a Science?' *The Guardian*, 6 November.

Shiller, Robert. 2020. *Narrative Economics: How Stories Go Viral and Drive Major Economic Events*. Princeton, NJ: Princeton University Press.

Shin, Hyun S. 2009. 'Reflections on Northern Rock: The Bank Run that Heralded the Global Financial Crisis'. *Journal of Economic Perspectives* 23 (1): 101–19.

Shonfield, Andrew. 1965. *Modern Capitalism: The Changing Balance of Public and Private Power*. London: Oxford University Press.

Simon, Herbert A. 1955. 'A Behavioral Model of Rational Choice'. *The Quarterly Journal of Economics* 69 (1): 99–118.

Simon, Herbert A. 1983. *Reason in Human Affairs*. Stanford, CA: Stanford University Press.

Sinn, Hans-Werner. 2009. *Kasino-Kapitalismus: Wie es zur Finanzkrise kam, und was jetzt zu tun ist*. Berlin: Econ.

Sinn, Walter, and Sebastian Thoben. 2019. *Deutschlands Banken 2019: Erst sanieren, dann konsolidieren*. Frankfurt: Bain & Company.

Soularue, Gérard, Abderrahim Doulazmi, and Fabienne Brilland. 2010. *Restaurer des relations de confiance entre les réaux bancaires et les TPE-PME*. Chambre de Commerce de l'Industrie de Paris. http://www.etudes.cci-paris-idf.fr/rapport/256-relations-de-confiance-entre-les-banques-et-les-tpe-pme (Accessed 10 February 2014).

Staats, Stefan. 2006. *Fusionen bei Sparkassen und Landesbanken: Eine Untersuchung zu den Möglichkeiten der Vereinigung öffentlich-rechtlicher Kreditinstitute*. Berlin: Duncker & Humblot.

Stappel, Michael. 2010. *Finanzverbund gestern und heute*. BVR. http://www.giz.bvr.de/giz/giz2006.nsf/B46CC85A8F406BF2C125778F0025966E/$FILE/Entstehung_Finanz Verbund.pdf (Accessed 17 January 2013).

Statistisches Bundesamt. 2018. 'Ausstattung privater Haushalte mit Informations- und Kommunikationstechnik'. https://www.destatis.de/DE/ZahlenFakten/GesellschaftStaat/EinkommenKonsumLebensbedingungen/AusstattungGebrauchsguetern/Tabellen/Infotechnik_D.html;jsessionid=9117C7E00589E3EE3A9975CABC8E317D.Internet Live1#tab221330No1 (Accessed 24 August 2018).

Steinbrück, Peer. 2008. *Regierungserklärung des Bundesministers der Finanzen, Peer Steinbrück, zur Lage der Finanzmärkte vor dem Deutschen Bundestag am 25. September 2008 in Berlin*. Bulletin der Bundesregierung, 97–1.

Steinbrück, Peer. 2010. *Unterm Strich*. Hamburg: Hoffmann und Campe.

Steinbrück, Peer. 2012. *Vertrauen zurückgewinnen: Ein neuer Anlauf zur Bändigung der Finanzmärkte*. https://www.spdfraktion.de/system/files/documents/konzept_aufsicht_und_regulierung_finanzmaerkte.pdf (Accessed 13 August 2020).

Stigler, George J. 1971. 'The Theory of Economic Regulation'. *The Bell Journal of Economics and Management Science* 2 (1): 3–21.

Stone, Deborah. 1989. 'Causal Stories and the Formation of Policy Agendas'. *Political Science Quarterly* 104 (2): 281–300.

Story, Jonathan. 1997. 'Globalisation, the European Union and German Financial Reform: The Political Economy of "Finanzplatz Deutschland"'. In *The New World Order in International Finance*, ed. Geoffrey R. Underhill. Basingstoke: Macmillan, 245–73.

Story, Jonathan, and Ingo Walter. 1997. *Political Economy of Financial Integration in Europe: The Battle of the Systems*. Manchester: Manchester University Press.

Strange, Susan. 1988. *States and Markets*. London: Pinter Publishers.

Streeck, Wolfgang. 2009. *Re-forming Capitalism: Institutional Change in the German Political Economy*. Oxford: Oxford University Press.

Streeck, Wolfgang. 2010. *E Pluribus Unum? Varieties and Commonalities of Capitalism*. MPIfG Discussion Paper, 10/12. http://www.mpifg.de/pu/dp_abstracts/dp10-12.asp (Accessed 2 August 2014).

Streeck, Wolfgang, and Kathleen A. Thelen, eds. 2005. *Beyond Continuity: Institutional Change in Advanced Political Economies*. Oxford and New York: Oxford University Press.

Tachdjian, Krystèle. 2012. 'La BCE presse le comité de Bâle d'alléger les contraintes de liquidité'. *Agefi Quotidien*, 29 August. http://www.agefi.fr/articles/la-bce-presse-le-comite-de-bale-d-alleger-les-contraintes-de-liquidite-1235177.html (Accessed 8 April 2014).

Tarullo, Daniel. 2008. *Banking on Basel: The Future of International Financial Regulation*. Washington, DC: Peterson Institute for International Economics.

Tavory, Iddo, and Nina Eliasoph. 2013. 'Coordinating Futures: Toward a Theory of Anticipation'. *American Journal of Sociology* 118 (4): 908–42.

Thelen, Kathleen A. 2004. *How Institutions Evolve: The Political Economy of Skills in Germany, Britain, the United States, and Japan*. Cambridge and New York: Cambridge University Press.

Thiemann, Matthias. 2018. *The Growth of Shadow Banking: A Comparative Institutional Analysis*. Cambridge: Cambridge University Press.

Thiveaud, Jean-Marie. 1997. 'Les évolutions du système bancaire francais de l'entre-deux-guerres à nos jours: spécialisation, déspécialisation, concentration, concurrence'. *Revue d'économie financière* 39: 27–68.

Tsingou, Eleni. 2014. 'Power Elites and Club-Model Governance in Global Finance'. *International Political Sociology* 8 (3): 340–2.

Tsingou, Eleni. 2015. 'Club Governance and the Making of Global Financial Rules'. *Review of International Political Economy* 22 (2): 225–56.

Turner, Adair. 2009. *The Turner Review: A Regulatory Response to the Global Banking Crisis*. London: FSA.

Turner, Adair. 2012. *Economics after the Crisis: Objectives and Means. The Lionel Robbins Lectures*. Cambridge, MA: MIT Press.

Underhill, Geoffrey R., ed. 1997. *The New World Order in International Finance*. Basingstoke: Macmillan.

Uterwedde, Henrik. 1988. *Wirtschaftspolitik der Linken in Frankreich. Programme und Praxis 1974–1986*. Frankfurt am Main: Campus Verlag.

van der Zwan, Natascha. 2014. 'Making Sense of Financialization'. *Socio-Economic Review* 12: 99–129.

van Evera, Stephen. 1997. *Guide to Methods for Students of Political Science*. Ithaca, NY: Cornell University Press.

vbw. 2012. *Auswirkungen der CRDIV auf die Unternehmensfinanzierung*. http://www.aecm.eu/servlet/Repository/auswirkung-der-crd-iv-auf-die-unternehmensfinanzierung.pdf?IDR=402 (Accessed 9 March 2014).

Vitols, Sigurt. 2004. *Changes in Germany's Bank-Based Financial System: A Varieties of Capitalism Perspective*. WZB. Discussion Paper, SP II 2004–03. http://papers.ssrn.com/sol3/papers.cfm?abstract_id=517984 (Accessed 14 November 2012).

Vogel, David. 1987. 'Political Science and the Study of Corporate Power: A Dissent from the New Conventional Wisdom'. *British Journal of Political Science* 17 (4): 385–408.

Vogel, Steven K. 1996. *Freer Markets, More Rules: Regulatory Reform in Advanced Industrial Countries.* Ithaca, NY: Cornell University Press.

Weber, Axel. 2009. *Perspektiven für den deutschen Finanzmarkt: Vortrag auf dem deutschen Steuerberaterkongress.* Hamburg, 4 May. https://www.bundesbank.de/resource/blob/688 906/50950f789f77938f5e9a21eb2d7b1c14/mL/2009-05-04-weber-perspektiven-fuer-den-deutschen-finanzmarkt-download.pdf (Accessed 13 August 2020).

Wendt, Alexander. 1999. *Social Theory of International Politics.* Cambridge and New York: Cambridge University Press.

White, Lindsey, and JahanZaib Mehmood. 2017. *Ten Years Later, World's Biggest Banks Keep Getting Bigger.* S&P Global Indicators. https://www.spglobal.com/en/research-insights/articles/ten-years-later-worlds-biggest-banks-keep-getting-bigger (Accessed 18 July 2020).

Widmaier, Wesley W., Mark Blyth, and Leonard Seabrooke. 2007. 'Exogenous Shocks or Endogenous Constructions? The Meanings of Wars and Crises'. *International Studies Quarterly* 51 (4): 747–59.

Williamson, John, and Molly Mahar. 1998. *A Survey of Financial Liberalization.* Department of Economics, Princeton University. Essays in International Finance, 211. http://www.princeton.edu/~ies/IES_Essays/E211.pdf (Accessed 12 November 2012).

Woll, Cornelia. 2005. *Learning to Act on World Trade: Preference Formation of Large Firms in the United States and the European Union.* MPIfG Working Paper, 05/1.

Woll, Cornelia. 2008. *Firm Interests: How Governments Shape Business Lobbying on Global Trade.* Ithaca, NY: Cornell University Press.

Woll, Cornelia. 2014. *The Power of Inaction: Bank Bailouts in Comparison.* Ithaca, NY: Cornell University Press.

Yee, Albert S. 1996. 'The Causal Effects of Ideas on Policies'. *International Organization* 50 (1): 69–108.

Young, Kevin L. 2012. 'Transnational Regulatory Capture? An Empirical Examination of the Transnational Lobbying of the Basel Committee on Banking Supervision'. *Review of International Political Economy* 19 (4): 663–88.

ZDH. 2011. *Basel III—Positionen des Handwerks.* http://www.zdh.de/fileadmin/user_upload/themen/wirtschaft/Basel_III/20110524_ZDH_Position_Basel_III.pdf (Accessed 10 March 2014).

Zentraler Kreditausschuss. 2010. *Stellungnahme des Zentralen Kreditausschusses zum Arbeitspapier der Dienststellen der Europäischen Kommission zu möglichen zusätzlichen Änderungen der Banken- und Kapitaladäquanzrichtlinie ('CRD').* http://ec.europa.eu/internal_market/consultations/2010/crd4_en.htm (Accessed 7 April 2014).

Zimmermann, Hubert. 2014. 'A Grand Coalition for the Euro: The Second Merkel Cabinet, the Euro Crisis and the Elections of 2013'. *German Politics* 23 (4): 322–36.

Zohlnhöfer, Reimut. 2011. 'The 2009 Federal Election and the Economic Crisis'. *German Politics* 20 (1): 12–27.

Zysman, John. 1983. *Governments, Markets, and Growth: Financial Systems and the Politics of Industrial Change.* Ithaca, NY: Cornell University Press.

Index